Empathonomics

Debarshi Roy

Empathonomics

The Economics of Empathic Behaviour

palgrave
macmillan

Debarshi Roy
Founder
SEAB - Empathy Diagnostic Systems
Siliguri, West Bengal, India

ISBN 978-981-95-4032-7 ISBN 978-981-95-4033-4 (eBook)
https://doi.org/10.1007/978-981-95-4033-4

Cover illustration: Debarshi Roy

This Palgrave Macmillan imprint is published by the registered company Springer Nature Singapore Pte Ltd.
The registered company address is: 152 Beach Road, #21-01/04 Gateway East, Singapore 189721, Singapore

Dedicated to Ma and Baba

Foreword

Empathonomics – The Economics of Empathic Behaviours connects a key aspect of human behaviour, empathy, with the selfish and calculating rational economic man in mainstream economics textbook. Economists are now moving beyond the stylised models of motivation based on a narrow view of *Homo economicus*, who solely values money and leisure, embracing a wider perspective that incorporates a richer set of motivations. This broader understanding includes pro-social motivations such as a commitment to a mission (Besley & Ghatak, 2018). Other non-pecuniary motivations include intrinsic motivation, reputational concerns and social norms, status rewards and pure altruism (Benabour & Tirole, 2006). Yet another approach has been the role of identity, and how individual behaviour in the economic domain is shaped by their social and professional identity (Akerlof & Kranton, 2010). All these approaches—and that is not an exhaustive list—provide explanations as to how individuals behave in a more pro-social way than the purely selfish rational economic agent.

Traditional economic models have, until recently, largely excluded psychological constructs from their core tenets. The book contributes to filling this gap. Its objective is not to present predetermined prescriptive models, but rather to encourage the recognition of empathy as a crucial element in economic activities and planning, thereby encouraging further discussion, research and theorisation for models that might enhance human wellbeing.

The book is broadly structured into two parts. The first part lays the conceptual groundwork, delving into the definition and historical perspectives of empathy, as well as its integration into broader economic thoughts and theories, including strategic decision-making in game theory. The second part then contextualises empathy within specific and vital areas of economic activity, such as management, welfare, health, education and migration. These areas are chosen due to their profound impact on socio-economic wellbeing and where empathic interventions are deemed both possible and necessary.

This is a timely and thought-provoking exploration of a critical, multi-faceted human trait within the economic sphere. It presents a broad range of viewpoints and empirical evidence. The book's strength lies in its balanced approach, acknowledging both the benevolent potential and the inherent limitations and strategic, sometimes manipulative, applications of empathy. By dissecting how empathy has intersected with economic thought and human behaviour across diverse contexts, it provides a robust framework for further dialogue and research. The insights offered are valuable for anyone seeking a deeper understanding of the complex interplay between human nature and the economic systems that shape our world. Given my own work in this area over two decades since I started working on NGOs from the point of view of organizational economics and subsequently got interested in a range of organizations that are neither state-run or for-profit, including social enterprise (see Ghatak, 2020), I am very happy to see a book devoted to exploring alternative drivers of human behaviour in the economic domain and hope it encourages further thinking and research along this direction.

References

Akerlof, G., & Kranton, R. (2010). *Identity economics: How our identities shape our work, wages, and well-being*. Princeton Univ. Press.

Benabou, R., & Tirole, J. (2006). Incentives and prosocial behavior. *American Economic Review, 96*(5), 1652–1678.

Besley, T., & Ghatak, M. (2018). Pro-social motivation and incentives. *Annual Review of Economics, 10*, 411–438.

Ghatak, M. (2020). Economic theories of the social sector: From non-profits to social enterprise. In W. W. Powell & P. Bromley (Eds.), *The nonprofit sector: A research handbook* (3rd ed.). Stanford University Press.

Professor Maitreesh Ghatak is Professor of Economics at the London School of Economics and a Fellow of the British Academy. He is the Director of the Development Economics research program at Suntory and Toyota International Centres for Economics and related Disciplines at the London School of Economics.

London School of Economics
London, UK

Maitreesh Ghatak,

Acknowledgements

The intersection of behavioural sciences and economics has inspired a diverse range of research projects in recent times. My interest in empathic behaviour inspired the research, thoughts and ideations that led to this monograph wherein I have attempted to contextualize empathy within the broader perspective of economic behaviour.

The journey of writing this book has been fairly long and often tedious; interspersed by moments of quiet reflection and long phases of limited progress. Throughout this long journey, I have been fortunate to receive the unwavering support of many individuals. Professor Hirak Ray, as always, has stood by me as a pillar of strength and a vital intellectual outlet. My uncle, Mr. Om Prakash Aggarwal, has been a lifelong source of inspiration, offering profound philosophical insight since my early years. I am especially grateful to Professor Maitreesh Ghatak for his consistent encouragement and motivational support. I am deeply indebted to him for most generously contributing the foreword to this work. I extend my sincere gratitude to Ms. Aparajita Singh from Palgrave Macmillan for her thoughtful guidance and help throughout the course of this publication.

No work of this nature is ever completed without the enduring support of family. My heartfelt thanks and love go to my wife Margaret, daughter Nayantara, our extended family member Sobha, and our beloved canine son Alex—for their patience, belief and steadfast presence.

This monograph is a product of individual reflection which was energized by the quiet strength of collective encouragement. I hope it contributes meaningfully to the important discourse around empathy and economic behaviour.

Competing Interests The author has no competing interests to declare that are relevant to the content of this manuscript.

Contents

PART I

Empathy – The Concept and Its Relation to Economic Thoughts and Theorizations

CHAPTER 1

Introduction

"Never judge another man until you have walked a mile in his moccasins"—the aphoristic native American proverb efficiently explains the fundamental nuance of empathic behaviour. While empathy is and will remain a complex polysemic psychological construct, a benevolent feeling with fellow humans is the fundamental and central ideation of empathy around which the ensuing discussions of this book will be woven. This ideation is not unique per se and most studies on empathy have been related to prosocial and altruistic behaviour (Maibom, 2017). What makes this discussion unique to an extent is its structured attempt to connect empathy with, arguably, one of the most unforgiving areas of social science-economics.

It is pertinent to note that the fields of economics and psychology have had a complex relationship. Empathy had been directly or tacitly recognized as a pertinent (and often important) part of economic thought and planning through many centuries spanning from the ideations of the ancient Indian polymath Chanakya and traversing through the discourses presented by utilitarian thinkers like Jeremy Bentham and the father of modern economics: Adam Smith. However, the introduction of a rationalist approach to the field of economics as advocated by the Italian polymath Vilfredo Pareto and later promoted by economists such as Paul Samuelson had led to economics being separated (in fact being divorced) from the field of psychology. It was only with the advent of John Maynard

D. Roy, *Empathonomics*,
https://doi.org/10.1007/978-981-95-4033-4_1

Keynes and the introduction of Keynesian economics that psychology was reintroduced within economic thinking and ideations. Moreover, Keynesian economics had also reintroduced empathy in modern economic thought. The importance of empathic economic thought was further championed by stalwarts like Gunnar Myrdal, Amartya Sen and Joseph Stiglitz. While the American economist and political scientist Herbert Simon had questioned the concept of *Homo economicus* and introduced the alternate model of bounded rationality in the 1950s, the active recognition of economics as a science that is closely connected with psychology found support and recognition within the works of a new set of experts, some of who were trained psychologists seeking to explore economic behaviour. The new field of study was named Behavioural Economics and the field was inspired by the works of wizards like Richard Thaler, Daniel Kahneman and Amos Tversky. Notwithstanding the overwhelmingly substantial role that benevolence plays within the relation between empathy and economics, empathy is connected to economics in myriad and often circuitous ways some of which cannot be described as benevolent. The competitive and sometimes Machiavellian aspects of empathic economic behaviour oftentimes manifest within the realms of strategic behaviour and the popular method for the analysis of such behaviour—game theory.

In a world that is overwhelmingly driven by ruthless competition where the ends define the means, concepts like altruism might seem redundant, more so when the concept is contextualized within the science and practice of economics. The concept of the economic man – *Homo economicus* describes an infinitely rational animal who takes all decisions to maximize his or her self-interest. Norman (2008) had opined that this approach to economics seeks "to promote a debased and narrow view of human beings as merely greedy and fearful profit-maximisers" (p. 74). In a similar vein Ransom and Baird (2009) had opined "economics should serve the needs of the people – not the other way around. But you could be forgiven for thinking that economics involves people being forced into some procrustean, mathematically defined framework – free-market liberalism, for example – simply because that's the way it's been for so many years" (pp. 8–9). Evidently, the traditional view of an infinitely rational economic man does not fully reveal the diverse and complex nature of human behaviour. It is therefore not surprising that traditional economic theories find it difficult to explain why some individuals sacrifice their self-interest for others. However, some economists attempt to distinguish between actions that are motivated by self-interest (self-regarding preferences) from those that are motivated by factors other than one's own interest (other-regarding preferences) (Huettel, 2014). Much of individual acts of generosity and sacrifice are witnessed within altruistic behaviour. Altruistic acts are those voluntary acts of compassion where no reciprocity is expected. If this definition of altruism is strictly adhered to, a significant part of overt social welfare activities like those emanating from corporate social responsibility initiatives cannot be termed as altruistic because they are neither voluntary nor are bereft of all elements of reciprocity. Altruistic behaviour is posited to be deeply connected to empathy, and numerous experts over the years have emphasized that empathy plays a fundamental role in motivating altruistic behaviour (Hoffman, 1976; Zahn-Waxler et al., 1984). Schramme (2017) seemed to agree with this point of view as he opined "empathy is identified with a 'feeling with' another person, or with 'empathic concern.' This then seems to straightforwardly account for altruism" (p. 205).[1]

Economic discussions on altruism are often placed within the context of public and common goods. Huettel (2014) had described public goods as "something that benefits many people, all of whom want the public good to continue to exist" (p. 131). Such public goods could be provided by the government (street lights, national defence, etc.) at little or no cost and mostly funded by taxes. In addition, public goods might also be funded by private donations and charity. However, such donations and charitable endowments may not necessarily be altruistic in nature. Andreoni (1990) had posited "When people make donations to privately provided public goods, such as charity, there may be many factors influencing their decisions other than altruism" (p. 464). These factors could include a desire to enhance prestige, respect, or even to avoid public derision and a feeling of guilt. Andreoni (1990) had explained this through the theory of warm glow altruism; warm glow represents the joy, satisfaction and selfish pleasure derived from the act of altruism. Andreoni (1990) had described this form of altruism as impure altruism. However, not all altruistic contributions to public goods are impure, as Banerjee (2021) had posited "Individuals who contribute to a public good are often part of a community and care about the other members that benefit from it" (p. 2). Such contributions no doubt have an empathic motive, and it is in this context that empathy might have a mediating role to play within the relationship between public goods and altruistic behaviour. Heal (2021) had emphasized that empathic considerations can influence private contributions to public goods. Heal (2021) had further posited that if individuals empathetically care about the wellbeing of others, then private contributions to public goods will be sufficient for the efficient provision of such goods. Further, when individuals become more empathic, it leads to an increase in the provision of public goods.

The concept of common goods presents within close ideational proximity of public goods.[2] A fairly simplistic but effective description of common good could be that which is beneficial to the overall wellbeing of society. Common good is shared by and is beneficial to all members of a society. Dupré (1993) had explained that the classical definition of common goods which was based on Aristotelian thoughts and principles related to a good that was achievable only by a community as a collective but was shared individually by the members of the community. Common good is rivalrous in nature (as opposed to public goods which are non-rivalrous) and might include a wide gamut of facilities that are available to the members of a community. Such facilities might comprise of amenities and services like roads, libraries, hospitals; law enforcement, justice systems, access to clean water and air and other aspects of wellbeing. (Waheed, 2018). Certain scholars (Simm, 2011; Held, 1970) have posited that the concept of common good is essentially objective and normative in nature. Consequently, there is no rational objection to the concept of common good. Moreover, if common good is taken to be an aggregation of individual good, then there should be no conflict between individual good and common good; however, if at all such conflicts arise, the common good prevails over individual good (Simms, 2011).

If empathic behaviour of an individual or a set of individuals towards another member (or a set of members) of the group is to be contextualized within the concepts of public and common goods, it would require an analysis of the decision-making dynamics within collective societal groups. The role of an empathic person (or a set of empathic persons within the collective) in the context of collective goods was explained by Batson et al. (1995a) wherein he suggested that the decision of an empathic person (or persons) towards a collective good would be influenced by three motives: self-interest of the person or persons, collective interest of the collective and the interest of the empathic targets (which would result in altruistic behaviour). If the altruism that was evoked by the empathic targets was strong enough, it would lead to the allocation of a certain amount of resources for the targets; this allocation would however come at a cost to the individual interest of the empathic persons, the collective or both. While prima facie such allocations might seem ethical, it might be perceived as unjust and unfair by a section of the community. The resultant dilemma was studied by Batson et al. (1995b) who posited that "empathy-induced altruism and the desire to uphold a moral principle of justice are independent prosocial motives that sometimes cooperate but sometimes conflict" (p. 1042). Thus, empathic decision making particularly within the context of resource allocation in respect of collective goods may not follow accepted principles of justice.

Altruistic and empathic economic systems which prioritize common good tend to focus on the deprived sections of the society. As Duchrow and Hinkelammert (2004) had opined "the perspective of the common good fundamentally starts with the weakest, most threatened members of the community. If they can live, all can live. And finally there is liberation from oppression; all are involved and all are given a living. Justice and life are the basic perspectives" (p. 157). Bullard (2009) had opined that within the context of common good a community not only consists of children, the elderly, the sick or the unemployed but also "landless farmers, indigenous peoples, the urban poor, underpaid and precarious workers, women in many situations, people of color and migrants. The list is long, and it adds up to the majority of humanity" (p. 156). Thus, inclusiveness presents as an important characteristic of empathic economic systems. It could be argued that the empathic allocation of resources to the deprived sections of the society comes at a cost to the more affluent members of the society and at times the collective at large. However, such allocations might be considered necessary for the empathic considerations of inclusive upliftment and wellbeing of all sections of society.

A discussion on empathic economic behaviour does not however begin and end with altruistic acts. The necessity for altruistic acts, at least those that we might describe as charitable acts meant to help the socio-economically backward sections of the society, find their fundamental reason within the inequalities in society. In a perfect world where every human might be deemed to have the same standards of living, the concept of altruism would be redundant; such a world is not only impossible but also unnatural. However, it is not utopian or even impertinent to envisage a world that is fair and just enough to ensure that even the poorest of the poor might live a life of dignity wherein they are not only able to fulfil their basic needs of food, clothing and shelter from their income but also provide education and good health to their children so that the next generation might have a chance at a better life through socio-economic upliftment. The real world is however inordinately inequal, and in recent years the K shaped growth pattern observed in many countries after the Covid pandemic has made it more so. A cursory visit to the International Monetary Fund website will acquaint the reader with a graph that has been shared from the World Inequality Report, 2022 (Chancel, 2022); the graph has a notification at the top which reads, "The richest 1 percent of the world's population is so much wealthier than the poorest half that the top 1 percent column does not fit on this graph" (https://www.imf.org/en/Publications/fandd/issues/2022/03/Global-inequalities-Stanley).

The world Inequality Report, 2022, broadly concludes that across the world "The richest 10% own around 60-80% of wealth. The poorest half typically owns less than 5% of wealth" (Chancel, 2022, p. 12).[3] In more specific terms it has been reported within the study that the bottom 50% of the population own 2% of the total wealth while the top 10% own 75.6% of the total wealth. Moreover, the share of the wealthiest group's wealth is growing at a rapid rate over time. The World Inequality Report, 2022, opines, "When the growth rate of a group is faster than the growth rate of the average, this group's share of total wealth increases. This is what happened among the wealthiest groups" (Chancel, 2022, p. 91). The high rate of growth among the wealthy would be accepted and appreciated if it had led to a comparable rate of growth among the other sections of the population, as Professor Joseph Stiglitz pointed out: "If the rich were growing richer and if those in the middle and at the bottom were also doing better, that would be one thing, especially if the efforts of those at the top were central to the successes of the rest. We could celebrate the successes of those at the top and be thankful for their contributions. But that's not what's been happening" (Stiglitz, 2012, p. 35). Pettifor (2009) had explained that since assets are mostly owned by the rich, inflation in value of the assets lead to the rich accumulating more wealth and growing richer over a period. The rich do not require to be involved in productive activity and the rent from their assets suffice. In contrast the salaried middle class, farmers or small business owners do not experience a comparative inflation in prices of their good, services, salaries or wages.

Experts have posited that the root cause of income inequality lies within wage stagnation among the middle and lower middle-class population (Stiglitz, 2012; Mishel et al., 2015). Such inequalities do not help the overall economic growth of a country, as Dabla-Norris et al. (2015) had reported within their study that "making the rich richer by one percentage point lowers GDP growth in a country over the next five years by 0.08 percentage points—whereas making the poor and the middle class one percentage point richer can raise GDP growth by as much as 0.38 percentage points." The researchers had conjectured on the reasons for the phenomenon and concluded that the middle class and the poor tend to spend a higher percentage of their income over the rich and thus they help in increasing demand and stimulating growth.

Numerous researchers have put forward their view on the reasons for wage stagnation and economic inequality; most have concluded that economic inequality results from causes that are not economic. Mishel et al. (2015) had opined "Wage stagnation for the vast majority was not created by abstract economic trends. Rather, wages were suppressed by policy choices made on behalf of those with the most income, wealth, and power." In fact, Professor Stiglitz (2012) had identified political causes to be the primary reason for economic inequality: "the inequality is cause and consequence of the failure of the political system, and it contributes to the instability of our economic system, which in turn contributes to increased inequality—a vicious downward spiral" (Stiglitz, 2012, p. 10). If political decisions are to be accepted as a significant cause for the inordinate socio-economic inequality that is witnessed in the world, then it might be surmised that such inequality is avoidable, manmade and results from an unempathic approach to decision making.

The problem with inequality is that it often results in intergenerational transmission. Those that graduate out of good universities and technical institutes have the best chance at well-paying jobs. It is however difficult and often expensive to secure admissions to good universities or institutes and study a course of one's choice. The preparatory courses for such entrances are often expensive too and out of reach of the poorer sections of society. The schools that cater to children from socio-economically backward sections of society lack infrastructure and adequate teachers. Such schools most often do not create the atmosphere that is fundamental to motivate children to dream of a better life and work to fulfil that dream.[4] Carter (2015) had explained, "many affluent families invest in strategic practices that not only heighten their children's competitive advantage and chances for upward mobility but also keep us wedded to a phenomenon that widens inequality—segregation" (p. 76). A similar problem occurs in the healthcare sector where the rich have the means to access the best healthcare possible while the poor are often treated in facilities with limited infrastructure and healthcare professionals.

Moreover, societies are not empathic to the poor and blame them for their predicament. Poverty is often presented as a consequence of laziness, delinquency, substance abuse or other such anti-social behaviour.

While economic inequality could be recognized as a fundamental outcome of unempathic economic systems, such inequal systems lead to further unfair practices, exploitation, injustice and oftentimes blatant unapologetic cruelty. The concentration of power in the hands of a few has led to dangerous levels of inhumane behaviour meted out for the weak. The terrible evils of the trans-Atlantic slave trade and the criminalities of colonization wherein humans were dehumanized and traded (as well as treated) like cattle were motivated by the objective of economic profit. The unempathic systems of corporate management that has evolved over the past century where profit has been prioritized over people and employees have been laid off in brutal and unempathic manner leading to psychological breakdowns and even suicide could be viewed as an extension of the same unempathic practices which have its roots within the slave driven economy of the yester years. In an overwhelming number of cases employees are not even provided with a notice of their being dismissed from their jobs and often learn about it when they reach their office for work or as in some cases try to log in to their official email accounts and find them blocked. The dystopian situation could be best described through the headline of a *Forbes* online article which reads: "CEO Who Fired 900 Employees Via A Zoom Video And Called His Employees 'Dumb Dolphins' Had A Mass Layoff—Some Workers Found Out By Seeing Their Bank Account" (Kelly, 2022).

Watanabe and Kosaki (2017) had posited that social equality and inequality have significant effects on empathic behaviour. Individuals belonging to socially equal groups experience similar emotions and often indulge in similar behaviours. Thus, social equality serves to strengthen bonds among the members of the social group through empathy. Contrarily social inequality leads to negative emotions like envy or schadenfreude which is described as the happiness that one feels at the misfortune of others. Watanabe and Kosaki (2017) explained the negative psychological reaction to another person's wellbeing as reverse empathy which was described as "a non-state-matching form of empathy in which distress results from observing the fortune of others" (p. 278). Watanabe (2011) had earlier described the phenomenon succinctly as "happiness of the others is a taste of acid" (p. 1).

If economic systems and processes are to be empathically designed with an objective to reduce inequalities in society, it would require an understanding of the empathic nature and disposition of the social classes involved. While the inequalities in socioeconomic conditions and its broad effects are well documented, it is imperative within the subject of the present discussion to explore the empathic dimensions of socioeconomic inequality from the perspective of social and individual psychology. Consequently, it would be pertinent at this stage to understand if empathic behaviour presents with variations across class divides. Some researchers have proposed it to be so (Kraus & Keltner, 2009; Kraus et al., 2010). In this regard Manstead (2018) had posited, "Working-class people score higher on measures of empathy and are more likely to help others in distress" (p. 267). Several reasons have been suggested to explain this differential. Kraus et al. (2010) had proposed that individuals from the higher classes of society tend to internalize their focus and emphasize upon their own unique capabilities and qualities; on the other hand individuals from the lower classes are more socially oriented and thus are more attentive to the emotions and behaviour of other people. Further, it has been posited that lower-class individuals are more interdependent on each other and such interdependency within relationships enhance empathy (Stinson & Ickes, 1992; Kraus et al., 2010). The sense of interdependency leads to a lower sense of personal control over events and encourages the analysis and explanation of such events in social and situational terms (Manstead, 2018).

It has often been proposed that economic inequality can be reduced by a redistribution of resources from the wealthy to the poor. However, as discussed earlier, such attempts at redistribution are bound to face opposition from the powerful wealthy class who are less empathic towards to the plight of the poor (Jia, 2023). According to Jia (2023), wealthy individuals are more empathetic towards the poor when they accept that the marginal utility of consumption for the poor is significantly higher than the rich. However, Jia (2023) acknowledged that a psychological phenomenon termed as motivated reasoning acts as a barrier to such acceptance. Motivated reasoning is a phenomenon wherein individuals allow biases to influence how they perceive new information and tend to accept evidences that support their extant beliefs while rejecting those that present a contrarian view (Kunda, 1990; Jia, 2023).

There is evidence however which suggest that an individual's experience does affect his or her views on redistribution and inequality. Jia

(2023) had posited that wealthy individuals who had grown up in poverty tend to be more supportive of redistributive policies. Similarly, Margalit (2013) had posited "personal experience of economic hardship, particularly the loss of a job, had a major effect on increasing support for welfare spending" (p. 80). In other words, an individual who has experienced poverty and hardship is likely to be more empathic towards those who are poor than an individual who has not experienced poverty. Jia (2023) in conclusion had remarked "self-serving bias can be mitigated by exposing individuals to more diverse personal experiences, leading to an increase in empathy towards the less fortunate and consequently promoting greater redistribution" (p. 33).

The discussion in this book involves an analysis of some of the core areas of economic life contextualized within the perspective of empathic (and unempathic) behaviour. The behaviour that is described and analysed include individual, group, societal and organizational behaviour as well as governmental policies and theories that affect the lives of the people.

The book is divided into two parts. The first part of the book consists of Chaps. 1–4 which discuss, in detail, the role of empathy within the broad ambit of economic behaviour. The objective of this part of the book is to present an overview of the concept of empathy and its various aspects in order to familiarize the reader with the idea of empathy, its history, scientific background as well as the diverse fields and contexts within which the concept is allied along with its limitations. The discussion in this part further proceeds to an in-depth exploration of empathy within the context of the various ideations, theories and schools that broadly constitute economic thought. The second part of the book consist of Chaps. 5–10 which attempt to contextualize the role of empathy within some important areas of economic activity. These areas are education, health, business management, the role of welfare in societies, societal behaviour and approach towards migrants and labour.

An honest attempt to analyse the role of empathy in economic behaviour requires a thorough analysis of the historical and present reality of human actions and their outcome. Unfortunately, many instances of such historical and current realities present with instances of inhumane cruelty which has no place for empathy. The industrial revolution and its aftermath colonization, slave trade and the consequent dehumanization of a large section of the human population (many of who belong to the colonizing country themselves) have left a lasting and almost permanent scar on the human race. The scar however is not merely a passive aesthetic blot but an active bleeding wound that manifests itself within the design and process of various socio-economic systems that are in operation around the world even today. The factory model of schooling, a healthcare system geared to favour the rich, an unempathic and cruel corporate management culture that does not value employees and wherein all processes and systems are meant to maximize efficiency at all cost leading to a maximization of the owners' wealth, skewed and exploitative land and labour policies,[5] all have their source within theories and practices that came into existence centuries ago. Such unempathic socio-economic behaviour provides a potent point-of-reference for what was (and is) and what could (and can) be and illustrate evidently an argument for an empathic economic system which benefits all humans by prioritizing their wellbeing. As a consequent to this line of argument the chapters in this book focus on some of the key areas of economic activity that present as areas of concern and need immediate empathic intervention. While a discussion on empathic economic systems might, without deliberate intent, evolve into a normative discourse, the primary objective of this discussion is to acquaint the reader with the prevailing circumstances; present the historical background for the circumstances; report on the theories, research findings and empirical evidences on the different socio-economic and behavioural patterns that are relevant to the topic of discussion and ideate on economic and behavioural policy interventions which might make economic systems more empathic, thus helping in the creation of a more equal, just and fair world.

The core thesis that is presented in this work revolves around the argument that empathy might be well regarded as a central driver of economic life rather than a discretionary peripheral virtue. As an extension of this line of thought it could be proposed that the science and art of economics is not limited to the study of markets but also involves the exploration of moral ecosystems which encourage human flourishing through the creation and sustenance of economic systems that inherently embed empathy to catalyse resilient, sustainable and equitable growth for all.

A significant part of traditional economic theory, however, finds its foundations on concepts such as rationality, self-interest and efficiency while at times deemphasizing the value of human connections. The discussions presented in the ensuing chapters delve deeper into the role of empathy in traditional economic theorizations and in the approaches to socioeconomic activities and behaviour like education, healthcare, migration, business management and social welfare. Consequently, the fundamental objective of this exercise involves the exploration and discussion of empathy as a potent force in shaping socio-economic choices, determining socio-economic outcomes and ensuring collective wellbeing. While the discussions presented herein do not claim to present new theorizations or models, they engage intimately with extant theory and body of research to weave a coherent network of narratives to highlight the importance of empathy in economic thought and activity.

Notes

1. An aspect of altruistic action presents itself within the phenomenon that people show more willingness to give to causes when they know that some specific and identifiable person will benefit from their help. So, people will be more willing to help a single child who needs money for treatment than to a group of 100000 people who are displaced by a cyclone. This is an empathy paradox which is discussed in later chapters. See Huettel (2014).
2. Even though the terms public good and common good are sometimes used interchangeably, there are some fundamental differences in the classical definition of the terms. For example, while both public good and common good are non-excludable, public good is non-rivalrous but common good is rivalrous. The differences however are dynamic and might be blurred or augmented by the nature and extrapolation in the meaning and usage of the terms.
3. The World Inequality Report, 2022, went further to report that the wealthy were associated with higher emissions of Green Houses gases (GHG). In the context of the United States, while the bottom 1% of the population emitted 9.7 tonnes of CO_2, the top 1% emitted 269.3 tonnes of CO_2 per capita.
4. In an interesting study panning over Ethiopia, India, Peru and Vietnam, Behrman et al. (2017) found that while an increase in income levels or in the levels of education (schooling) might lead to a reduction in poverty and inequality within the parent's generation, however the effects do not carry over to the children's generation.
5. The unempathic nature of labour relations in the USA was evident within the conspiracy doctrine which formed the basis of all labour relation issues in the eighteenth and early part of the nineteenth century. The conspiracy doctrine was a deterrent against all types of collective action by labour unions and prevented the workers from trying to improve their working conditions. Any forms of collective protest led to criminal action, prosecution and conviction of the workers and trade union leaders (Zimmer, 2003). Poulson (1986) explained "Labor law in America until the 1930s was for the most part established by the courts through common law, equity proceedings, or constitutional interpretations. The legal doctrines that were the

basis for labor law were, first, the criminal conspiracy doctrine, and, subsequently, injunctions and damage suits. Traditionally, labor historians have interpreted these legal doctrines in terms of class conflict. These writers maintain that the courts did not function as an independent judiciary, but rather as an appendage of propertied interests legitimizing their suppression of labor organizations. Judges drawn from the upper class reflected a pro-business ideology and were responsive to propertied interests in cases involving labor unions. The objective of labor law, in that view, was to create a hostile legal environment for labor unions making it difficult for unions to organize workers and bargain collectively with employers" (p. 212).

References

Andreoni, J. (1990). Impure altruism and donations to public goods: A theory of warm-glow giving. *The Economic Journal, 100*(401), 464–477. https://doi.org/10.2307/2234133

Banerjee, A. (2021). Contribution to a public good with altruistic preferences. *Working paper of the Max Planck Institute for Tax Law and Public Finance no. 2021-08*. https://doi.org/10.2139/ssrn.3864933

Batson, C. D., et al. (1995a). Empathy and the collective good: Caring for one of the others in a social dilemma. *Journal of Personality and Social Psychology, 68*(4), 619–631. https://doi.org/10.1037/0022-3514.68.4.619

Batson, C. D., et al. (1995b). Immorality from empathy-induced altruism: When compassion and justice conflict. *Journal of Personality and Social Psychology, 68*(6), 1042–1054. https://doi.org/10.1037/0022-3514.68.6.1042

Behrman, J. R., et al. (2017). Intergenerational transmission of poverty and inequality: Parental resources and schooling attainment and children's human capital in Ethiopia, India, Peru, and Vietnam. *Economic Development and Cultural Change, 65*(4), 657–697. https://doi.org/10.1086/691971

Bullard, N. (2009). To live well. In D. Ransom & V. Baird (Eds.), *People first economics*. New Internationalist Publications Ltd.

Carter, P. L. (2015). Educational equity demands empathy. *Contexts, 14*(4), 76–78. https://doi.org/10.1177/153650421561189

Chancel, L. (2022). *World inequality report 2022*. World Inequality Lab. Retrieved June 2, 2023, from https://wir2022.wid.world/www-site/uploads/2023/03/D_FINAL_WIL_RIM_RAPPORT_2303.pdf

Dabla-Norris, E., et al. (2015). *Growth's secret weapon: The poor and the middle class*. Retrieved June 3, 2023, from https://www.imf.org/en/Blogs/Articles/2015/06/15/growths-secret-weapon-the-poor-and-the-middle-class

Duchrow, U., & Hinkelammert, F. J. (2004). *Property for people, not for profit*. Zed Books and Catholic Institute for International Relation.

Dupré, L. (1993). The common good and the open society. *The Review of Politics, 55*(04), 687–712. https://doi.org/10.1017/s0034670500018052

Heal, G. (2021). Empathy and the efficient provision of public goods. *NBER working paper no. 29255.* Retrieved August 29, 2024, from https://www.nber.org/system/files/working_papers/w29255/w29255.pdf

Held, V. (1970). *The public interest and individual interests.* Basic Books.

Hoffman, M. L. (1976). Empathy, role-taking, guilt, and the development of altruistic motives. In T. Likona (Ed.), *Moral development and behavior.* Holt, Rinehart, and Winston.

Huettel, S. (2014). *Behavioral economics: When psychology and economics collide.* The Great Courses.

Jia, T. (2023). Empathy, motivated reasoning, and redistribution. *Stanford Digital Repository.* Retrieved August 29, 2024, from https://purl.stanford.edu/bs806zt3604. https://doi.org/10.25740/bs806zt3604

Kelly, J. (2022). *CEO who fired 900 employees via a zoom video and called his employees 'Dumb Dolphins' had a mass layoff—Some workers found out by seeing their bank account.* Retrieved June 6, 2023, from https://www.forbes.com/sites/jackkelly/2022/03/09/ceo-who-fired-900-employees-via-a-zoom-video-and-called-his-employees-dumb-dolphins-had-a-mass-layoff-some-workers-found-out-by-seeing-their-bank-account/?sh=44ed08ad25fe

Kraus, M. W., & Keltner, D. (2009). Signs of socioeconomic status: A thin-slicing approach. *Psychological Science, 20*(1), 99–106. https://doi.org/10.1111/j.1467-9280.2008.02251.x

Kraus, M. W., et al. (2010). Social class, contextualism, and empathic accuracy. *Psychological Science, 21*(11), 1716–1723. https://doi.org/10.1177/0956797610387613

Kunda, Z. (1990). The case for motivated reasoning. *Psychological Bulletin, 108*(3), 480–498. https://doi.org/10.1037/0033-2909.108.3.480

Maibom, H. L. (2017). Introduction to philosophy of empathy. In H. L. Maibom (Ed.), *The Routledge handbook of philosophy of empathy.* Routledge.

Manstead, A. S. R. (2018). The psychology of social class: How socioeconomic status impacts thought, feelings, and behaviour. *British Journal of Social Psychology, 57*, 267–291. https://doi.org/10.1111/bjso.12251

Margalit, Y. (2013). Explaining social policy preferences: Evidence from the great recession. *American Political Science Review, 107*(1), 80–103. https://doi.org/10.1017/S0003055412000603

Mishel, L., et al. (2015). *Wage stagnation in nine charts.* Retrieved June 3, 2023, from https://www.epi.org/publication/charting-wage-stagnation/

Norman, J. (2008). *Compassionate economics.* Policy Exchange, University of Buckingham Press.

Pettifor, A. (2009). Beyond the crash – A green new deal. In D. Ransom & V. Baird (Eds.), *People first economics*. New Internationalist Publications Ltd.

Poulson, B. W. (1986). Criminal conspiracy, injunctions and damage suits in labor law. *The Journal of Legal History, 7*(2), 212–227. https://doi.org/10.1080/01440368608530866

Ransom, D., & Baird, V. (2009). Introduction. In D. Ransom & V. Baird (Eds.), *People first economics*. New Internationalist Publications Ltd.

Schramme, T. (2017). Empathy and altruism. In H. L. Maibom (Ed.), *The Routledge handbook of philosophy of empathy*. Routledge.

Simm, K. (2011). The concepts of common good and public interest: From Plato to biobanking. *Cambridge Quarterly of Healthcare Ethics, 20*(04), 554–562. https://doi.org/10.1017/s0963180111000296

Stiglitz, J. (2012). *The price of inequality*. W.W. Norton and Company.

Stinson, L., & Ickes, W. (1992). Empathic accuracy in the interactions of male friends versus male strangers. *Journal of Personality and Social Psychology, 62*(5), 787–797. https://doi.org/10.1037/0022-3514.62.5.787

Waheed, H. (2018). The common good. In E. N. Zalta (Ed.), *The Stanford encyclopedia of philosophy* (Spring 2018 ed.). Retrieved June 13, 2023, from https://plato.stanford.edu/entries/common-good/

Watanabe, S. (2011). Empathy and reversed empathy of stress in mice. *PLoS One, 6*(8), e23357. https://doi.org/10.1371/journal.pone.0023357

Watanabe, S., & Kosaki, Y. (2017). Evolutionary origin of empathy and inequality aversion. In S. Watanabe et al. (Eds.), *Evolution of the brain, cognition, and emotion in vertebrates*. Springer Japan. https://doi.org/10.1007/978-4-431-56559-8_13

Zahn-Waxler, C., et al. (1984). The origins of empathy and altruism. In M. W. Fox & L. D. Mickley (Eds.), *Advances in animal welfare science* (pp. 21–41). The Humane Society of the United States.

Zimmer, M. J. (2003). Systemic empathy. *Columbia Human Rights Law Review, 34*, 575–603. Retrieved June 14, 2023, from https://lawecommons.luc.edu/cgi/viewcontent.cgi?referer=&httpsredir=1&article=1268&context=facpubs

CHAPTER 2

Empathy: An Overview of the Concept

The word empathy finds its roots within the Greek word 'pathos' which means suffering. The Greek word for empathy is *empatheia*, which translates to 'in suffering.'[1] Not much is written about empathy by the ancient Greek philosophers; however, the word empathes has been reported to have been mentioned in Aristotle's *On Dreams* and Plutarch's Lives (Agosta, n.d.; Roy, 2022a). The concept of empathy however was discussed in seriousness much later, during the times of the Scottish enlightenment, by David Hume who had posited that "the minds of men are mirrors to one another" (Hume, 1739–40, p. 214) and his fellow countryman Adam Smith who had proclaimed "How selfish soever man may be supposed, there are evidently some principles in his nature, which interest him in the fortunes of others, and render their happiness necessary to him, though he derives nothing from it, except the pleasure of seeing it' (Smith, 1759, p. 11). However, the phenomenon that had been narrated by Hume and Smith was described by the term sympathy, the word 'empathy' was formally coined over a hundred years later.

The precursor to the English word 'empathy' was the German word Einfühlung which was developed in the late nineteenth and early twentieth century. Einfühlung originated from the German words ein which meant into and fuhlung which meant feeling, thus Einfühlung meant feeling into (Roy, 2022a). Einfühlung, as a concept was rooted within the ideations of German aesthetics. It involved the assumption that objects

D. Roy, *Empathonomics*,
https://doi.org/10.1007/978-981-95-4033-4_2

had artistic appeal only when empathy was connected with it. Thus, aesthetic delight of an object was in reality the personal delight that was projected on those objects (Lanzoni, 2018; Roy, 2022a). Theodor Lipps, a psychologist and philosopher from Munich, had described Einfühlung as "the projection of inner feelings of striving and movement into objects" (Lanzoni, 2018, p. 15). This projection was posited to be the key to aesthetic experience (Lanzoni, 2018; Roy, 2022a). It was explained that the aesthetic connection between an observer and a work of art occurs at two distinct levels: at one level, "the observer feels into the situation that is portrayed in the painting and the other when the observer feels into the thoughts of the artist who has created the painting or artwork" (Roy, 2022a, p. 12; Ganczarek et al., 2018). Thus, the concept of Einfühlung recognized that humans could feel into inanimate objects like stones or inhuman entities like animals and plants (Roy, 2022a). It was within an extension of this line of thought that experts like Arthur Schopenhauer had commented on the importance of feelings in architecture (Watson, 2014), and in furtherance to this ideation, Lipps (1905) and Stueber (2019) had posited that objects are perceived to be beautiful when they are recognized as being similar to some human body, through an empathic connection.

Edward Titchener, an American psychologist from Cornell University, is credited with the first definitive English translation of the word Einfühlung in 1908; curiously James Ward an advocate of panpsychism[2] had proposed the word 'empathy' almost simultaneously at Cambridge University. The word empathy thus became a part of the regular terminology used in psychology and was included within textbooks by 1909 (Lanzoni, 2018; Roy, 2022a). The concept of empathy had inspired researchers both in Europe and in America. The approaches to the study of empathy were however different in the two continents; while the American researchers focussed on overt behavioural aspects like observable bodily movements (kinesthetics) and gestures, the researchers in Europe concentrated on the unobservable aspects of empathy that were dominated by the internalized mental processes (Lanzoni, 2018; Roy, 2022a). The relationship between kinesthetic action and empathy was studied in detail by an American psychologist Herbert Sidney Langfeld who posited that every external stimulus excites a response within organisms and that response might be functional or aesthetic. Functional responses are mostly practical in nature while aesthetic responses are synchronous (Langfeld, 1920, 1927, 1931; Lanzoni, 2018; Roy, 2022a). For example, if one observes a branch swaying in the wind, the responses might involve reaching out to stop the branch from swaying (functional) or sway along with the branch (aesthetic) (Lanzoni, 2018; Roy, 2022a).[3]

In addition to an influence on art and aesthetics, the concept of empathy also influenced the practice and study of medicine especially with regard to treatment of patients with mental disorders. It should be emphasized that in the nineteenth century, patients with mental illnesses were subjected to horrific inhuman treatment. They were mostly incarcerated within mental asylums in inhuman conditions with no access to medical treatment to cure them of their ailments. In fact, the society judged mental patients as morally depraved who were being punished by God for their sins (Lieberman & Ogas, 2015; Roy, 2022a). The situation changed appreciably when in the twentieth century a Swiss psychiatrist Adolf Meyer introduced the idea that behaviour and mental health had its origins within biology and introduced the concept of psychobiology (Lamb, 2015; Roy, 2022a). In addition, Adolf Meyer also coined the term 'psychopathy' to describe various mental disorders and socially deviant behaviour (Lanzoni, 2018). Medical technology was rudimentary at the time and tools of diagnosis were inadequate, thus most causes for mental illnesses could be discovered only after the patients' death when a post-mortem analysis was conducted. During that era, empathy was used in the differential diagnosis of schizophrenia and maniac depression. Similarly, Carl Jung had differentiated between hysterics and schizophrenics on the basis of empathy and proposed that hysterics had an overload of empathic feeling while the schizophrenics had little or no empathy. Similar thoughts on schizophrenia were put forward by an American physician Roy G Hoskins who had conducted a long-term (20-year) study of schizophrenic patients; Hoskins had described empathy as a "social capacity rooted in biology" (Lanzoni, 2018, p. 71). Thus, the concept of empathy had now traversed from art and architecture to facilitate medical diagnosis and therapy (Moreto et al., 2017; Lanzoni, 2018; Roy, 2022a).

The post-World War II era witnessed significant changes in the world; among these changes were an attitudinal shift in the manner that people perceived others. The war had caused severe traumas on the psyche of the people and the images of death and destruction as well as the horrors of the holocaust cast an indelible impression on the minds of the people in those post-Freudian years. It was during these years that empathy evolved as a popular word and was listed in the Webster's collegiate dictionary in 1944 (the Concise Oxford dictionary listed it thereafter) (Lanzoni, 2018;

Roy, 2022a). The change in human attitude towards others led to movements like American civil rights movements and the dissolution of oppressive colonial forms of government in many parts of the world.

The post-war years understandably witnessed increased importance for the practice of psychotherapy, especially in the treatment of post-traumatic stress disorders among soldiers who had witnessed the horrors of the war from close quarters. During that time an American psychologist named Carl Rogers pioneered an empathy-driven approach to the practice of psychotherapy. Rogers' approach was termed as client-centered approach (Rogers, 1951); it encouraged an understanding of the patients' problems and even co-experiencing them (Roy, 2022a) while discarding the traditional hierarchal models through which patients were judged and diagnosed (Lanzoni, 2018; Roy, 2022a). Carl Rogers described empathy within therapeutic context "as if one were the other person, but without ever losing the 'as if' condition" (Rogers, 1959, p. 210). Carl Rogers' method thus required the therapist to empathetically adopt the client's "frame of reference" (Lanzoni, 2018, p. 85). It was also around this time that the Swiss psychiatrist and psychoanalyst Carl Jung had coined the term wounded healer (Jung, 1951) which was based on the Greek mythology of Chiron. A wounded healer is a person who has faced some form of hardship or grief, as a result of which she is willing to help others facing such problems.

In the 1960s the concept of empathy was used within the analyses and study of child psychology especially within the context of developmental psychology. Jean Piaget (1896–1980), the noted Swiss developmental psychologist, had postulated that children below the age of seven were not capable of empathically connecting with others. Piaget had termed this phenomenon as egocentricism and clarified that such lack of empathy in children below seven was due to their inability to understand that other people could have thoughts, ideas or beliefs that were different to theirs (Anderman & Anderman, 2009; Roy, 2022a). Piaget had introduced two aspects of egocentricity in children: language and morality. He posited that the language aspect of egocentricity was apparent in children when they spoke to themselves while playing or when children surmised, when communicating with others that the audience knew the entire background of their discourse (Roy, 2022a). The moral aspect of egocentricity in children was evident in the fact that children are interested in the final outcomes of their action and tend to ignore the purpose and rationale of their actions (Fogiel, 1980; Roy, 2022a). Over the years, however, Piaget's postulates have been widely disputed and several studies have shown that even infants exhibit empathic connections and express reactions of distress when they hear the sound of another infant crying; this phenomenon has been described as reflexive crying or emotional contagion (McDonald & Messinger, 2011; Martin & Clark, 1982).

An extension of the influence of empathy in developmental psychology had been witnessed in the analysis of autism spectrum disorder. Developmental psychologists have reported a link between empathy and autism. It was in this regard that a British developmental psychologist Simon Baron-Cohen had proposed the mind-blindness theory of autism wherein he had posited that mind blindness is a state wherein individuals cannot put themselves in other person's shoes and thus cannot understand the other person's thoughts, feelings or even expressions on the other person's face (Baron-Cohen et al., 1985; Baron-Cohen, 1995). Over the years, the reaction to Baron-Cohen's theory has been mixed. Some studies had reported that autistic children, even those with high IQ levels, showed compromised performance levels in tasks requiring empathy (Yirmiya et al., 1992; Dyck et al., 2001; Roy, 2022a). However, certain other experts like Cook (2013) and Taylor (2017) had disagreed with Baron-Cohen and his theory of mind blindness.

If empathy was to be presented as an acceptable scientific construct, it was imperative that the physiological aspects of the phenomenon be studied and the results collated with acceptable medical explanations. The early approaches to the study of psychology involved the concept of dualism which posited that the mind and the body were distinctly separate entities. However, with advancements in medical science, it was clear to physicians that most aspects of human behaviour were connected to physiological processes. In 1822 a French physiologist François Magendie identified the difference between spinal nerves that transmit messages from the sensory receptors present in the skin (sensory nerves) and those that carry messages to the muscles for motor action (Motor nerves).[4] Further, researchers in the nineteenth century had begun to posit that different parts of the brain performed different functions (Gray, 2007; Roy, 2022a). In this context Pierre Paul Broca had presented the first definitive proof of localization of different brain functions (Roy, 2022a). During the early years of medical research on the brain and its functions, the research activities were severely constrained by the lack of technology. Illnesses of the brain were most often diagnosed during post mortem examinations when the patient had already died. The lack of technology made it impossible to study the functioning of a live brain. However, in the twentieth century as several advanced equipment like the CT scan, MRI and fMRI were invented, it was possible to study the functioning of the live brain. In fact, equipment like the functional Magnetic Resonance Imaging (fMRI) and Transcranial Magnetic Stimulation (TMS) can now study the functioning of the brain in real time, thus allowing psychologists to study and derive causal relationships between human behaviour and the different parts of the brain (Roy, 2022a). Understandably, the advancement of technology has noticeably aided empirical studies on the physiological aspects of empathy and has provided researchers in empathy with the much-needed scientific models that govern and regulate empathic behaviour.

Discussions on the physiological aspects of empathy are divided into two schools of thought: the theory of the mind and the simulation theory. Jankowiak-Siuda et al. (2011) described these theories as the top-down and bottom-up models of neural processing. The simulation theory, which is a bottom-up model, posits that when individuals observe others' behaviour or emotions, they replicate the same emotions or behaviour within themselves to try and understand how it feels (Lopez, 2010; Roy, 2022a). The physiological argument for the simulation theory was augmented through the discovery of a set of neurons that were termed as mirror neurons. The mirror neurons were discovered by an Italian Neurologist Giacomo Rizzolatti and his team (Rizzolatti et al., 1996; Rizzolatti & Craighero, 2004; Rizzolatti & Fabbri-Destro, 2010; Roy, 2022a). The unique feature of mirror neurons is that they are not only activated when individuals perform certain actions but also when the individuals observe others perform the same actions, thus mirroring the actions of others. Mirror neurons are automatic and do not need to be consciously activated and they not only mirror actions but also 'emotions and mental states' (Hamilton, 2013, p. 92). Numerous studies have been conducted on the role of the mirror neuron system on empathic human behaviour. Calvo-Merino et al. (2005) studied the effect of mirror neurons on expert dancers. The researchers divided a set of individuals into three groups: the first group consisted of individuals who were expert classical ballet dancers, the second group consisted of individuals who were expert capoeira dancers, while the third group consisted of individuals who were not experts in any form of dancing (the third group was included as the control group). The members of all the three groups were shown videos of ballet dancing and Capoeira dance, and their brain activities were studied through functional magnetic resonance imaging (fMRI). The researchers reported that the mirror neuron system in the individuals exhibited higher levels of activation when the individuals were shown videos of dances in which they were experts in contrast to videos of dances in which they were not proficient. Thus, experts of a dance form exhibited empathic connection with dancers of the same dance form due to the activation of the mirror neuron system (Calvo-Merino et al., 2005; Roy, 2022a). Lahav et al. (2007) conducted a similar study with a group of pianists and found that mirror neurons were activated when the pianists listened to a piece of music that they had recently learnt. The activation of the mirror neuron system is however not limited to dance and music. Sapolsky (2017) reported that the cells from an area of the brain known as the anterior cingulate cortex responds to an individual's pain; the cells from the same area of the brain are also activated when the individual witnesses another individual in pain. The anterior cingulate cortex is very closely connected to empathy. Sapolsky (2017) had commented, "when it comes to empathy, all neurobiological roads pass through the anterior cingulate cortex" (Sapolsky, 2017, p. 528). The concept of mirror neurons has also been used to explain autism spectrum disorder. The Broken Mirror Theory (Hamilton, 2013) posits that autism spectrum disorder could find its cause within a malfunction in the mirror neuron system. Ramachandran and Oberman (2006) had concurred with this posit and commented, "findings provide compelling evidence that people with autism have dysfunctional mirror neuron systems" (Ramachandran & Oberman, 2006, p. 67).

The alternate to the simulation theory is the top-down model of neural processing which is known as the Theory of the Mind (Jankowiak-Siuda et al., 2011; Roy, 2022a). The concept was first put forward by Premack and Woodruff (1978) after observing the phenomena in adult chimpanzees. The Theory of the Mind was described by Thompson (2017) as "understanding another person's knowledge, beliefs, emotions, and intentions and using that understanding to navigate social situations" (Thompson, 2017). The Theory of the Mind develops in children at around the age of four; however, children with autism spectrum disorder exhibit delays in such development (Roy, 2022a). An interesting characteristic of the Theory of Minds was proposed by Dvash and Shamay-Tsoor (2014) who posited that the Theory of Minds presents with two dimensions: cognitive and affective, while different areas of the brain are activated in relation to these two dimensions. The cognitive dimension is related to the awareness of intentions and mindset of the other person while the affective dimension is related to an understanding of the feelings. While the simulation theory and the theory of the mind are exclusive in nature, a third neurological model known as the dual route system (Yu & Chou, 2018) proposes that empathy exists within a dual neurological route: a lower route which is fast and automatic and is related to affective empathy and a higher route which is slower and complex and is related to cognitive empathy. The lower route is related to the mirror neuron system.

An alternate approach to the theory of mind is the empathizing-systemizing theory (Baron-Cohen, 2009). This theory introduces the concept of systemizing which is defined as "the drive to analyze or construct systems" (Baron-Cohen, 2009, p. 71). The individual propensity to systemize is evaluated by a measure known as the Systemization Quotient. A higher systemization score projects a higher propensity to systemize. Thus, individuals who tend to prioritize systemization through the recognition of rules and regulations score high on Systemization Quotient. It is empirically observed that individuals with Autism or Asperger's Syndrome sometimes score higher on the Systemization Quotient over the general population. Baron-Cohen (2009) reported that females are high on empathizing while males are better at systemizing.

Studies linking brain functions to empathic behaviour have found that different regions of the brain are involved in the complex process that leads to empathic behaviour (Roy, 2022a). A group of scientists from Cambridge University have reported that empathy is partly linked to genes; however, women were more empathic than men due to social and non-genetic factors (University of Cambridge, 2018; Warrier et al., 2018).

The operationalization of psychological constructs presents as a complex and often difficult exercise, frequently hindered by subjective interventions and differential interpretations of the construct. Empathy, being a fundamentally polysemic construct, presents with similar complexities and problems in its operationalization. Elmer Ernest Southard had developed a scale to measure in 1918, to assist in the differential diagnosis of schizophrenia (Roy, 2022a). In 1949 a Cornell university psychologist Rosalind Dymond attempted to operationalize empathy in a methodical and scientific manner. Her first attempt involved the measurement of empathy through the Thematic Apperception Test (TAT) that had been developed by Henry Murray and Christina D. Morgan (Morgan & Murray, 1938; Morgan, 1995). Later Dymond developed a rigorous instrument to evaluate empathy through a quantitative process. This test consisted of a questionnaire that contained four parts with six identical items:

self-confidence, superior-inferior, selfish-unselfish, friendly-unfriendly, leader-follower and sense of humour (Dymond, 1949). Subsequently, several scales were developed for measuring empathy; prominent among those were the Empathy Test (Kerr & Speroff, 1951), Diplomacy Test for Empathy (Kerr, 1960), Hogan Empathy Scale (Hogan, 1969), Questionnaire Measure of Emotional Empathy (Mehrabian & Epstein, 1972), Interpersonal Reactivity Index (Davis, 1980) and The Toronto Empathy Questionnaire (Spreng et al., 2009). At the organizational level, Roy (2022b) developed and successfully pilot tested an instrument named School Empathy Audit Battery (SEAB) to evaluate empathy within school organizations.

Modern discussions on empathy often revolve around the question as to whether empathy is a trait that is inherent in individuals and thus cannot be learnt and inculcated, or is it a skill-based behaviour that one learns and can be inculcated in individuals through training? Some experts describe it as both. Experts have variously described empathy as a capacity, ability and skill thus recognizing that empathic behaviour can be inculcated by individuals through training and learning processes. In this context, Ioannidou and Konstantikaki (2008) had presented an interesting difference between sympathy and empathy; the researchers described sympathy as "emotional reaction, immediate and uncontrolled" (Ioannidou & Konstantikaki, 2008, p. 119) while empathy was described as "a skill learned or an attitude of life" (Ioannidou & Konstantikaki, 2008, p. 119). However, when empathic behaviour is contextualized within the physiological neural processes and genetic dispositions that are supposed to influence and in fact control such behaviour, it becomes evident that empathic behaviour does present with at least some elements of inherent trait. Decety (2012) had described empathy as "natural capacity to share, understand, and respond with care to the affective states of others" (Decety, 2012 as quoted in van Dongen, 2020, p. 1). This description of empathy however explains empathy as a trait rather than a skill. Ratka (2018) had explained, "Neuroscience discoveries demonstrate that the human brain is hardwired for empathy" (Ratka, 2018, p. 1140); however, the researcher had recognized the malleable nature of empathy and its ability to be influenced by interventions such as education and training or other factors such as cultural differences and life experiences.

It is widely accepted that the progress of human civilization has been broadly driven by the mental capacity of humans to logically and rationally analyse problems and solve them; to understand complex thoughts and ideas; to learn from circumstances and experiences and to use the knowledge that is acquired through such learning within similar situations in future. This mental capacity of humans to engage in such advanced and complex cognitive tasks is commonly referred to as intelligence. While humans possess limited physical prowess as compared to other animals, the human race has survived and flourished mostly due to their higher levels of intelligence. Consequently, humans have utilised their intellectual capacities to create better quality of life with enhanced life expectancies for fellow humans. However, as the human race has evolved into an increasingly interconnected and complex entity, empathy has evolved as an important evolutionary mechanism which is essential for survival. The connection between the traditional concept of intelligence with that of empathy is complex and oftentimes bewildering. Freehill (1974) had reported that the correlation between empathy and intelligence was "commonly low, often low-negative" (Freehill, 1974, p. 248). In a contrasting note, Guo et al. (2019) reported that fluid intelligence is positively correlated to pro-social behaviour. While the connection between empathy and intelligence as described in its classical sense has been reported to be curious, the relation is however overwhelmingly dependent on the approach towards the description and definition of the concept of intelligence itself. In this regard it will be pertinent to note that intelligence has been described through many diverse ideations some of which have been closely connected with empathy. The prominent among these are emotional intelligence and the concept of multiple intelligences.

In his book *Frames of mind*, Dr Howard Gardner had proposed a Theory of Multiple Intelligences (Gardner, 2011). The Theory of Multiple Intelligences that Dr Gardner had proposed consisted of eight distinct areas of intelligences that were supposed to comprehensively constitute human intelligence. These areas were interpersonal, intrapersonal, naturalistic, logical, literary, spatial, musical and kinesthetic. A ninth area namely moralistic was added subsequently. Several influential studies have been conducted to ascertain the relationship between the model proposed by Gardner and empathic behaviour. It is widely posited that empathy is closely related to interpersonal intelligence. Dien and Wustqa (2018) had reported that three indicators of empathic behaviour, namely sensitivity towards others' feelings, providing attention to others and understanding the desires and wants of others were influencers of interpersonal intelligence. Berrocal et al. (2008) had opined "Interpersonal intelligence is the ability to relate to and understand others" (Berrocal et al., 2008, p. 127).

The researchers had further explained that interpersonal intelligence helps individuals to "try to see things from other individuals' perspectives in order to understand how the other person thinks and feels" (Berrocal et al., 2008, p. 127). Giannopoulou et al. (2016) had studied the relationship between musical intelligence and empathy among adolescents and found that the relationship was stronger for females over males.

Over the ensuing decades of the twentieth century, the traditional concept of intelligence was expanded to include several alternate ideations of the term. In this regard Michael Beldoch (1964) had introduced the concept of emotional intelligence. The Oxford Dictionary of Psychology described emotional intelligence as the "Ability to monitor one's own and other people's emotions, to discriminate between different emotions and label them appropriately, and to use emotional information to guide thinking and behaviour" (Colman, 2003, p. 246). However, the term emotional intelligence as its fundamental ideation was popularized by an American psychologist named Daniel Goleman. Daniel Goleman's book *Emotional Intelligence — Why It Can Matter More Than IQ* (1995) had helped to promote the concept among a wide range of audience, and emotional intelligence was mainstreamed as an important alternate measure of human competency (Roy, 2022a). Goleman's work encouraged further research in the area, and as a result three separate models of emotional intelligence were conceived and proposed by experts. The first of these was the trait model of emotional intelligence which was proposed by Konstantinos Vasilis Petrides. This model lay emphasis on self-reporting and thus emotional intelligence according to the trait model was essentially an individual's self-perception of his or her emotional abilities (Petrides & Furnham, 2001; Roy, 2022a). Later, in 2004, Mayer et al. developed the ability model of emotional intelligence and described emotional intelligence as "the capacity to reason about emotions, and of emotions to enhance thinking. It includes the abilities to accurately perceive emotions, to access and generate emotions so as to assist thought, to understand emotions and emotional knowledge, and to reflectively regulate emotions so as to promote emotional and intellectual growth" (Mayer et al., 2004, p. 197). The ability model described emotional intelligence as the ability to perceive, understand and manage emotions both in the context of one's own self and in reference to others (Roy, 2022a). The third model of emotional intelligence was presented by Daniel Goleman. The model presented by Goleman is often referred to as the mixed model; it uses five distinct constructs to describe emotional intelligence:

self-regulation, self-awareness, social skills, motivation and empathy (Goleman, 1995, 1998). According to Goleman, the five constructs present as skills which could be learnt and not inherent traits (Boyatzis et al., 2000). Several studies were conducted to explore the relationship between emotional intelligence and empathy. In one such study, Fernandez-Abascal and Martin-Diaz (2019) reported that emotional intelligence was positively related to empathic perspective taking and negative related to empathic personal distress.

The modern theorization of empathy often revolves around the model that was proposed by Paul Ekman. Within this model empathy includes three distinct dimensions: cognitive, affective and compassion (Ekman, 2003; Roy, 2022a). The cognitive dimension of empathic behaviour involves understanding a situation or problem from the other person's point of view while the affective or emotional dimension of empathy involves feeling as the other. The compassion aspect of empathy involves taking actionable steps to mitigate the suffering of the other person(s). The concept of cognitive empathy steps beyond mere benevolence to include strategic behaviour like negotiations and bargaining where it is important to understand a problem from the opponent's point of view. Affective empathy involves feeling like the other. It is often observed that feeling like the other in certain situations might have grave implications for the empath. If nurses continuously feel as the patient's kin, they could develop a mental condition known as compassion fatigue which leads to burn outs and mental trauma. Compassionate action might occur as a consequence of cognitive understanding of a person's situation even if affective empathy is absent. Thus, it is enough to understand a situation from the other's point of view in order to take steps to mitigate their suffering, feeling as the other is not necessary for compassionate action. This dimension is important while designing empathic social systems wherein the entities would require to understand a situation from the other's point view as a precursor to compassionate action often in absence of affective empathy.

It is pertinent, in the context of the topic which this book attempts to discuss, that the discussion on empathy be extrapolated from mere individual behaviour to the larger context of social systems. In fact, empathy is considered by many to be an evolutionary mechanism which has evolved among social beings like humans and primates to facilitate and ensure their survival in social groups. Charles Darwin is reported to have recognized sympathy as one of the strongest human instincts to evolve (Goetz et al.,

2010) and had posited that sympathy "will have been increased through natural selection; for those communities, which included the greatest number of the most sympathetic members, would flourish best, and rear the greatest number of offspring" (Darwin, 1871, p. 88). In the absence of a distinct concept of empathy during the Darwinian era, it could be argued that the phenomenon described by Darwin as sympathy was in fact empathy. Maibom (2017) had concurred "Darwin also thought that sympathy was the more proximate mechanism of altruistic action. Since he was inspired by Hume, and Hume's sympathy is what we now call empathy, we can assume that he had empathy in mind" (p. 4). De Waal (2009) had explained this succinctly, "Many animals survive not by eliminating each other or keeping everything for themselves, but by cooperating and sharing. This applies most definitely to pack hunters, such as wolves or killer whales, but also to our closest relatives, the primates" (pp. 6–7). Segal (2011) had described social empathy "as the ability to more deeply understand people by perceiving or experiencing their life situations and as a result gain insight into structural inequalities and disparities" (p. 266). Segal's model of social empathy consisted of three components: "individual empathy, contextual understanding, and social responsibility" (Segal, 2011, p. 266). The objective of social empathy is to gain useful insights into the socio-economic inequalities and disparities that exist within societal structures with view to improve the socio-economic conditions of the deprived sections of the society. Empathy might be important within social relationships too. Morelli et al. (2017) had reported within their study that people with high levels of empathy were central to social relationships and networks that were defined by trust. The researchers further reported that in case something bad happens people turn to individuals with higher levels of empathy for help. Further, empathy is found to increase individuals' engagement in pro-social activities like volunteering (Chung et al., 2021). Hoffman (1989) had argued that social situations that involve justice frequently include individuals or groups who could be in distress (emotional, economic or even physical) and that there is evidence to the effect that the common human response to others in distress involves an empathic element. The empathic distress that is created within such situations motivates compassionate behaviour to reduce the suffering of those in need. The motivation for such empathic behaviour however is triggered by the need to reduce one's own empathic distress or egotistical needs. Hoffman (1989) further explains that reactions in such situations may involve empathic anger at the culprit for causing the harm to the victim.

The example of a child getting angry and attacking a doctor who was administering an injection (and thus causing pain) to another child was given. Hoffman (1989) also explained that empathic reactions to situations involving justice might also produce as guilt. Empathic guilt manifests in situations when the empath has caused harm to a victim as also when the empath is innocent but has remained as a mere bystander when the victim was harmed.

While discussing the various aspects of empathy, it is necessary to recognize and deliberate upon the fact that empathy is not a wholly benevolent concept per se. While literature on the concept largely presents benevolence as the sine qua non for empathic behaviour, such a surmise only serves to oversimplify a complex construct. The first limitation of empathy lies within the understanding that awareness of a person's problem might not present as a potent motivator to help the person. David Brookes (2011) had explained this succinctly: "Empathy makes you more aware of other people's suffering, but it's not clear it actually motivates you to take moral action or prevents you from taking immoral action." In order to emphasize his point, Brookes (2011) had shared the case of certain Nazi soldiers who would weep while they carried on killing Jewish women and children. Brookes (2011) further described empathy as a "'fragile flower,' easily crushed by self-concern." An identical view of empathy was propounded by Prinz (2011) who had posited "empathy is not a major player when it comes to moral motivation. Its contribution is negligible in children, modest in adults, and non-existent when costs are significant" (p. 221).

It is recognized by many researchers that empathy can be used with malevolent intentions and cognitive empathy has been used to promote violence and fascism. The use of empathy with malevolent intentions has been termed as tactical empathy (Bubandt & Willerslev, 2015). Bubandt and Willerslev (2015) presented the case of Yukaghir hunters who masquerade as male moose to attract female moose to hunt them. The hunters use their empathic understanding of female moose behaviour to kill them. The researchers also cited the case of a religious riot in Indonesia where empathic understanding was used with malevolent intentions. The researchers commented, "The Siberian hunter and the Indonesian letter-writer are both using empathy to identify with the particular bodily states and experiences of a significant other in order to mimic, with varying degrees of fidelity, the senses and sensibilities of that other. Yet both turn the empathic faculty violently against that other" (Bubandt & Willerslev,

2015, p. 7). Wispé (1986) had thus commented, "empathy can be not only perverted but also abused. For example, it has been said that the Nazis attached howling devices to their dive bombers during World War II to create fear and panic among those about to be bombed. In this instance, their accurate use of empathy allowed them to predict the impact of their inventions" (Wispé, 1986, p. 319). As is evident from the cases cited, empathic understanding is sometimes connected with an objective to deceive and even harm. This phenomenon is also very common, albeit in a passive form, within the world of competitive gambling like poker where players adjust their games according to their empathic understanding of the opponent's behaviour (Roy, 2022a).

The recognition and use of the malevolent potential of empathy, especially cognitive empathy, is not new and there are examples of the malevolent use of empathy among some ethnic groups since ancient times (Roy, 2022a). Hollan and Throop (2008) had reported that members of the Yapese, highland Maya, Inuit and Torajan communities understand that intimate knowledge of their communities might be used by enemies to harm them and thus they consciously try to block such knowledge from others. Hollan and Throop (2008) had thus explained, "In the extreme, they may fear others will use empathic-like knowledge to physically harm or kill, as the highland Maya do. But even as in the case of the Inuit, where personal knowledge is used not to harm blatantly but to shame and humiliate with the ostensible purpose of teaching people how to behave properly, we see how potentially hurtful such information can be" (Hollan & Throop, 2008, p. 392).

Many a times, real-life situations present with serious paradoxes where, even when faced with grievous crimes it is difficult to wholly empathize with the victim. Some incidents of violent crime have retribution as a primary objective. Such crimes might have their source within some grievous harm that was caused to the accused by the victim. Most often such violent crimes create an empathic division with peoples' opinions being divided on the matter as to who to empathize with. Consequently, most acts of violence whether political, racial or even retributory in nature result in individuals and groups empathizing with one party in the conflict or the other. Roy (2022a) had posited "Empathy does not present with a clear black and white categorical division on ethical or humanitarian principles and very often the moral lines separating the oppressor and the oppressed are blurred by circumstances, biases and the weight of historical and experiences" (Roy, 2022a, p. 68). This aspect of empathic dilemma transcends into most situations which might encourage division in opinion. Thus, in every controversial case whether it be land acquisition, migration, green energy or abortion rights, opinion is strongly divided on one side or the other. Further empathy is not a fair and equitable phenomenon based on moralistic judgements, rather empathy is a biased emotion. Paul Bloom (2016) had explained, "We are not psychologically constituted to feel toward a stranger as we feel toward someone we love. We are not capable of feeling a million times worse about the suffering of a million than about the suffering of one" (Bloom, 2016, p. 81). In fact, humans tend to feel more empathic towards a friend rather than towards a stranger; this cognitive bias is known as friendship bias. Hoffman (2007) had explained friendship bias as "empathic distress toward the 'friend' than toward the 'acquaintance'" (Hoffman, 2007, p. 207). This aspect of empathy is further noted within the phenomenon of in-group empathy bias wherein individuals are more empathic towards others of their own group. Thus, for example, teachers are more empathic towards other teachers and doctors are more empathic towards other doctors. In addition, empathic behaviour is also influenced by a cognitive bias known as the here-and-now bias. The here-and-now bias had been described by Hoffman (2007) as "empathy is naturally biased in favor of victims in the immediate situation because the automatic, involuntary, and salient empathy-arousing processes (conditioning, association, mimicry) require situational and personal cues that are at their peak when a victim is present" (Hoffman, 2007, p. 209).

The discussion within this chapter sought to acquaint the reader with a brief but nevertheless comprehensive idea about the history and development of this interesting and important psychological phenomenon. The history of empathy began as an abstract polysemic concept which seemed to have influenced diverse fields of thoughts ranging from the aesthetic domains of visual arts and architecture to the emotional realms of poetry. Empathy, however, was not confined within the sphere of artistic and literary works and was used as a scientific basis to diagnose mental illnesses and conditions likes schizophrenia and autism. Over the decades, with the advancement of technology, it was possible to study and recognize the neurological basis of empathic behaviour and the discovery of mirror neurons helped to establish the scientific background for the phenomenon. The concept of empathy has been studied within the context of diverse fields like psychology, sociology, military strategy, business management and organizational behaviour, economics, political science, computer science, medicine and neurology, fine arts, architecture and literature. It is rare for what is fundamentally a psychological concept to have been studied and explored with the context of such diverse and multiple fields of thought. The reason for this could be the important evolutionary role that empathy plays in sustaining life among animals that live in social groups; in fact, empathy could be posited to be a fundamental driver for social existence. If the importance of empathy for social existence is to be recognized, it is essential to study that the role of empathy within the different social systems that account for humans living as a community. Economics is one such system and in the ensuing chapters this book will attempt to contextualize the important psychological phenomenon of empathy within the science of economics.

Notes

1. Sympathy translates to 'with suffering.'
2. Panpsychism, which is derived from the word 'pan' (meaning all) and 'psyche' (meaning mind) proposes that all objects possess consciousness.
3. In an interesting attempt, the American poet and psychologist June Downey had studied the relationship between empathy and poetry. She had explored in detail the reactions of readers to poetry and the mental images that were created within the minds of the readers as assisted by poetry. See Hogan and Broudy (2000).
4. This is known as the Bell–Magendie law in medical science.

References

Agosta, L. (n.d.). *Empathy and sympathy in ethics. Internet encyclopedia of philosophy.* Retrieved February 22, 2022, from https://www.iep.utm.edu/emp-symp/

Anderman, E. M., & Anderman, L. H. (*2009*). Egocentrism. In E. M. Anderman & L. H. Anderman (Eds.), *Psychology of classroom learning: An encyclopedia* (Vol. 1, pp. 355–357). Gale Cengage Learning.

Baron-Cohen, S. (1995). *Learning, development, and conceptual change. Mindblindness: An essay on autism and theory of mind.* The MIT Press.

Baron-Cohen, S. (2009). Autism: The empathizing-systemizing (E-S) theory. *Annals of the New York Academy of Sciences, 1156*(*1*), *68–80.* https://doi.org/10.1111/j.1749-6632.2009.04467

Baron-Cohen, S., et al. (1985). Does the autistic child have a "theory of mind"? *Cognition, 21*(1), 37–46. https://doi.org/10.1016/0010-0277(85)90022-8

Beldoch, M. (1964). Sensitivity to emotional expression in three modes of communication. In J. R. Davitz (Ed.), *The communication of emotional meaning*. McGraw-Hill.

Berrocal, P., et al. (2008). Assessment of emotional and multiple intelligences. In D. Martines (Ed.), *Multicultural school psychology competencies: A practical guide*. SAGE Publications, Inc. https://doi.org/10.4135/9781452231624

Bloom, P. (2016). *Against empathy. The case for rational compassion*. Harper Collins.

Boyatzis, R., et al. (2000). Clustering competence in emotional intelligence: Insights from the emotional competence inventory (ECI). In R. Bar-On & J. D. A. Parker (Eds.), *Handbook of emotional intelligence*. Jossey-Bass.

Brookes, D. (2011). *The limits of empathy*. Retrieved April 30, 2020, from https://www.nytimes.com/2011/09/30/opinion/brooks-the-limits-of-empathy.html

Bubandt, N., & Willerslev, R. (2015). The dark side of empathy: Mimesis, deception, and the magic of alterity. *Comparative Studies in Society and History, 57*(1), 5–34. https://doi.org/10.1017/S0010417514000589

Calvo-Merino, B., et al. (2005). Action observation and acquired motor skills: An FMRI study with expert dancers. *Cerebral Cortex, 8*, 1243–1249. https://doi.org/10.1093/cercor/bhi007

Chung, Y. W., et al. (2021). Can empathy help individuals and society? Through the lens of volunteering and mental health. *Healthcare, 9*(1406). https://doi.org/10.3390/healthcare9111406

Colman, A. M. (2003). *Oxford dictionary of psychology*. Oxford University Press.

Cook, R., et al. (2013). Alexithymia, not autism, predicts poor recognition of emotional facial expressions. *Psychological Science, 24*, 723–732. https://doi.org/10.1177/0956797612463582

Darwin, C. (1871). *The descent of man, and selection in relation to sex* (p. 2004). Barnes and Nobles Books.

Davis, M. H. (1980). A multidimensional approach to individual differences in empathy. *Journal of Personality and Social Psychology, 10*(85) Retrieved April 20, 2023, from https://www.researchgate.net/publication/34891073_A_Multidimensional_Approach_to_Individual_Differences_in_Empathy

De Waal, F. (2009). *The age of empathy*. Harmony Books.

Decety, J. (2012). *Empathy: From bench to bedside*. MIT Press.

Dien, C. A., & Wustqa, D. U. (2018). The interpersonal intelligence profile of seventh-grade students in mathematics learning. *Journal of Physics Conference Series, 1108*, 012080. https://doi.org/10.1088/1742-6596/1108/1/012080

Dvash, J., & Shamay-Tsoor, G. S. (2014). Mind and empathy as multidimensional constructs neurological foundations. *Topics in Language Disorders, 34*(4), 282–295. https://doi.org/10.1097/TLD.0000000000000040

Dyck, M. J., et al. (2001). Do autism spectrum disorders differ from each other and from non-spectrum disorders on emotion recognition tests? *European Child and Adolescent Psychiatry, 10*(2), 105–116. https://doi.org/10.1007/s007870170033

Dymond, R. F. (1949). A scale for the measurement of empathy. *Journal of Consulting Psychology, 13*, 127–133. https://doi.org/10.1037/h0061728

Ekman, P. (2003). *Emotions revealed: Recognizing faces and feelings to improve communication and emotional life*. Times Books.

Fernández-Abascal, G. E., & Martín-Díaz, D. M. (2019). Emotional intelligence, specific aspects of empathy, and non-verbal sensitivity. *Frontiers in Psychology, 10*, 1066. https://doi.org/10.3389/fpsyg.2019.01066

Fogiel, M. (1980). *The psychology problem solver: A complete solution guide to any textbook*. Research & Education Association.

Freehill, M. F. (1974). Intelligence, empathy and methodologic bias about teaching the gifted. *The Gifted Child Quarterly, 18*(4), 247–248. https://doi.org/10.1177/001698627401800405

Ganczarek, J., et al. (2018). From "Einfühlung" to empathy: Exploring the relationship between aesthetic and interpersonal experience. *Cognitive Processing, 19*(2), 141–145. https://doi.org/10.1007/s10339-018-0861-x

Gardner, H. (2011). *Frames of mind: The theory of multiple intelligences*. Basic Books.

Giannopoulou, P., et al. (2016). Relating musical intelligence to empathy and aggression in adolescence. *Collective Volume of the Scientific Conference Determinants and Prospects in Education, 1*(1), 67–76.

Goetz, J. L., et al. (2010). Compassion: An evolutionary analysis and empirical review. *Psychological Bulletin, 136*, 351–374. https://doi.org/10.1037/a0018807

Goleman, D. (1995). *Emotional intelligence: Why it can matter more than IQ*. Bantam Books.

Goleman, D. (1998). *Working with emotional intelligence*. Bantam Books.

Gray, P. (2007). *Psychology* (5th ed.). Worth Publishers.

Guo, Q., et al. (2019). Why are smarter individuals more prosocial? A study on the mediating roles of empathy and moral identity. *Intelligence, 75*, 1–8. https://doi.org/10.1016/j.intell.2019.02.006

Hamilton, A. (2013). Reflecting on the mirror neuron system in autism: A systematic review of current theories. *Developmental Cognitive Neuroscience, 3*, 91–105. https://doi.org/10.1016/j.dcn.2012.09.008

Hoffman, M. L. (1989). Empathic emotions and justice in society. *Social Justice Research, 3*(4), 283–311. https://doi.org/10.1007/bf01048080

Hoffman, M. L. (2007). *Empathy and moral development. Implications for caring and justice*. Cambridge University Press.

Hogan, R. (1969). Development of an empathy scale. *Journal of Consulting and Clinical Psychology, 33*(3), 307–316. https://doi.org/10.1037/h0027580

Hogan, D. J., & Broudy, S. M. (2000). June Etta Downey. *The Feminist Psychologist, Newsletter of the Society for the Psychology of Women*, Division 35 of the American Psychological Association, *27*(2).

Hollan, D., & Throop, J. (2008). Whatever happened to empathy? Introduction. *Ethos, 36*(4), 385–401. https://doi.org/10.1111/j.1548-1352.2008.00023.x

Hume, D. (1739–40). *A treatise of human nature.* Oxford University Press, 1978.

Ioannidou, F., & Konstantikaki, V. (2008). Empathy and emotional intelligence: What is it really about? *International Journal of Caring Sciences, 1*(3), 118–123.

Jankowiak-Siuda, K., et al. (2011). How we empathize with others: A neurobiological perspective. *Medical Science Monitor, 17*(1), RA18-24. https://doi.org/10.12659/MSM.881324

Jung, C. (1951). *Fundamental questions of psychotherapy.* Princeton University Press.

Kerr, W. A. (1960). *Diplomacy test of empathy, form "A", (manual).* Psychometric Affiliates.

Kerr, W. A., & Speroff, B. J. (1951). *Manual for the empathy test.* Psychometric Affiliates.

Lahav, A., et al. (2007). Action representation of sound: Audiomotor recognition network while listening to newly acquired actions. *Journal of Neuroscience, 27*(2), 308–314. https://doi.org/10.1523/JNEUROSCI.4822-06.2007

Lamb, S. (2015). Social skills: Adolf Meyer's revision of clinical skill for the new psychiatry of the twentieth century. *Medical History, 59*(3), 443–464. https://doi.org/10.1017/mdh.2015.29

Langfeld, H. S. (1920). *The aesthetic attitude.* Harcourt, Brace, & Howe.

Langfeld, S. H. (1927). Consciousness and motor response. *Psychological Review, 34*(1), 1–9. https://doi.org/10.1037/h0070746

Langfeld, S. H. (1931). A response interpretation of consciousness. *Psychological Review, 38*(2), 87–108. https://doi.org/10.1037/h0073454

Lanzoni, S. (2018). *Empathy – A history.* Yale University Press.

Lieberman, A., & Ogas, J. (2015). *Shrinks: The untold story of psychiatry.* Hachette UK.

Lipps, T. (1905). *Aesthetik* (Vol. 2). Voss Verlag.

Lopez, R. (2010). *Empathy 101. How do we empathize?* Retrieved March 3, 2020, from https://www.psychologytoday.com/intl/blog/our-social-brains/201007/empathy-101

Maibom, H. L. (2017). Introduction to philosophy of empathy. In H. L. Maibom (Ed.), *The Routledge handbook of philosophy of empathy.* Routledge.

Martin, G. B., & Clark, R. D. (1982). Distress crying in neonates: Species and peer specificity. *Developmental Psychology, 18*(1), 3–9. https://doi.org/10.1037/0012-1649.18.1.3

Mayer, J. D., et al. (2004). Emotional intelligence: Theory, findings, and implications. *Psychological Inquiry, 15*, 197–215. https://doi.org/10.1207/s15327965pli1503_02

McDonald, M. N., & Messinger, S. D. (2011). The development of empathy; how when and why. In A. Acerbi, J. A. Lombo, & J. J. Sanguineti (Eds.), *Free will, emotions and moral actions; philosophy and neuroscience in dialogue*. IF-Press.

Mehrabian, A., & Epstein, N. (1972). A measure of emotional empathy. *Journal of Personality, 40*(4), 525–543. https://doi.org/10.1111/j.1467-6494.1972.tb00078.x

Morelli, S. A., et al. (2017). Empathy and well-being correlate with centrality in different social networks. *Proceedings of the National Academy of Sciences, 114*(37), 9843–9847. https://doi.org/10.1073/pnas.1702155114

Moreto, G., et al. (2017). Assessing empathy among medical students: A comparative analysis using two different scales in a Brazilian medical school. *Educacion Medica, 19*(S2), 162–170. https://doi.org/10.1016/j.edumed.2017.07.019

Morgan, W. (1995). Origin and history of the thematic apperception test images. *Journal of Personality Assessment, 65*(2), 237–254. https://doi.org/10.1207/s15327752jpa65/02_2

Morgan, D. C., & Murray, A. H. (1938). Thematic apperception test. In H. A. Murray (Ed.), *Explorations in personality*. Oxford University Press, 2008.

Petrides, K. V., & Furnham, A. (2001). Trait emotional intelligence: Psychometric investigation with reference to established trait taxonomies. *European Journal of Personality, 15*, 425–448. https://doi.org/10.1002/per.416

Premack, D., & Woodruff, G. (1978). Does the chimpanzee have a theory of mind? *Behavioral and Brain Sciences, 1*(4), 515–526. https://doi.org/10.1017/s0140525x00076512

Prinz, J. (2011). Is empathy necessary for morality? In A. Cplan & P. Goldie (Eds.), *Empathy: Philosophical and psychological perspectives* (pp. 211–229). https://doi.org/10.1093/acprof:oso/9780199539956.003.0014

Ramachandran, S. V., & Oberman, L. (2006). Broken mirrors: A theory of autism. *Scientific American, 295*(5), 62–69. https://doi.org/10.1038/scientificamerican1106-62

Ratka, A. (2018). Empathy and the development of affective skills. *American Journal of Pharmaceutical Education, 82*(10), 1140–1143. https://doi.org/10.5688/ajpe7192

Rizzolatti, G., & Craighero, L. (2004). The mirror-neuron system. *Annual Review of Neuroscience, 27*(*1*), *169–192*. https://doi.org/10.1146/annurev.neuro.27.070203.144230

Rizzolatti, G., & Fabbri-Destro, M. (2010). Mirror neurons: From discovery to autism. *Experimental Brain Research, 200*(3–4), 223–237. https://doi.org/10.1007/s00221-009-2002-3

Rizzolatti, G., et al. (1996). Premotor cortex and the recognition of motor actions. *Cognitive Brain Research, 3*(2), 131–141. https://doi.org/10.1016/0926-6410(95)00038-0

Rogers, C. (1951). *Client-centered therapy: Its current practice, implications, and theory*. Houghton Mifflin.

Rogers, C. (1959). A theory of therapy, personality, and interpersonal relationships as developed in the client-centered framework. In S. Koch (Ed.), *Psychology: A study of a science* (Vol. 3, pp. 184–256, 210). McGraw-Hill.

Roy, D. (2022a). *Empathy driven school systems. nature, concept and evolution*. Routledge.

Roy, D. (2022b). *Auditing for empathy – The new trend in Indian schools*. Think pieces series no. 30, Education. Retrieved April 20, 2023, from https://educationsouthasia.web.ox.ac.uk/

Sapolsky, R. (2017). *Behave: The biology of humans at our best and worst*. Bodley Head.

Segal, E. A. (2011). Social empathy: A model built on empathy, contextual understanding, and social responsibility that promotes social justice. *Journal of Social Service Research, 37*(3), 266–277. https://doi.org/10.1080/01488376.2011.564040

Smith, A. (1759). *The theory of moral sentiments*. August M. Kelley Publishers, 1966.

Spreng, R. N., et al. (2009). The Toronto Empathy Questionnaire: Scale development and initial validation of a factor-analytic solution to multiple empathy measures. *Journal of Personality Assessment, 91*(1), 62–71. https://doi.org/10.1080/00223890802484381

Stueber, K. (2019). Empathy. In E. N. Zalta (Ed.), *The Stanford encyclopedia of philosophy* (Fall 2019 ed.). Retrieved February 22, 2022, from https://plato.stanford.edu/archives/fall2019/entries/empathy/

Taylor, S. (2017). Is autism really an "Empathy Disorder"? *Psychology Today*. Retrieved February 15, 2020, from https://www.psychologytoday.com/intl/blog/out-the-darkness/201705/is-autism-really-empathy-disorder

Thompson, N. B. (2017). *Theory of mind: Understanding others in a social world*. Retrieved March 11, 2020, from https://www.psychologytoday.com/us/blog/socioemotional-success/201707/theory-mind-understanding-others-in-social-world

University of Cambridge. (2018, March 12). Genes play a role in empathy. *ScienceDaily*. Retrieved August 26, 2020, from www.sciencedaily.com/releases/2018/03/180312085124.htm

van Dongen, J. D. M. (2020). The empathic brain of psychopaths: From social science to neuroscience in empathy. *Frontiers in Psychology, 11*, 695. https://doi.org/10.3389/fpsyg.2020.00695

Warrier, V., et al. (2018). Genome-wide analyses of self-reported empathy: Correlations with autism, schizophrenia, and anorexia nervosa. *Translational Psychiatry, 8*(1). https://doi.org/10.1038/s41398-017-0082-6

Watson, V. (2014). Colour sensation and Empathy: Arthur Schopenhauer's Negative Philosophy and colour theory as the basis of an elemental Colour Architecture. *Architectural Theory Review, 19*(2), 192–202. https://doi.org/10.1080/13264826.2014.967333

Wispé, L. (1986). The distinction between sympathy and empathy: To call forth a concept, a word is needed. *Journal of Personality and Social Psychology, 50*(2), 314–321.

Yirmiya, N., et al. (1992). Empathy and cognition in high functioning children with autism. *Child Development, 63*(1), 150–160. https://doi.org/10.2307/1130909

Yu, C., & Chou, T. (2018). A dual route model of empathy: A neurobiological prospective. *Frontiers in Psychology, 9*, 2212. https://doi.org/10.3389/fpsyg.2018.02212

CHAPTER 3

Empathy and Economic Thought

Chanakya (also known as Kautilya or Vishnugupta) was an ancient Indian teacher and philosopher who lived from 375 BC to 283 BC. In India he is regarded as one of the first proponents of the science of economics and its use in the art of statecraft. Chanakya wrote an influential work on political science titled *Arthashastra*; 'Arthashastra' literally means economics or the science of economics. Chanakya's vision of political governance relied heavily on economics; in fact, he had proposed that kings should learn the subject from experts. Chanakya understood that economics was the most vital component of politics, and if the citizens of a country were not provided with the means to procure basic amenities like food, clothing and shelter, the state would invariably fail and collapse. Conversely, Chanakya however also appreciated that the kings could remain powerful only by amassing wealth and power. Thus, the economic function of a Kautilyan state was two pronged: to provide its citizens with a comfortable life and to amass wealth through taxation and other economic means to enhance its power. The economy that Chanakya proposed was a mixed economy which promoted both state and private activities. Interestingly in a Kautilyan state, the king was not the owner of all the lands (as was the norm of the times), even private entities could own land alongside the king (Olivelle, 2013).

Importantly, a Kautilyan state was described as a form of what is now known as a welfare state with an empathic foundation. Chanakya had

D. Roy, *Empathonomics*,
https://doi.org/10.1007/978-981-95-4033-4_3

explained, "In the happiness of his subjects lies the king's happiness; in their welfare his welfare. He shall not consider as good only that which pleases him but treat as beneficial to – him whatever pleases his subjects" (Kautilya, 4th Century BC, p. x).[1] It might be argued that Chanakya's emphasis on an empathic king in a welfare state had strategic undercurrents and was fundamentally a master plan to thwart rebellions among the subjects. Chanakya had argued that "Discontented and impoverished people might be provoked to revolt; they may then kill their king or go over to the enemy" (Kautilya, 4th Century BC, p. 90). Thus, a king who was driven by self-interest would promote public interest but only as a mean to enhance his own self-interest. However, since a Kautilyan state involved a system wherein predominantly the self-interest of the king was in sync with the public interest, the citizens would enjoy better standards of living even as the king was promoting his self-interest. Fundamentally, Chanakya did emphasize on the importance of wealth and prosperity. He decried poverty and argued that ethical values can be preserved only when society is prosperous (Sihag, 2005). Thus, it might seem and not wholly without reason that Chanakya's dislike of poverty was not motivated by the predicament of the poor but by the threat that their suffering might present to the ruler. However, within the discourse in Arthashastra the king is often advised to rule as a father figure and importance is laid on just procedures. The empathic nature of the Kautilyan state is emphasized within the advice given to the king with regard to the governance of newly acquired territory wherein it is stated to the king that: "He shall adopt the way of life, dress, language and customs of the people [of the acquired territory], show the same devotion to the gods of the territory [as to his own gods] and participate in the people's festivals and amusements" (Kautilya, 4th Century BC, p. 741). The empathic advice however is not bereft of strategic intentions; if the king dresses and behaves like his subjects, he will be able to understand them better and put himself in their proverbial shoes. Chanakya had thus woven an intricate strategic thread around empathic governance where the wellbeing of the subjects was the not ultimate aim but rather just a means to consolidate and enjoy power.

Chanakya's ideations on governance might be placed within the view point of utilitarianism which is essentially a normative theorization of ethical actions that attempt to maximize happiness and wellbeing of the relevant party; the relevant party could be the ruler or the ruled as the situation and direction of perception demanded. The concept of Utilitarianism is fundamentally based on the concept of utility. Jeremy Bentham

(1748–1832), the English philosopher and economist, who is widely regarded as the founder of utilitarianism had explained: "By the principle of utility is meant that principle which approves or disapproves of every action whatsoever, according to the tendency which it appears to have to augment or diminish the happiness of the party whose interest is in question: or, what is the same thing in other words, to promote or to oppose that happiness. I say of every action whatsoever; and therefore not only of every action of a private individual, but of every measure of government" (Bentham, 2007, p. 14). In this regard, Bentham (2007) had explained that individual utility is anything that adds to the sum total of an individual's pleasure or diminishes the individual's pain and promotes his or her interest. In the context of a community, the interest of a community can be described as the aggregate interests of the members of the community. However, as some experts like Sugden (2002) have argued, if rational decision making within the realms of utilitarianism entails the maximization of individual pleasure and minimization of individual pain, then a common 'currency' for the measurement of such pain and pleasure has to be developed; in the absence of which, pleasure and pain, as is but natural, will present with divergent interpretations in relation to the parties concerned. Utilitarian theorizations involve a model wherein a dual framework of the individual and the community is involved. While individual decision making involves the maximization of individual pleasure and minimization of individual pain, community decisions involve a maximization of the aggregate pleasure of the community or minimization of the aggregate pain. The question thus arises as to whether individual decisions are strictly confined to the maximization of individual pleasure within the individual frame, or do individual decision makers exhibit empathic understanding and take into account the best interests of the community to which they belong? Sugden (2002) confirms that while at least some utilitarian thinkers propose that individual decisions are taken keeping in mind the larger interests of the community, utilitarian economists however feel that individual decisions by economic agents "are approximately rational with respect to the individual frame" (Sugden, 2002, p. 65). The discussion when juxtaposed against the concept of the Kautilyan state leads to a conundrum, does the state act with the objective of maximizing its own utility as a community (deciding either as individual members or as a community of the ruling class)? It definitely constitutes an action that Chanakya had not termed untenable. Alternatively, the state could exist with the sole objective to serve the people and maximize their utility, which some would argue would represent the truest definition of a welfare state. Such states however could be unsustainable or weak without revenue and would ultimately face the possibility of a collapse which ironically would not present as the best outcome in the peoples' interests since the state in question was an empathic/welfare state. Given the complexities Lyons (2003) had explained that within Bentham's ideas of utilitarianism: "The basic principle of utility may be understood as saying, roughly, that one ought to promote the happiness of those under one's 'direction', that is, those subject to one's direction, influence, or control" (p. 31). In other words, according to Lyons (2003), utilitarian theory promotes the normative directive that governments should uphold the interests of the people that they govern. However, Lyons (2003) explained that there might be a differential between those that are under ones' direction, influence or control and others who might be the actual ones affected. In the broader sense Lyons' posit could be interpreted as a caution towards the difference between those that a government serves such as the people under its command and those who might be affected by its decisions even though they are beyond its formal authority of power. International trade, environmental practices, military interventions might all present as relevant examples of this predicament. However, a narrower interpretation might present the argument that governments might define and recognize those that it serves only as those that are keeping it in power. This could be political interest groups, wealthy donors or even sections of voters.

Jeremy Bentham's ideas on utilitarianism are dichotomous. While Bentham's model of an individual rational decision maker is one who takes decisions to maximize his or her utility, his framework for the community involves individuals who might sacrifice their own wellbeing for that of the community. Lyons (2003) explains this problem succinctly: "Bentham's view of human nature implies that it is impossible for me to do things that his principle of utility requires me to do, such as sacrifice my own happiness for the sake of others" (p. 12). According to Lyons (2003) Bentham does posit that individuals ought to augment the happiness of the community members in general thus essentially proposing that individuals ought to do what they inherently cannot do. Consequently Lyons (2003) argues that "Bentham violates the fundamental principle that 'ought implies can'" (p. 12). The principle posits that moral, social or political obligations must be feasibly achievable. It is thus inconsistent and irrational to claim that an agent should achieve what is beyond their capacity to achieve. Bentham requires individuals to act beyond their normal human nature. At a broader level, Bentham requires governments to maximize the happiness of all those that they serve and thus obligates governments to achieve far beyond what they can reasonably and practically achieve. It is not possible for governments to fully predict or control the consequences of its actions, especially when the effects occur beyond its boundaries of power or in the distant future. Consequently, the utilitarian requirement for an exhaustive maximization of utility sets an impossible standard which no government can achieve and might at best approximate this ideal standard.

Jeremy Bentham's contemporary, the Scottish philosopher and thinker Adam Smith (1723–1790) is widely regarded as the father of modern economics; however, it is a popularly held view among economists that he was not a utilitarian in the classical sense of the term. Witztum and Young (2013) argued that Smith's conception of utility differed fundamentally from utilitarianism. Even as Smith acknowledged the pursuit of pleasure as a possible driver of human behaviour, his concept of pleasure was not the quantifiable pleasure which is central to utilitarian thought, nor was utility, for him, a guide to action or a tool for moral evaluation. Brady (2015) had argued that within Adam Smith's postulates utility has a simplistic meaning: usefulness. Thus, utility is that which is used towards the achievement of a desired purpose. The means that are used however should present with fitness for the ends that are desired and the consequent sense of harmony leads to pleasure. Importantly, Smith valued the harmonious relationship between the means and the ends, holding that the fitness or apt arrangement of means could itself yield satisfaction and sometimes even more than the attainment of the end itself (Smith, 2004). In the same vein, Macfie (1959) noted that Smith treated utility as a means or mediate good, which was sufficient as the basis of economic science. By contrast, the utilitarian perspective is almost exclusively outcome-focused, concentrating on the maximization of pleasure and minimization of pain, with little concern for the nature or fitness of the means employed.

Smith wrote two sensational books during his lifetime; *The Theory of Moral Sentiments* (1759) and *The Wealth of Nations* (1776); his first book (*The Theory of Moral Sentiments*) was largely ignored by utilitarian thinkers like Bentham who considered the discussion of utility presented within the book as largely insignificant (Rosen, 2000). Brady (2015) had argued that within the discourse in the Wealth of Nations, Smith had rejected the utilitarian line of thought by recognizing the importance of uncertainty and rejecting mathematical models of probability; utilitarianism, the author argued was heavily dependent on the knowledge about future consequences of individual actions to compare cost with benefits and thus required accurate calculations of probability. Smith's works were the subject of endless debates among experts, and the seemingly divergent ideas that the books presented resulted in the formulation of the term 'The Adam Smith Problem' (Montes, 2003). It was perceived that while his earlier work discussed normative social propriety of *Homo sapiens*, the later work dealt with the rational and cold *Homo economicus*. Several experts have suggested that the root cause of the Adam Smith problem lay within the divergent interpretation of the terms sympathy and empathy as is used in modern times. Ken Binmore (1998) had asserted that "we must look to the modern distinction between empathy and sympathy in order to achieve a reconciliation between his two books" (p. 364). Adam Smith had used the word sympathy instead of empathy in order to describe actions that were fundamentally empathic in nature (the concept of Einfühlung was developed later only in the late nineteenth and early twentieth century).

Adam Smith's work *The Theory of Moral Sentiments* recognized the importance of what Smith termed as sympathy. Macfie (1959) acknowledged this aspect and noted that Smith regarded sympathy as the fundamental social bond and a seminal source of moral sentiments. Adam Smith began his book (*Theory of Moral Sentiments*) with the words "How selfish soever man may be supposed, there are evidently some principles in his nature, which interest him in the fortune of others, and render their happiness necessary to him, though he derives nothing from it except the pleasure of seeing it" (Smith, 2004, p. 11). Thus, in his opening arguments, Smith (2004) had commented upon the fundamental human tendency to be happy at the wellbeing and good fortunes of others. The term sympathy as used by Smith throughout his discourse actually described what was subsequently defined as empathy. Adam Smith's description of 'sympathy' clarifies this further: "That this is the source of our fellow-feeling for the misery of others, that it is by changing places in fancy with the sufferer, that we come either to conceive or to be affected by what he feels, may be demonstrated by many obvious observations, if it should not be thought sufficiently evident of itself. When we see a stroke aimed and just ready to fall upon the leg or arm of another person, we naturally shrink and draw back our own leg or our own arm; and when it does fall, we feel it in some measure, and are hurt by it as well as the sufferer" (Smith, 2004, p. 12). Importantly thus, Smith's notion of sympathy stepped beyond mere passive concern and involved an active process of imaginatively placing oneself in another's situation and sharing their feelings. This was aptly illustrated in his description of instinctively recoiling when seeing someone about to be struck. This conception of sympathy aligns closely with what is now described as empathy. Fontaine (1997) highlighted that Smith's active interpretation of sympathy contrasted sharply with utilitarian thinkers like Hume,[2] who viewed it as a more passive transmission of feelings.

Fontaine (1997) suggested that within the sphere of Adam's Smith's discourse, empathic identification was necessary for sympathy (explained as the concern for others' wellbeing); such empathic identification would present with enhanced vigour and frequency among members of related groups or families. However, Fontaine (1997) was categorical in explaining that it would not be correct to assume that "Smithian economic agents would be willing to sacrifice their own interests to contribute personally to the welfare of those who belong to the same intimate group, it is altogether reasonable to argue that economic agents gain some knowledge about each other's preference patterns thanks to the frequent transactions characteristic of small communities of exchangers" (p. 268).

Fontaine (1997) claimed that Smith had also introduced a form of identification that was different from the unselfish empathic identification. This form was self-centred, and as Fontaine (1997) described, it merely involved "putting oneself in someone else's situation and conceiving what one should feel in like circumstances" (p. 268). This form of identification involving only a change of circumstance was described by Fontaine (1997) as partial empathic identification. The difference between complete empathic identification and partial empathic identification was that while in the first case individuals adopted the other person's preferences, in the latter case individuals kept their personal individual preferences (Kirman & Teschl, 2010). Thus, within Smith's discourse, there was a distinction between imagining oneself in the other person's circumstance (partial empathic identification) and imagining oneself as the other person (complete empathic identification). Fontaine (1997) explained "For Smith, the concern for the welfare of others can be said to be selfish only if in bringing someone else's case home to oneself, one has imaginatively taken on only his or her circumstances" (p. 266). Fontaine (1997) had explained the limitation of partial empathic identification with an illustrative example of an honest brewer and a dishonest butcher. It would be fallacious if the honest brewer evaluated the transaction behaviour of the dishonest butcher by anticipating what she as an honest butcher would do when dealing with an honest brewer (partial empathic identification); she would have better assessment of the situation if she evaluated what she as a dishonest butcher would do when dealing with an honest brewer. Conversely the dishonest butcher would be better off with an empathic identification of how she as an honest brewer would act when dealing with a dishonest butcher. Thus, within this example, partial empathic identification does not lead to enhanced knowledge about the other's behaviour. While it might be evidentially apparent at this stage that complete empathic identification could help economic agents in situations where one party is prone to dishonesty. Adam Smith however had approached the problem from a different point of view. In his later work *The Wealth of Nations,* Adam Smith (1977) claimed that "All systems either of preference or of restraint, therefore, being thus completely taken away, the obvious and simple system of natural liberty establishes itself of its own accord. Every man, as long as he does not violate the laws of justice, is left perfectly free to pursue his own interest his own way, and to bring both his industry and capital into competition with those of any other man, or order of men" (p. 914). Smith's views have been interpreted by Fontaine (1997) to mean that Smithian economic agents were governed by rules of justice in exchange to relations and thus avoided hurting the other's interests. Fontaine (1997) presented the argument that empathic identification would help in cases when the economic agents were strangers to each other or when one party was prone to dishonesty; a functional aspect of empathic identification which was seemingly not addressed by Smith.

The Wealth of Nations has often been described as the work that helped to establish economics as a distinct field of study; it is also a widely held belief that within the discourse in The Wealth of Nations, self-interest was presented as the fundamental guiding principle for economic agents (Postigo, 2014). Stigler (1976) had proclaimed "Smith had one overwhelmingly important triumph: he put into the center of economics the systematic analysis of the behavior of individuals pursuing their self-interest under conditions of competition. This theory was the crown jewel of The Wealth of Nations, and it became, and remains to this day, the foundation of the theory of the allocation of resources" (p. 1201). This interpretation of Adam Smith's second work is not without critics, and very influential economists (Coase, 1976; Elster, 1989; Smith, 2013) have opined that interpreting Adam Smith's ideas as advocation of unbridled self interest in human behaviour was misguided and wrong. Postigo (2014) had argued, "Nowhere in WN does Smith state that self-interest is the *only or the best* motivation for human action, not even of the economic sort" (p. 137). Postigo (2014) subsequently argued that Adam Smith himself had begun his first work (*Theory of Moral Sentiments*) with words that evoked benevolent fellow feelings among humans; that first book should be viewed as the philosophical and intellectual foundation for his second work. In the Wealth of Nations, Smith did focus on the importance of empathic identification in exchange relations; it has been proposed that economic offers are made in such ways that they appeal to the others' self-love, in order to make such offers one has to put oneself in the proverbial shoes of the other and reflect as to what would generate the required temptation for the acceptance of such offers (Fontaine, 1997). The fundamental question that emerges from a discourse on Smith's views on sympathy and empathic identification is whether altruistic behaviour which focuses on the welfare of others is at odds with the concept of self-interest. An attempt to answer the question might involve a discussion on the nature of the Smithian approach to the concept of self-interest (or self-love). Smith's concept of self-interest was founded on principles of mutual welfare; he recognized that the self-interest of economic agents was best served in recognizing and appealing to the self-interests (Smith termed it as self-love) of others. Smith (1977) thus conceded that within civilized society an economic agent "stands at all times in need of the co-operation and assistance of great multitudes" (p. 30). Postigo (2014) explained that within Smith's ideations an exchange or trade is meant to maximize one's self interest through the acquisition of goods that one does not possess but someone else does; the process however leads one to recognize what the other person might desire and offer that in exchange. For Adam Smith, exchange and trade were based on the pursuit of self-interest, wherein individuals sought goods they lacked by offering in return what others desired. Smith argued that all successful exchanges depended on appealing to the self-love of others and demonstrating mutual advantage (Smith, 1977). Postigo (2014) clarified that Smith's notion of self-interest was not analogous to the radical individualism which was later associated with Ayn Rand, but rather a recognition of mutual interdependence which made cooperation between agents possible. Contrarily, Randian self-interest, which is rooted in Ayn Rand's philosophy of objectivism, revolves around the ideation that individuals should rationally and unapologetically pursue their own personal happiness and goals as their highest moral purpose. Nevertheless, however, Smith's framework does raise questions about the potential dangers of unrestrained self-interest. In this context, Evenksy

(2005) had posed the dilemma of how a liberal society, founded on the fundamental principle of individuals' freedom to pursue their own interests, could avoid descending into a Hobbesian struggle of all against all. The answer, according to Holler and Leroch (2008), lies in the fundamental natural constraint that humanity presents upon selfishness: the capacity for sympathy, or the ability to view situations from the other person's perspective. The sympathy that Holler and Leroch (2008) had mentioned in the Smithian sense is now described as empathy.

In the late nineteenth century, the existing economic discourse was fundamentally challenged by a shift in economic thought that was brought about by the postulations of the Italian polymath Vilfredo Federico Damaso Pareto (1848–1923). Pareto was instrumental in advocating a theory that separated the field of economics from that of psychology; this shift is often described as the 'Paretian turn' (Sugden, 2002; Bruni & Sugden, 2007). As explained by Bruni and Sugden (2007), "This shift, initiated by Vilfredo Pareto and completed in the 1930s and 1940s by John Hicks, Roy Allen and Paul Samuelson, eliminated psychological concepts from economics by basing economic theory on principles of rational choice" (p. 146). In the deduction of economic theories, Pareto argued for the prioritizing of observable and objective postulations over those that were subjective and metaphysical (Bruni, 2013). Pareto had emphasized on the ordinal nature of utility; thus, the Paretian approach stressed on which options are preferred over others. This line of thinking was evident in the indifference curve analysis that Pareto had helped to develop; an indifference curve is a curve which represents different combinations of two goods between which a consumer is indifferent. Thus, a consumer does not prefer one combination of the two goods (known as commodity bundle) over the other along an indifference curve. Paretian analysis did not involve a study into the reasons for such indifference (which would have involved a digression into the realms of psychology) but just the observable fact of preference or indifference.[3] Pareto had thus developed a common currency for the analysis of utility, preference; it was deemed as an alternate to the subjective nature of the currency that the utilitarian theorists had advocated; pleasure (Sugden, 2002).

However, psychology was reintroduced into mainstream economic thinking when in the early parts of the twentieth century a British economist named John Maynard Keynes had put forward his macroeconomic theorizations; Keynes had developed his theories in the backdrop of the great depression. Although debatable and controversial, Keynes' views on macroeconomic policies would encourage a new direction of economic thought and the consequent genre would be recognized as Keynesian economics. Keynesian economics focused primarily on what is known in the field of economics as the short-run.[4] Keynes (2013) had famously said, "But this long run is a misleading guide to current affairs. *In the long run* we are all dead. Economists set themselves too easy, too useless a task if in tempestuous seasons they can only tell us that when the storm is long past the ocean is flat again" (p. 65). Prior to Keynes, classical economists had encouraged a cyclical economic model wherein it was posited that if aggregate demand in an economy fell, it would lead to low production levels and consequently low wages. However, as wages fell it would restimulate economic growth because lower wages would lead to lower inflation and that would act as a motivator for employers to increase investment and provide more employment thus leading to economic recovery. Keynes however disagreed with the classical economists and posited that during recession the general atmosphere of gloom and pessimism in the economy leads to a further decline in demand for goods and thus businesses cut down on production and avoid further investments. Keynes had proposed way out of such a crisis; he had advocated increased government spending during recession to make up for the decline in investment during the times; the increased government spending along with a reduction in taxes would lead to an increase in consumer spending which would in turn lead to an increase in demand, consequently encouraging investments and leading to more employment and ultimately resulting in economic recovery. Keynes' view on government interventions in economy was in stark contrast to the concept of laissez faire economies that was popular during the times. Keynes' thoughts and writings were technical and used cold mathematical formulations to put forward the logic and rationale of the arguments. Keynes' emphasis on quantitative analyses had led Franklin Delano Roosevelt to comment to his labour secretary Frances Perkins: "I saw your friend Keynes. He left a whole rigmarole of figures. He must be a mathematician rather than a political economist" (as quoted in Cassidy, 2011, p. 52). However, if Keynes' theories are contextualized within the despondent real-life scenarios within which they were formulated, the empathic disposition of Keynes' arguments would be obvious as would the real nature of the statement "in the long run we are all dead." Desperate times require desperate measures, and while it might be argued that economies that are facing a recession will ultimately recover in the long run, interventional measures to hasten that recovery might be conceived as an empathic attempt to help people in distress. Mann (2017) explained Keynesian economic thought as a science and sensibility that allows us to name ""the crisis"—poverty, unemployment, inequality—when everything hangs in the balance and "something must be done"" (p. 18). It might be argued that John Maynard Keynes' theories and works were influenced in no small part by a fundamental empathic understanding of human behaviour and psychology. The argument finds support in Keynes' work on consumption behaviour, particularly within Keyne's words describing his psychological law of consumption wherein he explained "the prevailing psychological law seems to be that when aggregate income increases, consumption-expenditure will also increase but to a somewhat lesser extent. This is a very obvious conclusion. It simply amounts to saying that an increase in income will be divided in some proportion or another between spending and saving, and that when our income is increased it is extremely unlikely that this will have the effect of making us either spend less or save less than before. This psychological law was of the utmost importance in the development of my own thought, and it is, I think, absolutely fundamental to the theory of effective demand as set forth in my book" (Keynes, 1937, pp. 219–220). Keynes theorizations had influenced a school of economic thought which came to be known as post-Keynesian. Post-Keynesian economics was not restricted to the ideations put forward by Keynes but was influenced by numerous brilliant economists such as the Polish Marxist economist Michał Kalecki.[5] Post Keynesian economists recognize the uncertainties that are inherent in economic activities thus rejecting a basic axiom of classical economics: ergodicity. In the process Post Keynesian economists acknowledge the situational and social variables that influence human behaviour. Post Keynesian economics fundamentally adheres to the postulate that employment (and unemployment) is not determined in the labour market but in the product market. Consequently, the phenomenon of involuntary unemployment (a common outcome of the post-Covid economies especially in developing countries like India) is a stark reality which has its roots in the insufficient demand (King, 2013).

Keynesian economics was in limelight during the financial crisis of 2007–2008 when Keynes and his thoughts were resurrected, and in line with Keynesian postulates, presidents George W. Bush and Barrack Obama cut taxes and increased spending to stimulate economic growth; lessons had been learnt from Roosevelt's policy of ignoring Keynesian postulates and increasing taxes (as well as curtailing government spending) in 1937 leading to a further collapse of the recession hit American economy at that time.

Just as Keynes' thoughts were apparently founded on a basic empathic understanding of the predicament of the socio-economically challenged especially during hard times like depression, Karl Gunnar Myrdal, a Swedish economist, was particularly known for his work on poverty and race relations which were intricately connected with an empathic understanding of people, their predicaments and the role of racial diversities in socio-economic outcomes. In fact, Myrdal's works have played important roles in catalyzing several watershed moments in human history. These include the establishment of the Swedish welfare state and the abolishment of the racially segregated school system in the USA. Myrdal's works on economic theory were in sync with that of Keynes; however, he had published his thoughts in Swedish and German several years before Keynes. In this context Barber (2008) had remarked, "If his contribution had been available to readers of English before 1936, it is interesting to speculate whether the 'revolution' in macroeconomic theory of the depression decade would be referred to as 'Myrdalian' as much as 'Keynesian'" (p. xi).

Myrdal had promoted the idea of empirical economics through a study of human behaviour, motivation, conditioning and the effect of social environment on such behaviour. Moreover, he recognized the effect of individual researchers' psychological disposition, personality and life experiences on their research and thinking. As such he was the first economic thinker to raise the issue of cognitive biases and their role in research. Myrdal (1973) had thus explained, "Adam Smith, Ricardo, List, Marx, John Stuart Mill, Marshall, Wicksell, Veblen, and Keynes, to mention only a few—have all been strikingly idiosyncratic, and it would be hard to believe that their personality traits did not set their mark on the direction and character of their contributions. I see here a large field for intensive psychological research, which must, however, situate the individual author in the social setting where he lived and worked" (p. 58). Interestingly thus it might be inferred that Myrdal did not constrain his thoughts to an empathic understanding of the subject of an economic study but also to an empathic understanding of the researchers and economists too who would interpret the studies through the prism of their own socio-psychological experiences, cognitive biases and inherent psychological disposition.

Gunnar Myrdal firmly believed in egalitarian economic reforms and did not agree with the notion that such reforms led to lower economic growth.

Myrdal (1973) wrote, "well-planned egalitarian reforms would be preventive, prophylactic, and thus productive. The fact that forty years of steadily speeded up social reform has not stopped economic growth and progress, as the older economists were continually warning, but that in Sweden these forty years have proved an outstanding success even in 'economic' terms, has now in hindsight given a pragmatic confirmation that we were right, even though behind this development were also other forces" (p. 9). Myrdal's economic thought laid importance on the fundamental human right to equality of opportunity as well as the right to be helped when needed (Myrdal, 1973). He had recognized that these basic concepts that defined human dignity had survived "many centuries of blatant inequality and oppression" (Myrdal, 1973, p. 34). It would thus not be very surprising to note that Myrdal was not impressed by Benthamite utilitarianism which he described as an "opportunistically biased way of thinking" (Myrdal, 1973, p. 35). Myrdal (1973) had identified four great dangers to the wellbeing of mankind: nuclear weapons, environmental pollution, drug addiction and abject poverty within which a significant section of the world population live.[6] Myrdal opined that while poverty was widely recognized as a serious problem in economic literature, the analysis for the reasons for poverty were often marred by opportunistic distortion and often merely presented the views of the dominant groups in society.

Myrdal (1973) had argued that the differential levels of development witnessed between developed and underdeveloped countries were not only dimensional but also qualitative in nature. Thus, he was fundamentally against categorizing the development differentials as a mere time lag. Myrdal's views thus presented as an antithesis to the views of Karl Marx who had opined, "The country that is more developed industrially only shows, to the less developed, the image of its own future" (Marx, 1867, pp. 6–7). Myrdal's had concluded that variables like climatic conditions and rate of population growth played important roles in the economic development of a region.

Gunnar Myrdal had applied and promoted a concept that was termed as circular cumulative causation to explain underdevelopment. Myrdal had explained "If things were left to market forces unhampered by any policy interferences, industrial production, commerce, banking, insurance, shipping and indeed almost all those economic activities which in developing economy tend to give a bigger than average return and, in addition, science, art, literature, educational higher culture generally – would cluster in certain localities and regions, leaving the rest of the country more or less in a backwater" (Myrdal, 1957, p. 26). Myrdal had earlier applied this line of thought in his seminal work on racial discrimination and segregation in the United States of America wherein he empathically analysed the problems that African Americans faced in that country. Myrdal had noted, "A deeper reason for the unity of the Negro problem will be apparent when we now try to formulate our hypothesis concerning its dynamic causation. The mechanism that operates here is the "principle of cumulation," also commonly called the "vicious circle." This principle has a much wider application in social relations. It is, or should be developed into, a main theoretical tool in studying social change. Throughout this inquiry, we shall assume a general interdependence between all the factors in the Negro problem. White prejudice and discrimination keep the Negro low in standards of living, health, education, manners and morals. This, in its turn, gives support to white prejudice. White prejudice and Negro standards thus mutually "cause" each other" (Myrdal, 1944, p. 75). Gunnar Myrdal was one of the first economists to empathically study the causes of poverty and underdevelopment; he had expanded on the concept of a welfare state to introduce the idea of a welfare world. Myrdal (1960) had opined, "As regards international relations, national economic planning has not had effects in line with those ideals. The Welfare State is nationalistic. Internationally the ideals of liberty, equality, and brotherhood can be attained only by a political development towards a Welfare World, which would imply rather fundamental changes in the trend towards economic planning in the individual countries" (pp. 13–14).

The end of World War II led to wide spread changes in the existing world order; the near elimination of the colonial system and the consequent emergence of the post-colonial economies, particularly in Asia, Africa and Latin America, led to new areas of ideations within the field of economic thought. It could be argued that empathic understanding of the predicaments of the poor provided the motivation for at least some of these ideations. The objectives of this new area of research and theorization within economics were largely benevolent and included models to attempt; reduction of poverty, increase per capita income, provide to the poor access to quality healthcare and education. The most prominent of these new areas of study within economics were development economics and welfare economics. Over the years many prominent development economists have contributed enormously to the design and implementation of public policy to reduce poverty; prominent among them is Amartya

Sen, the Nobel laureate economist from West Bengal, India, whose works have introduced a fresh empathic dimension to economic discourse.

While Sen's contributions to economic thought, especially within the context of human development and wellbeing, are diverse and extensive, the empathic nature of his ideations can be observed within his theorization of what is known as the capability approach. The capability approach was introduced by Sen and Martha Nussbaum in the 1980s; it is a normative theoretical framework which empathically recognizes that while the freedom to achieve a better standard of life is essential and fundamental to socio-economic development, such freedom should be contextualized within the capabilities of the people concerned to enhance their wellbeing. Such capabilities are provided by real opportunities to achieve such wellbeing. Thus, capability approach studies the capability of the people to better their standard of living over and above a right which enables them to do so (Robeyns, 2016). The word capability in this context is not used to define a measure of individual talent but describes a wider context. Robeyns (2009) had explained, "we should focus on people's real or effective opportunities to do what they want to do, and to be who they want to be, instead of focusing on people's holdings of social primary goods or their mental states (as in certain forms of utility). These beings and doings are called a person's functionings, and include such basic functionings as being healthy, being sheltered, not being mentally ill, engaging in social relations, and more complex and specific functionings such as combining a career with a gender-egalitarian family life. Capabilities are the effective opportunities that a person has to attain these functionings" (p. 403). Sen (1999) had thus surmised, "I argue in favour of focusing on the capability to function, i.e., what a person can do or can be" (p. ix).

Sen's capability approach fundamentally recognizes the differentials between mere statutory freedom to achieve one's wellbeing and the real-life constraints that might serve as impediments towards that goal. Most post-colonial political systems provide the legal and statutory freedom to individuals in order that they might take decisions with regard to their wellbeing; however, such statutory freedom might often present as insufficient for such decisions. Real-life opportunities for individual decision choices are constrained by numerous circumstantial and situational factors, some of which could be access to education or skills training, quality of health, sociocultural constraints which affect decision choices and even gender equality. A relevant example could be cited from the tea estates of West Bengal in India where some of the best tea in the world is produced.

The tribal workers in the tea gardens of the area were victims of colonial oppression for generations. They are now provided with reservations in educational institutions and government jobs in India. However, the tribal schools that cater to the children of the workers still witness very high school dropout rates. The reasons could be learned helplessness, risk aversion or the pressure of socio-economic conditions; all of which act as constraints to severely compromise the actual capacity of the tea estate children to continue their education and seek better standards of living outside the tea gardens (Roy, 2021). It is witnessed that discussions within the larger sections of society (and governments) present an unempathic view of such situations often indulging in blaming and judging the actors while remaining unaware of the fact that the capabilities of individuals to take decisions towards their wellbeing are often constrained greatly by factors beyond their control. It is in this context Sen's approach attempts to develop an empathic understanding of the predicaments that disadvantaged people face. Sen's approach "is much concerned with the opportunities that people have to improve the quality of their lives. It is essentially a 'people-centred' approach, which puts human agency (rather than organizations such as markets or governments) at the centre of the stage. The crucial role of social opportunities is to expand the realm of human agency and freedom, both as an end in itself and as a means of further expansion of freedom" (Drèze & Sen, 2002, p. 6).[7]

Amartya Sen's capability approach has encouraged what is known as the human development approach in economics. The World Development Report (1991) of the World Bank explained the concept of economic development from the perspective of this approach: "Economic development is defined in this Report as a sustainable increase in living standards that encompass material consumption, education, health and environmental protection. Development in a broader sense is understood to include other important and related attributes as well, notably more equality of opportunity, and political freedom and civil liberties. The overall goal of development is therefore to increase the economic, political and civil rights of all people across gender, ethnic groups, religions, races, regions and countries. This goal has not changed substantially since the early 1950s, when most of the developing world emerged from colonialism" (World Bank, 1991, p. 31).

The capability approach thus provides the fundamental basis for the United Nation's Human Development Index which was developed by the Pakistani economist Mahbub ul Haq. The Human Development Index is used by the United Nations to measure a country's development. The Index presents an alternative to the mere analysis of development through studies of economic growth through GDP. Robert Kennedy (1968) had illustrated the limitations of studying development through GDP in a speech at the University of Kansas wherein he had stated: "Our Gross National Product, now, is over $800 billion dollars a year, but that Gross National Product – if we judge the United States of America by that – that Gross National Product counts air pollution and cigarette advertising, and ambulances to clear our highways of carnage. It counts special locks for our doors and the jails for the people who break them. It counts the destruction of the redwood and the loss of our natural wonder in chaotic sprawl. It counts napalm and counts nuclear warheads and armored cars for the police to fight the riots in our cities. It counts Whitman's rifle and Speck's knife, and the television programs which glorify violence in order to sell toys to our children. Yet the gross national product does not allow for the health of our children, the quality of their education or the joy of their play. It does not include the beauty of our poetry or the strength of our marriages, the intelligence of our public debate or the integrity of our public officials. It measures neither our wit nor our courage, neither our wisdom nor our learning, neither our compassion nor our devotion to our country, it measures everything in short, except that which makes life worthwhile."

Over the past decades a significant section of influential economists has begun to appreciate the complexities of human behaviour and the unreal paradigms that promote the concept of the infinitely rational "homo-economicus" or the economic man. The new era of thinking has led to the recognition of a new field of economics that combine the fields of psychology and economics to analyse economics from the perspective of human behaviour; this new area of study is now known as behavioural economics. More than half a century ago the American economist and political scientist Herbert Simon (1955) had questioned the concept of the rational man wherein he had written: "Recent developments in economics, and particularly in the theory of the business firm, have raised great doubts as to whether this schematized model of economic man provides a suitable foundation on which to erect a theory—whether it be a theory of how firms do behave, or of how they 'should' rationally behave" (p. 99). Alternately Simon had stressed on the concept of bounded rationality, wherein it was recognized that human rationality is not infinite but is limited by constraints such as limitation of time, lack of knowledge and inherent human ability. Over the years as the field of behavioural economics emerged, the challenge to the concept of an infinitely self-centred rational man was supported by alternative theories and ideations on the role of cognitive biases in human decision making; consequently, behavioural economists like Daniel Kahneman and Richard Thaler have been awarded Nobel prizes or their contribution to the field.

As the role of human behaviour in economic decision making was accepted by mainstream economists, the field of psychology now played a prominent if not dominant role in economic thought. The field of development economics too witnessed a change in the traditional approach wherein new views which were based on true to life psychological theories with empirical foundations were inculcated in the discourse. The field of behavioural development economics however does not attempt to replace traditional models of developmental economics but only "seeks to augment existing theories of development economics by capturing systematic and relevant aspects of human behavior, often using parsimonious extensions of existing models" (Kremer et al., 2019, p. 351). Moreover, behavioural development economics while appreciating the need for institutions and economic policy in economic development does not blame the poor for their poverty (Kremer et al., 2019). The blame and shame approach is avoided through the encouragement of a philosophy that emphasizes on psychological factors that are universal in nature and avoids attributing blame for biases. Behavioural development economics thus inculcates the fundamental requirement for empathic understanding of people, that of creating a non-judgmental model which does not prima facie blame individuals or groups for their predicament. The advent of psychological analysis in development economics ushered in an era of alternate introspection on the reasons for human behaviour. Thus, while economists noticed that farmers in certain economies held on to obsolete and inefficient farming equipment, the analysis of the reasons for this behaviour was presented within divergent ideations; while a section of the developmental economists viewed this behaviour from the classical viewpoint of economics and declared that the farmers were absolutely rational and thoroughly aware of the advantages of traditional farming equipment, others found the behaviour irrational and attempted to change it through coercion or rewards (Kremer et al., 2019). A prominent chain of discussion in this specific context was initiated by the influential development economist Theodore Schultz (Nobel laureate, 1979). Schultz had posited that farmers in developing countries were "efficient but poor," Schultz's posit was in consonance with the thoughts proposed by the traditional development economists of the time who believed that farmers made rational choices even when they were operating in developing economies with limited income and means. However, some developmental economists have challenged the efficient but poor hypothesis stating that numerous variables such as land tenancy in developing economies do not present with efficient models (Alber & Sukhatme, 2006). Theodore Schultz had made some touching observations in the context of empathic understanding of the poor in his Nobel acceptance speech wherein he said, "[W]ho are rich find it hard to understand the behavior of poor people. Economists are no exception, for they too, find it difficult to comprehend the preferences and scarcity constraints that determine the choices that poor people make" (Schultz, 1980, p. 639).

Even if one momentarily assumes that humans are unboundedly rational, it would still be quite reasonable to maintain that the poor would think differently from the rich. Esther Duflo (2006) had thus posited, "Poverty thus affects behavior, even if the decision maker is 'neoclassical': unboundedly rational, forward-looking, and internally consistent" (p. 367). The *Homo economicus*, in Duflo's words, "would behave differently if he were poor than if he were rich" (p. 367). This difference in behaviour results in inconsistencies between real-life behaviour and that which is often predicted by certain economists who find it difficult to put themselves in the shoes of the poor to empathically understand them. Consequently, such inconsistent behaviour is often subsequently discarded as being foolish, ignorant or mere outliers which should be ignored. Herein it might be argued that development economics would gain immensely and produce results when economists can put themselves psychologically in place of the poor that they are attempting to serve and understand situations from their point of view (complete empathic identification). Such attempts might tend to slow down the research process, but in absence of calamitous conditions like economic depression, war, famine or pandemic, research in development economics might attempt to prioritize efficacy over efficiency.

Empathic understanding of situations is fundamental to the design of adequate solutions to the problems. The importance of this aspect of human behaviour was recognized by thinkers like Adam Smith even as the science of economics was in its nascent stage of development. Over the past decades the field of economics has been enriched immensely by the inculcation of ideas and theories from psychology. Such enrichment has been possible in so small measure through the recognition, directly or otherwise, of the importance of empathic understanding of human behaviour in the design of economic models. In order that economic models are designed to improve the lives of the people, it is imperative to study the behaviour of the poor (as well as the rich) in order to understand how humans behave under different conditions. Such studies would yield the most accurate results only when researchers can have a complete empathic identification with the subjects of the study. Moreover, empathic identification would remove the paternalistic approaches that are often witnessed in economic research. It might be interesting to note herein that over the large part of the twentieth century, economists have regularly inculcated empathy in their ideations and have thus helped the world to understand the reasons for cataclysmic economic situations like famines and depression. Empathic understanding of difficult situations by economists have also helped countries to discard grotesquely racist practices like segregated schools, encourage the idea and philosophy of welfare states, develop a human development index that steps beyond mere economic growth to analyse the living conditions of the people.

Empathic economics does not discard institutions but the focus of empathic economics is on the betterment of the people and institutions are just a means to that effect. Consequently, empathic economics could focus on empirical and experimental research and create models based on rigorous empathic identification with the actors in the model. Empathy in economic thought provides a power that helps in optimal outcomes of numerous economic processes whether in collective bargaining, trade negotiations, welfare and development, or in creating a fair and just world while ensuring for all humans the dignity that they deserve.

Notes

1. The original words being *"Praja sukhe sukham raja, prajanam tu hitey hitam, Natma priyyam hitam rajanaha prajanam cha hitam priyam." See* Kautilya, V. C. (4th Century B. C.).
2. In fact, the Scottish utilitarian thinker David Hume was sceptical about the fundamental process of empathy which required individuals to place themselves in the proverbial shoes of the other. This was evident from Hume's argument, "No force of imagination can convert us into another person, and make us fancy, that we, being that person, reap benefit from those valuable qualities, which belong to him. Or, if it did, no celerity of imagination

could immediately transport us back, into ourselves, and make us love and esteem the person, as different from us." See Hume (1983, p. 51).

3. In a letter to the French mathematician Hermann Laurent dated 19th January 1899, Pareto had written, "I am not interested in the reason why man is indifferent between [one thing and another]: I notice the pure and naked fact." See Bruni (2013, p. 51).
4. In the field of economics short run is a period wherein one factor of production is fixed. Long-run conversely refers to a time period wherein all the factors of production are variable.
5. Both Kalecki and Keynes had stressed on the importance of effective demand for employment as well as output. It has been claimed by several economists that Kalecki had published his principle of effective demand in 1933 around three years before Keynes who published his work in 1936. See Sawyer (1985).
6. The United Nations definition of poverty steps beyond mere lack of income to include hunger, malnutrition, lack of access to basic needs like education and healthcare as well as social discrimination. In 2015 it was estimated that 736 million people in the world lived below the international poverty line while 10% of the world's population lived in extreme poverty. These are pre-pandemic figures and the UN estimates that the Covid 19 pandemic could increase global poverty by half a billion people or 8% of the global human population. See https://www.un.org/en/global-issues/ending-poverty.
7. Martha Nussbaum had proposed that capabilities could be differentiated into intrinsic capabilities which described a person's intrinsic abilities and combined abilities which could be "defined as internal capabilities plus the social/political/ economic conditions in which functioning can actually be chosen" (Nussbaum, 2011, p. 22).

References

Alber, D. G., & Sukhatme, V. A. (2006). The "Efficient but Poor" hypothesis. *Review of Agricultural Economics, 28*(3), 338–334. https://doi.org/10.1111/j.1467-9353.2006.00296.x

Barber, W. J. (2008). *Gunnar Murdal. An intellectual biography.* Palgrave Macmillan.

Bentham, J. (2007). *An introduction to the principles of morals and legislation.* Dover Publications.

Binmore, K. (1998). *Game theory and the social contract volume 2. Just playing.* The MIT Press.

Brady, M. E. (2015). On Adam Smith's anti-utilitarianism in the wealth of nations. *SSRN Electronic Journal.* https://doi.org/10.2139/ssrn.2615211

Bruni, L. (2013). The Paretian turn. The foundation of the theory of rational choice, and its discontents. *Revue européenne des sciences sociales [Online], 51*(2), 47–64. https://doi.org/10.4000/ress.2510

Bruni, L., & Sugden, R. (2007). The road not taken: How psychology was removed from economics, and how it might be brought back. *The Economic Journal, 117*(516), 146–173. https://doi.org/10.2307/4121912

Cassidy, J. (2011, October 10). The demand doctor. *The New Yorker*, 46–57.

Coase, R. H. (1976). Adam Smith's view of man. *Journal of Law and Economics, 19*(3), 529–546. https://doi.org/10.1086/466886

Drèze, J., & Sen, A. (2002). *India: Development and participation*. Oxford University Press.

Duflo, E. (2006). Poor but rational? In A. Banerjee, R. Benabou, & D. Mookherjee (Eds.), *Understanding poverty*. Oxford University Press.

Elster, J. (1989). *Nuts and bolts for the social sciences*. Cambridge University Press.

Evenksy, J. (2005). *Adam Smith's moral philosophy: A historical and contemporary perspective on markets, law, ethics, and culture*. Cambridge University Press.

Fontaine, P. (1997). Identification and economic behavior sympathy and empathy in historical perspective. *Economics and Philosophy, 13*(2), 261–280. https://doi.org/10.1017/S026626710000451X

Holler, M. J., & Leroch, M. (2008). Impartial spectator, moral community, and some legal consequences. *Journal of the History of Economic Thought, 30*(03), 297–316. https://doi.org/10.1017/S1053837208000308

Hume, D. (1983). *An enquiry concerning the principles of morals*. Hackett Publishing Company.

Kautilya, V. C. (4th Century B. C.). *The Arthashastra, edited, rearranged, translated and introduced by L. N. Rangarajan*. Penguin Books, 1992.

Kennedy R. F. (1968). Remarks at the University of Kansas, March 18, 1968. Retrieved 28 December, 2021 from https://www.jfklibrary.org/learn/about-jfk/the-kennedy-family/robert-f-kennedy/robert-f-kennedy-speeches/remarks-at-the-university-of-kansas-march-18-1968

Keynes, J. M. (1937). The general theory of employment. *The Quarterly Journal of Economics, 51(2), 209–223*. https://doi.org/10.2307/1882087

Keynes, J. M. (2013). *The collected writings of John Maynard Keynes Volume IV. A tract on monetary reform*. Cambridge University Press for The Royal Economic Society.

King, J. E. (2013). A brief introduction to post Keynesian macroeconomics. *Wirtschaft und Gesellschaft - WuG, 39*(4), 485–508.

Kirman, A., & Teschl, M. (2010). Selfish or selfless? The role of empathy in economics. *Philosophical Transactions of the Royal Society, B: Biological Sciences, 365*(1538), 303–317. https://doi.org/10.1098/rstb.2009.0192

Kremer, M., et al. (2019). Behavioral development economics. In D. Bernheim, S. DellaVigna, & D. Laibson (Eds.), *Handbook of behavioral economics:*

Applications and foundations (Vol. 2). North Holland. https://doi.org/10.1016/bs.hesbe.2018.12.00

Lyons, D. (2003). *In the interest of the governed. A study in Bentham's philosophy of utility and law*. Oxford University Press.

Macfie, A. L. (1959). Adam Smith's moral sentiments as foundation for his wealth of nations. *Oxford Economic Papers, New Series, 11*(3), 209–228. https://doi.org/10.2307/2661906

Mann, G. (2017). *In the long run we are all dead*. Verso.

Marx, K. (1867). *Capital. A critique of the political economy volume 1*. Retrieved April 24, 2025, from https://www.marxists.org/archive/marx/works/download/pdf/Capital-Volume-I.pdf

Montes, L. (2003). Das Adam Smith problem: Its origins, the stages of the current debate, and one implication for our understanding of sympathy. *Journal of the History of Economic Thought, 25*(1), 63–90. https://doi.org/10.1080/1042771032000058325

Myrdal, G. (1944). *An American dilemma. The Negro problem and modern democracy*. Harper Brothers and Publishers.

Myrdal, G. (1957). *Economic theory and under-developed regions*. G. Duckworth.

Myrdal, G. (1960). *Beyond the welfare state*. Bantam Books.

Myrdal, G. (1973). *Against the stream*. Palgrave Macmillan.

Nussbaum, M. (2011). *Creating capabilities. The human development approach*. Harvard University Press.

Olivelle, P. (2013). *King, governance, and law in ancient India. Kautilya's Arthasastra*. Oxford University Press.

Postigo, G. Z. (2014). Adam Smith on sympathy: From self-interest to empathy. In D. F. Hardwick & L. Marsh (Eds.), *Propriety and prosperity new studies on the philosophy of Adam Smith*. Palgrave Macmillan.

Robeyns, I. (2009). Justice as fairness and the capability approach. In K. Basu & R. Kanbur (Eds.), *Arguments for a better world* (Vol. 1). Oxford University Press.

Robeyns, I. (2016). The capability approach. In E. N. Zalta (Ed.), *The Stanford encyclopedia of philosophy* (Winter 2016 ed.). Metaphysics Research Lab, Stanford University. Retrieved December 26, 2021, from https://plato.stanford.edu/archives/win2016/entries/capability-approach/

Rosen, F. (2000). The idea of utility in Adam Smith's The Theory of Moral Sentiments. *History of European Ideas, 26*(2), 79–103. https://doi.org/10.1016/s0191-6599(01)00002-x

Roy, D. (2021). The role of swarm intelligence in school dropouts among tribal students in the tea estates of West Bengal, India. In *Think pieces series no. 22. Education*. University of Oxford. Retrieved December 27, 2021, from https://educationsouthasia.web.ox.ac.uk/article/thinkpiece22

Sawyer, M. (1985). *The economics of Michal Kalecki*. Macmillan.

Schultz, T. W. (1980). Nobel lecture: The economics of being poor. *Journal of Political Economy, 88*(4), 639–651. https://doi.org/10.2307/1837306
Sen, A. (1999). *Commodities and capabilities.* Oxford University Press.
Sihag, B. S. (2005). Kautilya on ethics and economics. *Humanomics, 21*(3), 1–28. https://doi.org/10.1108/eb018902
Simon, H. A. (1955). A behavioral model of rational choice. *The Quarterly Journal of Economics, 69*(1), 99. https://doi.org/10.2307/1884852
Smith, A. (1977). *An inquiry into the nature and causes of the wealth of nations.* University of Chicago Press.
Smith, A. (2004). In K. Haakonssen (Ed.), *Theory of moral sentiments.* Cambridge University Press.
Smith, V. (2013). Adam Smith: From propriety and sentiments to property and wealth. *Forum for Social Economics, 42*(4), 283–297. https://doi.org/10.1080/07360932.2013.798241
Stigler, G. J. (1976). The successes and failures of Professor Smith. *Journal of Political Economy, 84*(6), 1199–1213. https://doi.org/10.2307/1831274
Sugden, R. (2002). Beyond sympathy and empathy: Adam Smith's concept of fellow-feeling. *Economics and Philosophy, 18*(1), 63–87. https://doi.org/10.1017/S0266267102001086
Witztum, A., & Young, J. T. (2013). Utilitarianism and the role of utility in Adam Smith. *The European Journal of the History of Economic Thought, 20*(4), 572–602. https://doi.org/10.1080/09672567.2011.592846
World Bank. (1991). *World development report. The challenge of development.* Oxford University Press.

CHAPTER 4

Empathy in Strategic Decision Making

The discussion in this chapter finds its fundamental rationale within the essential difference between sympathy and empathy. While sympathy presents as a behaviour wherein individuals feel for others with a sense of kindness, consolation or solace, empathy can be described as feeling as the other. Sinclair et al. (2016) had explained that sympathy is an "emotional reaction of pity toward the misfortune of another, especially those who are perceived as suffering unfairly. In contrast, empathy has been defined as an ability to understand and accurately acknowledge the feelings of another, leading to an attuned response from the observer" (p. 438). The fundamental difference between the two constructs sometimes leads to differential outcomes; while sympathy may involve shallow and distant responses to others' sufferings (Sinclair et al., 2016), it is most often overwhelmingly benevolent whereas empathy might not necessarily present with a benevolent intention. Chismar (1988) had explained that sympathy "entails having a positive regard or a non-fleeting concern for the other person. This would explain why to say, 'I sympathize with you' seems to suggest more support and compassion than, 'I empathize with you'" (p. 257). Thus, empathy towards the other need not be compulsorily rooted within the objective of support and help; rather, it could also be encouraged by competition, rivalry and even self-preserving or selfish motives. Allot (1992) had opined, "Empathy was a neutral mode of perception, in the sense that it could be used in relation to enemies or

D. Roy, *Empathonomics*,
https://doi.org/10.1007/978-981-95-4033-4_4

potential enemies, family or friends, or simply as a mode of obtaining information" (p. 354). The link between empathic disposition and non-altruistic behavioural outcomes is observed not only within adults but also in children. Barnett and Thompson (1985) had suggested that children who present with an enhanced awareness of others' feelings (cognitive empathy) but do not present with the tendency to share the feelings (affective empathy) "might be expected to be especially Machiavellian in his or her dealings with others" (p. 296). It might be emphasized at this point that cognitive and affective empathy is stressed upon in the discussions within this chapter. The strategic implications of empathy are wired within the evolutionary dimensions of empathy. Gierer (2000) had posited, "cognition-based empathy, perspective-taking linked to vicarious emotions, has evolved as a secondary effect of the evolution of strategic thought" (p. 577). The efficiency of all strategic thoughts and decisions depends upon a thorough understanding of the possible emotional and mental states of the others; such understanding allows for the prediction of the others' behaviour and the analysis of the differential outcomes arising from such behaviour. According to Gierer (2000), "This is best achieved if representations of others are connected to one's own emotional centres. Therefore, the evolution of the human brain is assumed to have established the capability of representations with such linkages" (p. 577). The preceding ideation stresses on the competitive nature of empathic behaviour wherein humans struggle and compete with each other in order to survive as per the dictum "survival of the fittest" and empathic disposition presents as a weapon to be deployed in this war for survival. While the term "survival of the fittest" has often been used to describe Darwinian evolution, Darwin himself had not coined the term.[1] In fact Darwin had stressed on the importance of sympathy as essential to evolutionary fitness; he had opined, "Species which are not social, such as lions and tigers, no doubt feel sympathy for the suffering of their own young, but not for that of any other animal. With mankind, selfishness, experience, and imitation, probably add, to the power of sympathy; for we are led by the hope of receiving good in return to perform acts of sympathetic kindness to others; and sympathy is much strengthened by habit. In however complex a manner this feeling may have originated, as it is one of high importance to all those animals which aid and defend one another, it will have been increased through natural selection; for those communities, which included the greatest number of the most sympathetic members, would flourish best, and rear the greatest number of offspring" (Darwin,

1871, p. 82). While Darwin had stressed on 'sympathy,' several scholars have posited that Darwin had actually used the word to describe what is known as empathy in recent times. Ekman (2010) opined that Darwin's sympathy "today would be termed empathy, altruism, or compassion" (p. 557).

Consequently, if the concepts of empathy, strategy and evolution are analysed in conjunction with the resultant discussion leads to two distinct chains of thought. The first of these chains concerns the fact that certain aspects of Darwinism seemingly reject the idea of survival of the fittest. In fact, Darwin himself had declared, "I probably attributed too much to the action of natural selection or the survival of the fittest" (Darwin, 1871, p. 152). This rejection could at least be related to the form in which the idea has been popularized (competition and confrontation). Darwin had opined that the evolutionary triumph of the human civilization can be attributed in some part to the evolution of empathy (Kukk, 2017). Thus cooperation, benevolent empathic disposition as well as altruism and compassion might present as a strategy in itself for survival and growth. The second chain of thought relates to the non-altruistic and competitive aspects of strategic empathy and its evolution as a self-preserving defensive or offensive instinct to protect oneself or attack the other. This chain of thought might be connected at least in part with the idea of survival of the fittest in its limited but popular form. The discussion in this chapter will involve analyses of both the emergent chains of thought.

The efficiency of strategic thinking processes depends largely on memory functions, the ability to learn from experiences (both from one's own and that of others) as well as the prediction/simulation of future outcomes and the assessment or appraisal of such outcomes in relation to one's desired state. However, as Gierer (2000) argued, "Learning from past experience alone could lead to predictions concerning future behaviour, but such predictions would be relatively time-consuming and liable to error" (p. 582). Thus, Gierer (2000) suggested that an efficient system utilizes the physiological similarities of human brains to create representations of others' present and future mental states within one's own mental self. Such empathic representations are moderated over time through accumulation of experience and knowledge to enhance the accuracy and the efficiency of the process. Since every human contains an identical copy of the neural circuitry of another human, Mafessoni and Lachmann (2019) posited that every human activates his or her "own decision making apparatus or neural circuitry, which can be used to extrapolate inferences concerning others' behavior. Information acquired over evolutionary time and information acquired through individual learning can thus be used to speed up adaptation to social encounters" (p. 1).

Cognitive and affective empathy is often presented within the concept of mind reading; Gallese and Goldman (1998) had defined mind reading as the "activity of representing specific mental states of others, for example, their perceptions, goals, beliefs, expectations, and the like" (p. 495). There are two approaches which seek to explain the phenomenon of mind reading, namely the Theory Theory (TT) and the Simulation theory (ST). The Theory Theory (TT) is founded on the proposition that mind reading is achieved by applying posits of a naïve or common-sense theory to explain and predict others' behaviour. Since mental states are considered unobservable, theoretical posits are applied to predict and explain the overt observable behaviour. Thus, according to this approach, "the theory of mind possessed by ordinary people consists of a set of causal/explanatory laws that relate external stimuli to certain inner states (e.g. perceptions), certain inner states (e.g. desires and beliefs) to other inner states (e.g. decisions), and certain inner states (e.g. decisions) to behavior" (Gallese &Goldman, 1998, p. 496).

Simulation theory posits that humans use their mental mechanisms to simulate the mental state of the other in order to explain or predict others' behaviour. The two approaches might be explained within the context of an example. Two gentlemen Anil and John are called for a job interview at XYZ Corporation; however, they are given two different time slots: Anil at 12 noon and John at 12:30 PM. They find themselves caught in a traffic jam on the way and thus are late, both reach at 12:35. Now the pertinent question would arise as to who would be angrier at being late. In a similar experiment conducted by Daniel Kahneman and Amos Tversky (1982) with regard to missing a flight, respondents overwhelmingly (96%) said that the person who missed the flight by a mere 5 minutes would be angrier. If that result is transferred to this example, it wouldn't be irrational to suppose that John would be angrier. Gallese and Goldman (1998) proposed that according to Theory Theory (TT), the surmise that John would be angrier could be reached either through the use of some prior information like a psychological law which predicts the behaviour (or even through Kahneman and Tversky's findings). On the other hand, the simulation theory would posit that the surmise was reached after the respondents put themselves in John's and Anil's shoes and imagined how they would react if they were in their place. This simulation would be possible through the activation and use of the neural pathways for such simulations that exist in humans.

The preceding discussion might be included within the precincts of strategic economic behaviour; such an inclusion will lend a theoretical rationale to the extended discussion on the role of empathy within such behaviour. Strategic behaviour within the purview of economics and beyond is most popularly studied through a set of mathematical techniques of analysis known as game theory. The winner of the 2007 Nobel memorial prize for economic sciences Roger Myerson had defined game theory as "the study of mathematical models of conflict and cooperation between intelligent rational decision-makers" (Myerson, 1991, p. 1). Game theory includes both the cooperative and non-cooperative aspects of strategic behaviour. While several scholars had worked on the concept previously, modern game theory has been conceptualized and popularized to a large extent through the seminal book *Theory of Games and Economic Behaviour* by John von Neumann and Oskar Morgenstern (1944). Myerson (1991) presents the argument that game theory provides an opportunity to understand human behaviour particularly within conflicts to compliment the advances made within the realm of physical sciences; this aspect is a prime motivator for game theorists to work and develop models that have useful applications within social sciences and beyond. A game can be considered to be an economic, social or political situation which involves more than one individual.[2] The individuals (also known as players) are assumed to be rational; rational players are those that act with the intention of maximizing their own gains. The expected utility theory has often been used to explain the decision choice of such rational players; it is proposed that when rational decision makers are faced with situations where the outcome is uncertain (probabilistic), they will act to maximize their expected utility. In order to explain the concept of expected utility, it is necessary to understand the concept of expected value. Expected value of an outcome is the probability weighted average of the outcome. Within a hypothetical situation wherein a person purchases a lottery ticket for ₹500, the prize is ₹100000 and the chances of winning the lottery is .25. The expected value of the lottery ticket is ₹100000 × .0025 = ₹250. The expected value of the lottery is less than its price; thus a decision to purchase it might be described as irrational. Similarly, a degree in medicine might lead to an income of ₹2,00,00,000 in one's lifetime; with a 70% chance of achieving that outcome. In such a case the medical degree will have an expected value of ₹ 1,40,00,000 in purely economic terms. The expected utility maximization theorem posits that a rational player will choose an alternative which will maximize his or her utility. If, for example, Anil derives 0 utils[3] from 0 shots of vaccine A, 2 utils from 1 shot of vaccine A, 3 utils from 2 shots of vaccine A. His expected utility from a 50:50 decision between 0 shots and 2 shots of the vaccine = 0(0 utils) + .5 (3) = 1.5 utils. However, his util from 1 sure shot of the vaccine is 1(2 utils) = 2 Utils. If Anil is a rational player, he will choose 1 sure shot of the vaccine rather than gamble on the decision between 0 and 2 shots. Economists had traditionally preferred the concept of subjective welfare to evaluate game theoretic decisions. Subjective welfare refers to one's own psychological dispositions and preferences to make judgements in order to evaluate relative welfare. Relative welfare is the valuation of one's situation as compared (or in reference) to another; this approach relies on psychological fulfilment and is thus often non-empirical and abstract in nature. If Anil prefers Mangoes over Apples, he will enjoy higher utility in a place where there is an abundance of Mangoes over Apples to consume over one which presents the reverse; the reason for such a preference is wholly psychological, subjective and cannot be empirically identified. Behaviourists had opposed this approach due to its non-empirical nature which relied on implicit psychological disposition; the noted economist Paul Samuelson thus put forward a theory that sought to define utility in purely technical terms devoid of psychological abstractions. Utility was herein described as "whatever it is that the agent's behavior suggests her to consistently act so as to make more probable" (Ross, 2019). Consequently, an economic agent was described as one who would act to maximize his or her utility function. Ross (2019) posits that within Samuelson's ideation, a player in game theoretic situation could be anyone or anything (human being, rat, dog, country, firm). An alternate approach to game theory however exists which emphasizes on game theory as a normative human strategic reasoning process. According to this approach, agents' actions are oftentimes motivated by the fact that "game-theoretic logic recommends certain actions as the 'rational' ones" (Ross, 2019).

While within the preceding examples Anil was a single player intending to take a decision with regard to a specific situation, problems however present with enhanced complexity when such decisions depend on the behaviour of two or more individuals. Thus, if there are two players A and B and A's decision depends on the decision that B will take with regard to a situation, then A has to place himself in B's proverbial shoes to understand what decision B might take; therein lies the importance of cognitive empathy in game theory. One of the earliest recorded instances of empathic understanding at work in a real-life game theoretic situation relates to the conquest of the Spanish explorer Hernán Cortés. In 1519 when Cortés led an expedition against the Aztecs to seize their treasures, he was hopelessly outnumbered; Cortés however had a deep empathic connection with his soldiers and he knew that when faced with certain defeat a significant number of them (if not all of the living ones) would try to escape in his ships. Cortés thus ordered his own ships to be burnt, when some of his soldiers queried as what would then comprise their modes of return, Cortés had declared that they would use their enemies' ships. Cortés in his action was not motivated solely by his own point of view but the rational analysis of what his solders might decide as the best action on their part under the circumstances. Iterative strategic empathy (I know that you know that I know that you know....) constitutes the essence of game theory within both competitive and cooperative strategic situations.

While economists have stressed on the necessity of rational players within the realm of game theory, it is important to understand that rationality often presents as a paradox when outcomes of strategic human behaviour is analysed. Frank (1988) had elaborated this aspect with an anecdote about two friends Jones and Smith: Jones had a briefcase worth $200 which Smith coveted, if Smith stole Jones' briefcase Jones had two choices, either to approach law enforcement to recover his suitcase (such a decision would cost Jones $300 in lost time and court fees) or to let his suitcase go since he was leaving town anyway so chances of future theft by Smith were non-existent. If Jones was a rational player, he would let the briefcase go without any action; however, if Jones was an irrational player, he would take punitive action. The paradox lies within the fact that Smith would steal the briefcase only if his empathic understanding of Jones projects him to be a rational player; if he realizes that Jones is capable of irrational reactions, he will not steal the briefcase. The paradox is often (mis) used in numerous situations involving economic transactions. Unscrupulous internet companies sell low-cost products which are spurious or defective to unsuspecting buyers; the time, effort and the resultant cost of replacement or legal recourse is many times higher than the cost of the product. Thus, these firms leverage on the rational decision-making capabilities of the buyers to cheat them. Low value transactions are thus prime targets for elements who game the rational decision-making capabilities of players to their advantage. Hernán Cortés too presented an aberration to rational behaviour by burning the very ships on which he and his army planned to return home with their loot. If he had acted rationally, he might have found himself stranded alone on the foreign shores while his soldiers fled on his ships. Irrational behaviour or at least an overt threat of such behaviour is thus an efficient strategy in some situations. The strategic aspect of irrationality has been used often in international politics; wherein it is euphemistically named the madman strategy. Richard Nixon had used the madman strategy during the Vietnam war by deploying nuclear armed bombers and threatening an all-out nuclear war. Several other leaders have used the same strategy over the years, most prominent being the successive leaders of Pakistan (Pervez Musharraf being the most vocal) who have threatened nuclear war against India in the eventuality of an armed conflict. Steven Brams, a professor of politics at New York University, explained, "It's an argument that there's a kind of method in the madness – that there's a rationality to appearing to be mad to force another player to back down in a confrontational situation" (As quoted in Garver, 2017). The argument presented does not propose that irrationality is strategically functional within all conflict situations; oftentimes conflict itself is irrational; countries have fought wars at the cost of countless lives and economic ruin for territories and land which are unfertile, desolate, uninhabitable with severely inhospitable climatic conditions. The money spent on such worthless conflicts could have been spent on education and healthcare of citizens. Likewise, organizations have sued opponents for miniscule sums of money and governments have prosecuted tax evaders for sums that were paltry when compared to the cost of such prosecution.

On the flipside of confrontational irrationality lies the human tendency of benevolent irrationality; wherein humans are kind, altruistic and compassionate towards others even at the cost of their own wellbeing. During the Covid-19 pandemic, doctors and nurses worldwide had displayed unthinkable selflessness while trying to save human lives. On 30 December 2019, Dr Li Wenliang had first warned his colleagues about the outbreak from corona virus. He had taken this step knowing that it could lead to repercussions from the Chinese regime. He was thereafter forced to admit that he was lying. Dr Li died on 7 February 2020 at the age of 33. Dr Roberto Stella, aged 67, an Italian general practitioner died on 10 March 2020 due to complications from Covid-19 infection. Dr Stella had contracted the virus while taking care of patients. A 68-year-old retired French doctor Jean-Jacques Razafindranazy volunteered to return to service to help the medical fraternity that was overwhelmed by the sheer number of patients; he subsequently died from Covid-19 that he had contracted while trying to save other's lives. Several healthcare workers have been known to commit suicide when diagnosed with Covid-19 in order to prevent further transmission (Pandey & Sharma, 2020). Humans are often selfless in their simple daily dealings too; guests tend to leave large tips at hotels or restaurants that they might never visit again, individuals tend to donate anonymously for causes that they care for or to people who they don't know. Humans have braved cyclones, forest fires, icy cold waters and even pandemic to render help to other humans and even animals. In India the police force in several states were seen to be feeding stray dogs and even landing up at senior citizen's houses with birthday cakes during extended lockdowns caused by the Covid-19 pandemic; a lady named Ms. Lokamani who worked as a support staff at a private school bought some policemen cold drinks with her meagre resources while they performed their duties in the blazing sun. At times humans have been known to remain honest under extreme temptation even when acts of misdemeanour would hardly have a chance of detection. Most of these actions of honesty, benevolence, altruism and compassion are performed without any expectation of quid pro quo; thus, the notion of unbounded human self-interest might present as questionable in these circumstances. Frank (1988) had described such aspects of seemingly irrational behaviour within a commitment model. He proposed that humans made a commitment in those situations and did not waver from it; such behaviour within the commitment model was overwhelmingly motivated by emotions.

The converse to the commitment model is the self-interest model wherein players act to protect their self-interest. The motivation for this behaviour is rational analysis. It is supposed within this model that humans act in self-interest even when they are seemingly altruistic and selfless. In this regard, it should be noted that honesty, loyalty and truth are also strategically efficient behaviour; people would like to associate, employ or even partner with individuals who present with these behavioural qualities. Thus altruism, honesty and even compassion can be deployed with self interest in mind. Adam Smith in his seminal work *The Wealth of Nations* had argued, "It is not from the benevolence of the butcher, the brewer, or the baker that we expect our dinner, but from their regard to their own interest. We address ourselves, not to their humanity but to their self-love, and never talk to them of our necessities but of their advantages" (Smith, 1776, p. 30). The American evolutionary biologist Robert Trivers (1971) put forward an interesting aspect of human altruism which he termed reciprocal altruism.[4] The concept of reciprocal altruism explains that altruistic behaviour often presents in conjunction with an expectation that the behaviour will be reciprocated by the recipient in future. In other words, reciprocal altruism is an academic version of the saying, "you scratch my back and I scratch yours." If the altruistic behaviour is not reciprocated by the beneficiary, then similar acts of altruistic behaviour towards that individual will cease. Subsequently an American mathematical psychologist Anatol Rappaport introduced the tit-for-tat strategy in game theory which was based on reciprocal altruism; the tit-for-tat strategy used an algorithm wherein both players in a game cooperated as long as one did not defect. Once one player defected the other would flow suit to punish him or her. A forgiving version of the tit-for-tat strategy allows one player to defect twice before retaliation, thus forgiving the defection once.

The role of empathy among players within diverse game situations have been studied in detail over the past decades. In this context numerous studies have involved one of the more notable games in game theory that was developed in 1950 by two scientists Merrill Flood and Melvin Dresher from the Rand Corporation. The game was later named Prisoner's dilemma by Albert Tucker.[5] Prisoner's dilemma involves the parable of two thieves A and B who are caught and kept in two separate rooms by the police without any chance of interacting with each other. The police present the two thieves with a set of choices and corresponding outcomes of the choices: if they both remain silent, they will have to spend one year each in prison; if they both betray each other, they will have to spend two years each in prison; if A betrays B but B remains silent, then A goes free but B will have to spend five years in prison; if B betrays A but A remains silent, then B goes free and A will have to spend five years in prison. The payoffs are presented in Fig. 4.1 in the matrix form. Prisoners' dilemma is observed in diverse real-life situations from international politics and conflicts to trade and commerce. In order to further analyse the strategic choices of this game, one needs to study the works of the American mathematician and economist John Nash. Nash in his PhD thesis submitted to the Department of Mathematics at Princeton University had introduced the

Fig. 4.1 Prisoners' dilemma

1,1	0,5
5,0	2,2

idea of what is now known as the Nash equilibrium, wherein he proposed "finite non-cooperative game always has at least one equilibrium point" (Nash, 1951, p. 286). Nash equilibrium describes a situation wherein a player does not have any incentive to change his or her strategy given that the other player(s) too do not change their strategy. In the prisoner's dilemma, the Nash equilibrium is obtained when both the players betray each other. If the prisoners' dilemma game is analysed closely, it will be evident that the players have strong motives not to cooperate (Axelrod, 1984; Sautter et al., 2007). Axelrod (1984) had explained, "it is better to defect if you think the other player will cooperate, *and* it is better to defect if you think the other player will defect. So no matter what the other player does, it pays for you to defect" (p. 9). However, if both the players in a prisoner's dilemma game defect (betray), they will both have worse outcomes than if they had both cooperated; that presents as the dilemma. Intriguingly it is often witnessed that players in a prisoners' dilemma game do cooperate even if such cooperation is essentially irrational (Raihani & Bshary, 2015). The reason for such irrational cooperation might lie within the empathic disposition of the players as Sautter et al. (2007) posited, "Empathy as a prosocial emotion could be a key to understanding the psychological underpinnings of why and who tends to cooperate in a collective act" (p. 154). In fact, the Nash equilibrium itself would arguably be rendered infructuous without factoring the empathic disposition of the players; Cory (2004) had explained, "The essential condition of a Nash equilibrium is a social exchange relationship – or a social game as implied and treated by the terminology of formal and mathematical game theory. And there could be no social exchange without empathy" (Cory, 2004, p. 90).

Empirical studies which explored the influence of empathic disposition on decisions to cooperate or betray in prisoners' dilemma yielded interesting results. Sautter et al. (2007) in their study found that "an empathetic disposition does not lead to a higher rate of cooperation but interacts with environmental conditioning to produce either a highly cooperative or highly uncooperative personality type" (p. 154). Consequently, high levels of empathy in individuals produced two polar outcomes: high levels of cooperation or high levels of non-cooperation. Sautter et al. (2007) reported that players from smaller towns and those with lesser income were more cooperative than their counterparts from large cities or those who had higher income levels. While larger cities induced a sense of anonymity which led to non-cooperative behaviour, smaller cities diminished the anonymity and people cooperated with each other. The researchers concluded that empathic disposition was mediated through social conditioning to produce the polarized outcomes. Sautter et al. (2007) thus posited that empathy does not present with a positive linear relationship with an inclination for just and egalitarian outcomes, but "an empathetic emotional disposition likely cultivates a sensitivity to social decisions, which, depending on an individual's social conditioning, leads to a more intense display of cooperation and defection" (p. 167). It is within the ambit of common-sense logic to assume that the behavioural dynamics of the players in one shot prisoner's dilemma may be different from that which is witnessed in the iterative versions of the game. While the tit-for-tat strategy and its derivatives might present as efficient strategies in iterative games, one shot prisoner's dilemma games provide no opportunities to learn from experiences and modify one's strategy accordingly. Thus, it would be prudent to surmise that players would overwhelmingly defect in such situations. However, as Rossi et al. (2017) reported from their studies, "A significant level of cooperation is observed in the experimental one-shot game" (p. 1) and that "a significant level of cooperation is observed among the users who are positively partially empathetic" (p. 30). Interestingly, the researchers also reported that "The experiment reveals not only positive affect of empathy but also a dispositional negative affect (spiteful or malicious) of empathy in the decision-making of some of the participants" (Rossi et al., 2017, p. 3). Thus, the results that Rossi et al. (2017) reported echoed in part at least the results of Sautter et al. (2007) in terms of polarity of behavioural outcomes resulting from empathetic disposition.

A situation similar to the prisoner's dilemma emerges within the game of public goods. A public goods game essentially presents a model for cooperative behaviour which includes an incentive for enjoying the benefits for free. A set of players are asked to contribute money to a pot and resultant money that is collected is distributed among the players equally. If a player does not contribute, he or she still reaps the benefits of the distribution, thus the Nash equilibrium in a public goods game involves defecting and not cooperating. Even though the rational self-interest-driven player should desist from contributing, the best outcome of the public goods game presents within cooperative behaviour. Batson et al. (1995) had explained that the social dilemma presented within the public goods game arises due to three fundamental reasons: "(a) each individual in a group or collective has a choice about how to allocate scarce resources (e.g., money, time, energy), and (b) allocation to the group as a whole provides more total benefit than does allocation by each individual to self, but (c) allocation by each individual to self provides more personal self-benefit than does allocation to the group as a whole" (p. 619). In a public goods game, however, if individuals keep maximizing their own self-interests, it results in a bad outcome where everyone stops contributing, thus leading to a collapse (Nash equilibrium presents as zero contribution). However, overwhelming evidence suggests that many people chose to maximize the benefit of the group rather than their own and seek to allocate their resources accordingly (Batson et al., 1995; Tomassini & Antonioni, 2020).

Several explanations have been put forward as reasons for such cooperative behaviour; prominent among them being enlightened self-interest which seeks to factor in long-term consequences of cooperation as well as avoidance of unwanted side effects like censure, guilt or shame and desire for positive side effects like praise and respect (Batson et al., 1995). However, Batson et al. (1995) had argued that in addition to enlightened self-interest, individuals might be prone to help others due to altruistic motivation that finds its basis in empathy. In this context, Batson et al. (1995) had explained, "If empathic emotion evokes altruistic motivation, then feeling empathy for another member of the collective should introduce an entirely new motive into a social dilemma (alongside self-interest and group-interest), a motive to benefit that individual" (p. 621). Several researchers have attempted to attribute the cooperation that is witnessed in public goods game to confusion, misunderstanding and error in judgement (Burton-Chellew et al., 2016; Goeschl & Lohse, 2018). However, experts like Andreoni (1995) echoed Batson et al. (1995) and posited that players in a public goods game often acted out of kindness and altruism rather than confusion when cooperating.

The role of empathy is evidently important within the ultimatum game which was developed by Güth et al. (1982) as an experimental form of an ultimatum bargaining situation. In the standard form of the game, a sum of money is to be divided among two players: one of who is a proposer and the other a responder. The proposer is in control of the money and has to make an offer to the responder for a split in the sum. If the responder accepts the offer, the money is split in the accepted manner or else no one gets any share of the sum. The ultimatum game provides no scope for negotiations between the players for a better outcome. Theoretically, rational players whose objectives are to maximize their utility should accept any positive offer as responders and thus rational proposers should make the smallest possible offer to the responders. In real-life scenarios, however, it has been reported that a majority of proposers offer between 40% and 50% of the sum in their control and that offer is most often accepted by the responders. However, the responders reject half the offers which are around 20% of the sum; the rates of such rejection increase further when the offers are around or below 10% of the sum (Page & Nowak, 2002; Houser & McCabe, 2014). It has been reported that if the players in an ultimatum game are empathic, they will strategize their offer based on their understanding of the amount that they themselves would accept in the scenario as the responder, in such cases non-rational offers which are above the lowest thresholds will be offered (Iranzo et al., 2012). Empathic strategists offer higher amounts as proposers thus empathy leads to the evolution of fairness (Page & Nowak, 2002; Iranzo et al., 2012). Behaviour of players in the ultimatum game does not seem to be predicted by age, sex or education; even the amount of money involved has little effect on the players' behaviour (Sigmund et al., 2002). In Indonesia when the ultimatum game was played with stakes that involved three times the average monthly income of the players, they still did not play the selfish strategy and rejected the game theoretic predicted outcome (Cameron, 1999).[6]

A popular criticism of the ultimatum game relates to the fact the experiment does not involve money that is earned but is given free without any work done for it; hence, the notion of fairness or unfairness does arise in such windfall gain. Several researchers have studied this aspect of ultimatum games and concluded that offers within ultimatum games are reduced significantly when the proposers have earned a right to propose through some action or competition rather than from situations where the proposer have just been endowed with a windfall gain. Interestingly when proposers have earned a right to propose, responders too accept far lower offers than when proposers are endowed with a windfall (Hoffman & Spitzer, 1985; Houser & McCabe, 2014). This aspect of participants' behaviour could also be explained through empathic disposition of the players. When a player earns a right to propose, the responder places himself in the proverbial shoes of the proposer and appreciates that if he/she would have earned a right to propose, he/she too would have offered a substantially lesser sum to the responder and thus accepts the offer.

The human behaviour observed within the ultimatum game exposes the divergence between an economic man (*Homo economicus*) and the emotional man (*Homo emoticus*). The economic man would have definitely played the game theoretic strategy of offering and accepting the minimal because any positive gain is better than no gain; however, such a rational decision would have been devoid of emotions. The decisions and behaviour of the emotional man is influenced by factors that affect such rational decision making; feelings of self-respect, fairness and justice, all of which find their source within empathic disposition. The rationale choice in an ultimatum game is often avoided not only in scenarios when individuals take decisions about their personal choices but even within macroeconomic decision making when national economies are at stake. *The New York Times* (Kanter & Alderman, 2015) reported that the Greek government was handed an ultimatum by its European lenders to agree to an extension of its bailout program or lose the funding; the decision was to be made by a strict deadline (Friday). The Greeks were reeling under severe economic crisis and were stressed, but even then, they did not acquiesce. The article quoted the Greek finance minister Yanis Varoufakis as declaring, "In the history of the European Union, nothing good has ever come out of ultimatums."

In real-life situations which play out beyond experimental setups (with artificial constraints), the dynamics of ultimatum games change drastically. The game is often not played between strangers but among people who know each other and thus bring their biases, affinity or dislike for each other to the game scenario. Moreover, knowledge about the other player and an experience of past interactions influence game decisions. In real-life situations, ultimatum games are not one-shot games without iterations and scope for negotiations.

The ultimatum game is often played out in real-life situations particularly within relationships involving asymmetric power distributions. Employers as well as employees play the ultimatum game when situations favour them; large corporations, monopolies and oligarchies often play the ultimatum game wherein the respondents are left with unjust take-it-or-leave-it choices. In divorce suits the powerful spouse attempts to throttle the other with vengeful ultimatums. Experiments on the ultimatum game have been played out in several complex corporate situations. An experiment was modelled on how certain corporates downsize their workforce even when they are making profit. The game involved a situation wherein either one player proposed how a given sum of money would be divided among two other players or two players co-operated to drive the third player put of the game and keep the sum to themselves and thus increase their profit. Another interesting experiment involved eBay wherein the experimenters introduced a buyer's protection insurance. It was seen that when a buyer's protection insurance was introduced, the buyers did not pay much attention to how the sellers were rated on eBay by previous purchasers; consequently, instances of fraud (which is an existing problem for eBay) increased (Grötker, 2009).

Studies and discussion of strategic behaviour have often been contextualized within the premises of violent human conflicts and their empathic causal analysis. In order to develop an empathic understanding of violent human conflicts, it is essential to study the motivations of each side within the conflict. Violent large scale human conflicts are broadly of two types: inter-state wherein two or more nations wage a war or even a limited conflict against each other and intra-state in which case the violent conflict is most often witnessed among two or more groups within a nation in the form of a civil war, riots or limited skirmishes.

It is an increasingly accepted argument that much of violent human conflicts in recent times have been perpetuated by economic factors; whether lopsided economic growth resulting in a wide gap between haves and have-nots, unimaginable poverty within a country or a group and even mad greed among oligarchs to control scarce and precious natural resources like oil or minerals. However, as Humphreys (2003) had opined, the instances of civil war in the world had increased in the twentieth century after the Second World War even as global economic prosperity increased; the reasons cited for this phenomenon by Humphreys (2003) were inequalities in the distribution of wealth and an increase in population. Curiously, a World Bank study however reported that wars in the current context have been "systematically related to a few economic conditions, such as dependence upon primary commodity exports and low national income. Conversely, and astonishingly, objective measures of social grievance, such as inequality, a lack of democracy, and ethnic and religious divisions, have had no systematic effect on risk" (Collier, 2000, p. 1). Homer-Dixon (1994) had posited that environmental scarcities could lead to violent conflict especially in poorer countries that are facing scarcity of water, aquatic and marine resources like fish, forest resources and fertile cultivable land.

Humphreys (2003) had used World Bank data to present an obvious relationship between a nation's wealth and its chances of a civil war. The model had proposed that while an individual living in country where the GDP per individual was $250 had a 15% probability of facing a war in the next five years another individual living in a country where the GDP per individual was \$1250 would face less than 4% chance of facing a war in the same time frame (the risk reducing to less than 1% in those countries having a per individual GDP of \$5000 or more). Since conflicts in poorer nations often spill over to affect even rich countries, it is in the strategic interest of the rich countries to exhibit empathic concern and help the poorer nations to promote economic growth there (Humphreys, 2003). A game theoretic analysis in such cases leads to a model wherein decision makers from rich countries are motivated to help poorer countries (GDP $\leq$ \$250) which have the highest threat of conflict rather than the developing countries which have a moderate level of threat (since the resources for such help are limited and would require a strategy wherein the minimum amount of resource would lead to the maximum positive change in terms of ushering peace through prosperity). It has also been proposed that a rise in international trade has led to lesser number of international wars and that countries which are involved in higher levels of trade with other countries are less likely to go to war (Jackson & Nei, 2015). It is evident from a cursory study of modern world politics that rich nations seldom go to war with each other. However, it is pertinent to note at this point that while the correlation between poverty and war is widely understood, the direction of the causal relationship is however not clear; thus, the jury is out on the issue of whether poverty leads to war or does war cause poverty.

There have however been arguments in favour of violence when violence is used as means of protecting property and wealth from predators, thus enhancing social welfare and productive activities (Bates et al., 2001). In the Weberian model (Weber, 1958), states have the monopoly of using violence to maintain order. This monopoly on violence can be used for welfare and social development or it might be predatory. Even governments that are voted in by the public might later turn predatory towards the very people who voted them to power or conversely a government that assumed power through predatory means might enhance social welfare of the citizens; Bates et al. (2001) expanded this argument to create a model of a stateless state (according to them since the behaviour of a state cannot be predictable, it might be assumed not to exist) wherein citizens could engage in production, violence and entertainment. The resultant game theoretic model that the researchers developed concluded that in a stateless society poverty was the price of peace while violence could present as the price of prosperity. This predicament, the researchers argued, could be offset by the systemic processes of a formal state; therein lies the attraction of political states. Skaperdas (2001) had concurred with this line of thought and posited, "Organized crime emerges out of the power vaccuum that is created by the absence of state enforcement" (p. 173).

Marxist ideologues propose that socio-economic inequalities often lead to violent conflicts. The World Bank report cited earlier however refutes that premise; nevertheless, experts like Humphreys (2003) have explained that while the World Bank study analysed inequalities among individuals (overall inequality), it is the inequalities among regional or ethnic groups of people (horizontal inequality) that often lead to conflicts. Gurr and Moore (1997) had emphasized that "systematic and selective limitation of peoples' access to economic opportunities or political positions based on their ascriptive characteristic" (p. 1084) have often led to ethnopolitical rebellions. Similarly, Muller and Seligson (1987) had posited, "the effect of income inequality on political violence is found to hold in the context of a causal model that takes into account the repressiveness of the regime, governmental acts of coercion, intensity of separatism, and level of economic development" (p. 425). Violent conflicts related to economic inequalities have been most vividly witnessed within instances of agrarian rebellions all over the world. Midlarsky (1982) had pondered on the reason as to why "major revolutions almost always occur in predominantly agrarian societies but almost never in industrial ones" (p. 3). The researcher had reasoned that industrial societies are more egalitarian and prosperous than agrarian societies. Consequently, while Marxists have often predicted that political revolution would be brought about by the working class, it has been the peasantry that has emerged as the core of violent political conflicts in many parts of the world. Several influential scholars such as Samuel Huntington (1968) and Manus Midlarsky (1982) have propounded what is described as discontent theories and opined that maldistribution of agrarian land was at the core of most mass political violence and revolution (Huntington, 1968; Midlarsky, 1982). However certain other theorists have proposed a contrarian view (resource allocation hypothesis) to explain political violence which clarifies that such violence and revolts are not a result of discontent per se (which is common in any society) but the ability of the agrarian society to mobilize resources and organize the revolt. Muller and Seligson (1987) had taken a broader view of the discontent hypothesis and opined that the main cause for political violence was "inequality in the distribution of income rather than maldistribution of land" (p. 427).

The role of empathy in violent human conflicts is curious. It is reported that humans feel more empathetic towards their own kind; thus, in a conflict between peasants and the government peasants will be more empathic towards their own kind and peasants of a particular group (e.g., rice cultivators) will be more empathically disposed towards their group rather than others. This behavioural phenomenon described as intergroup empathy bias was explained by Cikara et al. (2014) as "the tendency not only to empathize less with out-group relative to in-group members, but also feel pleasure in response to their pain" (p. 110). Thus, while perceived injustice and violence against a co-member of a group might lead other members to perpetuate violence as a motive to avenge the wrong; the violence might also be motivated by the urge to witness the members of an out-group suffer.[7]

Human reaction to violence and conflict is mediated by several complex behavioural phenomena. Josef Stalin is said to have proclaimed, "The death of a single Russian soldier is a tragedy. A million deaths is a statistic."[8] The statement, though cold and insensitive, exemplifies a tendency to deindividualize and sometimes dehumanize violence. Notwithstanding the various posits on the influence of empathy in violent conflicts, it is often observed that emphatic disposition towards individual identifiable victims of a conflict is far more potent than that for anonymous victims or mere statistical listings of victims. This phenomenon is termed as identifiable victim effect (Jenni & Loewenstein, 1997). A closely related behavioural phenomenon is the compassion fade (Västfjäll et al., 2014) where it is observed that human compassion for a single individual in distress fades when there are groups of distressed people. In fact, it has been reported that donors are willing to donate more money to a single child in need than to two needy children (Västfjäll et al., 2014). The behavioural patterns were recently observed in the outpouring of grief and sorrow that resulted from the photo of the dead body of the three-year-old Syrian child Alan Kurdi who tragically died while his family was trying to reach Europe during the refugee crisis. A similar empathic reaction was observed with regard to the photo of a young Afghan girl skipping with joy on reaching Melsbroek military airport in Belgium, her parents having successfully escaped from Taliban-controlled Afghanistan. When tragedy meets a face, it results in greater empathic reactions.

However, the complexities of human behaviour ensure that such behaviour cannot be constrained within certain set theories and phenomenon; thus, contrary to the previous discussion it has also been witnessed that human violence may not necessarily lead to morbid bitterness among the rival entities. Hartman and Morse (2015) in a study conducted among groups involved in the Liberian civil war found evidence of empathic behaviour among the warring factions; the researchers concluded "violence-affected individuals and communities host more refugees, do so for longer, host more outgroup refugees – even those co-ethnic to their wartime rivals – and host a higher share of refugees with health problems or fleeing direct violence" (p. 1).

Thomas Schelling, an American economist and recipient of the 2005 Nobel Memorial Prize in Economic Sciences for "having enhanced our understanding of conflict and cooperation through game-theory analysis,"[9] has worked extensively on the issue of game theory and conflicts. His approach to conflict resolution assumes that the two parties in a conflict (even in a violent conflict like war) present with interests that are in conflict to each other as well as those that are mutually dependent. Schelling (1980) explained, "'winning' in a conflict does not have a strictly competitive meaning; it is not winning relative to one's adversary. It means gaining relative to one's own value system; and this may be done by bargaining, by mutual accommodation, and by the avoidance of mutually damaging behaviour" (Schelling, 1980, pp. 4–5). Essentially Schelling proposes an empathic model of conflict resolution where even war and war-like situations might be viewed as non-zero-sum game situations where an efficient outcome might be achieved through negotiations and bargaining. Schelling's commendable work on deterrence and the use of credible threat of war to avoid actual war involved the use of strategic empathy without an overt mention of the term. He explained his strategy of conflict as "conditioning of one's own behaviour on the behaviour of others" (Schelling, 1980, p. 15).

The discussions in this chapter involved an analysis of empathic behaviour in situations that involve strategic decisions whether in everyday life or in dire unwelcome conflict situations involving violence. The role of empathy in such situations help in understanding the role and behaviour of the other party and calibrating a response based on one party's prediction of how the other will respond. Such predictions are efficiently moderated through an empathic understanding of the other. Thus, empathy is used as a strategic tool to enhance an understanding of a rival, a foe or even a collaborator or friend to design responses for maximization of ones' self-interest or as is often the case, the fulfilment of mutual objectives.

Notes

1. The term survival of the fittest was first used by English philosopher and biologist Herbert Spencer in his book *Principles of Biology* (Spencer, 1864).
2. A single player game is called a decision problem.
3. An imaginary unit of measuring utility that is derived from the consumption of a particular good or service.
4. Reciprocal Altruism is also observed in other animals such as vampire bats. (Wilkinson, 1984) and the naked mole rat (Jarvis, 1978).
5. Albert Tucker was a noted Canadian mathematician who had significant contributions to economics and game theory. Nobel laureates John Nash and Lloyd Shapley were his PhD students.
6. However, in an interesting analytical study on the Ultimatum game, Grohn et al. (2014) had presented a model wherein they had proposed that a proposer with high levels of empathy would offer the lowest value that the responder would be willing to accept; the researchers claimed, "Therefore, in the ultimatum game, the empathetic type will on average offer less than the non-empathetic type." See Grohn et al. (2014)
7. The German term to describe a feeling of joy in others' suffering is Schadenfreude.
8. As quoted in Nisbett and Ross (1980, p. 43).

References

Allot, R. (1992). Evolutionary aspects of love and empathy. *Journal of Social and Evolutionary Systems, 15*(4), 353–370. https://doi.org/10.1016/1061-7361(92)90023-7

Andreoni, J. (1995). Cooperation in public-goods experiments: Kindness or confusion? *The American Economic Review, 85*(4), 891–904. https://doi.org/10.2307/2118238

Axelrod, R. (1984). *The evolution of co-operation*. Basic Books.

Barnett, M. A., & Thompson, S. (1985). The role of perspective taking and empathy in children's machiavellianism, prosocial behavior, and motive for helping. *The Journal of Generic Psychology, Research and Theory on Human Development, 146*(3), 295–305. https://doi.org/10.1080/00221325.1985.9914459

Bates, R., et al. (2001). Organizing violence. *Journal of Conflict Resolution, 46*(5), 599–628. https://doi.org/10.1177/002200202236166

Batson, D. C., et al. (1995). Empathy and the collective good: Caring for one of the others in a social dilemma. *Journal of Personality and Social Psychology, 68*(4), 619–631. https://doi.org/10.1037/0022-3514.68.4.619

Burton-Chellew, M. N., et al. (2016). Conditional cooperation and confusion in public-goods experiments. *Proceedings of the National Academy of Sciences, 113*(5), 1291–1296. https://doi.org/10.1073/pnas.1509740113

Cameron, L. A. (1999). Raising the stakes in the ultimatum game: Experimental evidence from Indonesia. *Economic Inquiry, 37*(1), 47–59. https://doi.org/10.1111/j.1465-7295.1999.tb01415.x

Chismar, D. (1988). Empathy and sympathy: The important difference. *The Journal of Value Inquiry, 22*(4), 257–266. https://doi.org/10.1007/bf00136928

Cikara, M., et al. (2014). Their pain gives us pleasure: How intergroup dynamics shape empathic failures and counter-empathic responses. *Journal of Experimental Social Psychology, 55*, 110–125. https://doi.org/10.1016/j.jesp.2014.06.007

Collier, P. (2000). *Economic causes of civil war and their implications for policy*. World Bank Group. Retrieved September 9, 2021, from http://documents.worldbank.org/curated/en/272561468780312524/Economic-causes-of-civil-war-and-their-implications-for-policy

Cory, A. G. (2004). *The consilient brain*. Springer Science + Business Media.

Darwin, C. (1871). *The descent of man, and selection in relation to sex*. Princeton University Press, 1981.

Ekman, P. (2010). Darwin's compassionate view of human nature. *JAMA, 303*(6), 557–558. https://doi.org/10.1001/jama.2010.101

Frank, H. R. (1988). *Passions with reason*. W.W. Norton & Company.

Gallese, V., & Goldman, A. (1998). Mirror neurons and the simulation theory of mind-reading. *Trends in Cognitive Sciences, 2*(12), 493–501. https://doi.org/10.1016/s1364-6613(98)01262-5

Garver, R. (2017). *What game theory tells us about Trump's 'Madman' approach to North Korea*. Retrieved April 7, 2021, from https://www.thefiscaltimes.com/2017/08/11/What-Game-Theory-Tells-Us-About-Trump-s-Madman-Approach-North-Korea

Gierer, A. (2000). Evolution of empathy as a source of human altruism. In H. Cruse, J. Dean, & H. Ritter (Eds.), *Prerational intelligence: Adaptive behavior and intelligent systems without symbols and logic, Volume 1, Volume 2 prerational intelligence: Interdisciplinary perspectives on the behavior of natural and artificial systems, Volume 3. Studies in cognitive systems, Volume 26*. Springer. https://doi.org/10.1007/978-94-010-0870-9_65

Goeschl, T., & Lohse, J. (2018). Cooperation in public good games. Calculated or confused? *European Economic Review, 107*, 185–203. https://doi.org/10.1016/j.euroecorev.2018.05.007

Grohn, J., et al. (2014). A note on empathy in games. *Journal of Economic Behavior & Organization, 108*, 383–388. https://doi.org/10.1016/j.jebo.2014.01.008

Grötker, R. (2009). A game for life. *Max Plank Research, 2*, 80–85. Retrieved August 8, 2021, from https://www.mpg.de/794224/W006_Culture-Society_080-085.pdf

Gurr, T. R., & Moore, W. H. (1997). Ethnopolitical rebellion: A cross-sectional analysis of the 1980s with risk assessments for the 1990s. *American Journal of Political Science, 41*(4), 1079–1103. https://doi.org/10.2307/2960482

Güth, W., et al. (1982). An experimental analysis of ultimatum bargaining. *Journal of Economic Behavior & Organization, 3*(4), 367–388. https://doi.org/10.1016/0167-2681(82)90011

Hartman, A. C., & Morse, B. S. (2015). Wartime violence, empathy, and intergroup altruism: Evidence from the Ivoirian refugee crisis in Liberia. *British Journal of Political Science, 50*(2), 731–755. https://doi.org/10.1017/S0007123417000655

Hoffman, E., & Spitzer, M. L. (1985). Entitlements, rights, and fairness: an experimental examination of subjects' concepts of distributive justice. *The Journal of Legal Studies, 14*(2), 259–297. https://doi.org/10.2307/724430

Homer-Dixon, T. F. (1994). Environmental scarcities and violent conflict: Evidence from cases. *International Security, 19*(1), *50–40*. https://doi.org/10.2307/2539147

Houser, D., & McCabe, K. (2014). Experimental economics and experimental game theory. In P. W. Glimcher & E. Fehr (Eds.), *Neuroeconomics* (2nd ed.). Academic press. https://doi.org/10.1016/b978-0-12-416008-8.0

Humphreys, M. (2003). *Economics and violent conflict.* Retrieved September 9, 2021, from https://hhi.harvard.edu/publications/economics-and-violent-conflict

Huntington, S. P. (1968). *Political order in changing societies.* Yale University Press.

Iranzo, J., et al. (2012). Empathy emerges spontaneously in the ultimatum game: Small groups and networks. *PLoS One, 7*(9), e43781. https://doi.org/10.1371/journal.pone.0043781

Jackson, M. O., & Nei, S. (2015). Networks of military alliances, wars, and international trade. *Proceedings of the National Academy of Sciences, 112*(50), 15277–15284. https://doi.org/10.1073/pnas.1520970112

Jarvis, J. U. M. (1978). Energetics of survival in Heterocephalus glaber (Rüppell), the Naked mole-rat (Rodentia: Bathyergidae). *Bulletin of Carnegie Museum of Natural History, 6*, 81–86.

Jenni, K. E., & Loewenstein, G. (1997). Explaining the "Identifiable Victim Effect". *Journal of Risk and Uncertainty, 14*, 235–257. https://doi.org/10.1023/a:1007740225484

Kahneman, D., & Tversky, A. (1982). The simulation heuristic. In D. Kahneman, P. Slovic, & A. Tversky (Eds.), *Judgment under uncertainty.* Cambridge University Press.

Kanter, J., & Alderman, L. (2015). *Meeting on Greek debt produces an ultimatum.* Retrieved August 8, 2021, from https://www.nytimes.com/2015/02/17/business/international/greece-debt-eurozone-finance-ministers-meeting.html
Kukk, L. C. (2017). *The compassionate achiever.* Harper One.
Mafessoni, F., & Lachmann, M. (2019). The complexity of understanding others as the evolutionary origin of empathy and emotional contagion. *Scientific Reports, 9*(1). https://doi.org/10.1038/s41598-019-41835-5
Midlarsky, M. I. (1982). Scarcity and inequality: Prologue to the onset of mass revolution. *The Journal of Conflict Resolution, 26*(1), 3–38. https://doi.org/10.2307/173670
Muller, E. N., & Seligson, M. A. (1987). Inequality and insurgency. *The American Political Science Review, 81*(2), 425–452. https://doi.org/10.2307/1961960
Myerson, R. (1991). *Game theory. Analysis of conflict.* Harvard University Press.
Nash, J. (1951). Non-cooperative games. *The Annals of Mathematics, Second Series, 54*(2), 286–295. https://doi.org/10.2307/1969529
Neumann, J. V., & Morgenstein, O. (1944). *Theory of games and economic behaviour.* Princeton University Press.
Nisbett, R., & Ross, L. (1980). *Human inference: Strategies and shortcomings of social judgment.* Prentice-Hall, Inc.
Page, K., & Nowak, M. (2002). Empathy leads to fairness. *Bulletin of Mathematical Biology, 64*(6), 1101–1116. https://doi.org/10.1006/bulm.2002.0321
Pandey, K. S., & Sharma, V. (2020). A tribute to frontline corona warriors—Doctors who sacrificed their life while saving patients during the ongoing COVID-19 pandemic. *Indian Journal of Ophthalmology, 68*(5), 939–942. https://doi.org/10.4103/ijo.IJO_754_20
Raihani, N. J., & Bshary, R. (2015). Why humans might help strangers. *Frontiers in Behavioral Neuroscience, 9.* https://doi.org/10.3389/fnbeh.2015.00039
Ross, D. (2019). Game theory. In E. N. Zalta (Ed.), *The Stanford encyclopedia of philosophy* (Winter 2019 ed.). Retrieved April 6, 2021, from https://plato.stanford.edu/archives/win2019/entries/game-theory/
Rossi, G., et al. (2017). *Empathy in one-shot prisoner dilemma.* arXiv:1702.05361v2. Retrieved April 16, 2021, from https://arxiv.org/abs/1702.05361v2
Sautter, J. A., et al. (2007). A dual-edged sword: Empathy and collective action in the prisoner's dilemma. *The Annals of the American Academy of Political and SocialScience,614(1),154–171.*https://doi.org/10.1177/0002716207306360
Schelling, T. C. (1980). *The strategy of conflict.* Harvard University Press.
Sigmund, K., et al. (2002). The economics of fair play. *Scientific American, 286*(1), 82–87. https://doi.org/10.1038/scientificamerican01
Sinclair, S., et al. (2016). Sympathy, empathy, and compassion: A grounded theory study of palliative care patients' understandings, experiences, and preferences. *Palliative Medicine, 31*(5), 437–447. https://doi.org/10.1177/0269216316663499

Skaperdas, S. (2001). The political economy of organized crime: Providing protection when the state does not. *Economics of Governance, 2*(3), 173–202. https://doi.org/10.1007/pl00011026

Smith, A. (1776). *The wealth of nations. An inquiry into the nature and causes of the wealth of nations.* University of Chicago Press, 1977.

Spencer, H. (1864). *Principles of biology* (Vol. 1). William and Norgate.

Tomassini, M., & Antonioni, A. (2020). Public goods games on coevolving social network models. *Frontiers in Physics, 8*(58). https://doi.org/10.3389/fphy.2020.00058

Trivers, R. L. (1971). The evolution of reciprocal altruism. *The Quarterly Review of Biology, 46*(1), 35–57. https://doi.org/10.1086/406755

Västfjäll, D., et al. (2014). Compassion fade: Affect and charity are greatest for a single child in need. *PLoS One, 9*(6), e100115. https://doi.org/10.1371/journal.pone.0100115

Weber, M. (1958). Politics as a vocation. In H. H. Gerth & C. W. Mills (Eds.), *From Max Weber*. Oxford University Press.

Wilkinson, G. S. (1984). Reciprocal food sharing in the vampire bat. *Nature, 308*(5955), 181–184. https://doi.org/10.1038/308181a0

PART II

Empathy – In the Context of Specific Economic Activities

CHAPTER 5

Empathy and Business Management

The period between 1760 and 1850 ushered in massive changes in the socio-economic structure of England. The British historian Eric Hobsbawm (1996) had described the changes as: "for the first time in human history, the shackles were taken off the productive power of human societies, which henceforth became capable of the constant, rapid and up to the present limitless multiplication of men, goods and services" (p. 28). In fact, Hobsbawm (1996) went further and described the happenings of the times as "probably the most important event in world history, at any rate since the invention of agriculture and cities" (p. 29). Similarly, Wyatt (2009) had compared the events and changes of the times to that of the Neolithic revolution when humans had undergone a transition from being hunter gatherers to adopting agriculture as the means of sustenance. The comparison is not without reason; the changes brought forth during these times fundamentally altered the nature of human society that was prevalent for thousands of preceding years. In the beginning of this period, England was a largely agrarian and self-sufficient economy; however, the English society changed rapidly during these times to become a largely industrialized economy wherein even staple food and raw materials were being imported while exports included factory manufactured goods and textiles. The period saw a massive increase in the population supplemented by an improved standard of living[1] (Clark, 2010). This period of socio-economic change has been termed by historians as the industrial

D. Roy, *Empathonomics*,
https://doi.org/10.1007/978-981-95-4033-4_5

revolution.[2] Hobsbawm (1996) concurred: "To call this process the Industrial Revolution is both logical and in line with a well-established tradition" (p. 28).

While experts like Wyatt (2009) have presented the argument that the industrial revolution was the result of the "dramatic discoveries of the Scientific Revolution" (p. xi), others like Farr (2003) have asserted that industrial revolution was a product of an increase in economic demand and was not a direct result of an enhanced supply of scientific methods. The argument might be aptly placed in the context of the cotton industry. In the years preceding the industrial revolution, the demand for cotton was far higher than the corresponding supply. Consequently, machines were invented to increase the production of cotton during the times. Several legendary inventors such as Richard Arkwright (1732–1792), James Hargreaves (1720–1778), Samuel Crompton (1753–1827), Edmund Cartwright (1743–1823) contributed to the design and production of the new machines to enhance production in the cotton industry; thus, it is widely recognized that the cotton industry in England had played a major role in catalyzing the industrial revolution. Hobsbawm (1996) presented the argument that the British advancement in industries was not a consequent of superiority in science and technology; rather Britain lagged in the pursuits of natural and social sciences when compared with the European nations like France and Germany at that time. Hobsbawm (1996) further argued that the industrial revolution was not the result of intellectual and scientific refinements and the technologies used in the machines that were invented during the times were not beyond the reach of common artisans and their makeshift workshops. In the light of such arguments, it is interesting to explore the reasons for Britain's dominance as an industrial nation during the times. Hobsbawm (1996) posited that Britain provided the right environment for such transformation "since private profit and economic development had become accepted as the supreme objects of government policy" (p. 31). The agrarian pursuits in Britain were monopolized by few large landlords whose lands were cultivated by tenant farmers who in turn employed the landless workers to work in the fields. Hobsbawm (1996) explained that the agricultural activities in Britain during the times had three fundamental objectives: to feed the masses who worked in the factories, to provide cheap labour in large quantities to work in the factories and to provide a surplus which could be used as capital for other non-agrarian enterprises. More importantly Britain's dominance in the industrial revolution was augmented by the role of its colonies and in no small way the inhuman practices of slave trade as well. Adam Smith (1776) had posited that colonies prospered when 'plenty of good land' (p. 746) was available; however, as Williams (1944) posited, "land and capital were both useless unless labor could be commanded. Labor, that is, must be constant and must work, or be made to work, in co-operation" (p. 4). The attitude of the colonizers towards slavery was apparent in Adam Smith's words wherein he posited that the interests of the "superior orders obliges them to treat the inferior one with more generosity and humanity; *at least where that inferior one is not in a state of slavery*" (p. 746; emphasis added). Thus, it was accepted within the intellection of the times that slaves did not deserve the empathy, humanity or compassion of their so-called masters.

The colonial economies reaped massive benefits from such an inhuman practice mostly within labour intensive plantation-based industries like tobacco, sugar, tea and cotton. An appropriate example could be found within the cotton industry which was a flourishing British industry of the times and was predominantly founded on slave trade. Slaves from West African countries were shipped to colonies where they provided free labour for the cotton plantations. The colonies were not allowed to process the cotton into finished products, and the cotton was shipped to England where it was processed and sold to the African colonies at a humungous profit along with other finished products like alcohol or weapons. The ships carrying the products to Africa returned with a macabre human cargo of slaves for the Americas. The resultant model of the three-way passage has been termed as triangular trade (Lordshaughn, 2020). The profit from the triangular trade was reinvested in slave trade as well as the cotton industry and formed the basis of what is described as the Atlantic economy. While cities like London, Birmingham and Manchester witnessed incredible growth and development arising from the triangular trade (Lordshaughn, 2020), other port cities like Glasgow, Bristol and Liverpool were at the centre of the slave trade (Hobsbawm, 1996). The transatlantic passage from Africa to America was euphemistically termed as the middle passage. The passage involved ships carrying dehumanized human cargo in the form of slaves who were bought by slave traders from Africa and shipped to work in America (Walker, 2004). The Africans were treated worse than cattle on the slave ships; they were chained to each other and often had to lie on each other's faeces and urine. Women were sexually abused and the unhygienic conditions coupled with the barely breathable air led to outbreak of diseases like smallpox and yellow fever (Johnson et al., 1998). Slave trade, however, was not restricted to Africa; in India, poor tribal folk were sold as bonded labour to the expanding tea industry in Bengal and Assam. In fact, after the abolition of slavery in 1834, the British began the system of using indentured labour from India (called Girmitiya or Jahajis) to work in their plantations in Mauritius, Fiji and the Caribbean. The notorious system continued for over 80 years before being abolished in 1917 and involved the transportation of over two million Indians who were sent to around 20 British colonies of the times (Kumar, 2017).

A profound outcome of the industrial revolution was the introduction of the factory system; prior to the industrial revolution, manufacturing units were mostly situated within domestic homes. Thus, the factory essentially brought about a segregation between the points of consumption and production (Mokyr, 2001). When viewed within the socio-economic context, the factory represented an organization where the tools and machines of manufacture belonged to the owner of the factory who decided the rules of engagement. This was in stark contrast to the previous system wherein the tools and machines were owned by the artisans who worked according to rules which were set by themselves. Max Weber (1961) argued, "As between the domestic system and the factory the volume of fixed capital was decisive. Where fixed capital was not necessary the domestic system has endured down to the present; where it was necessary, factories arose" (p. 136). Consequently, a factory represented an organized system of mass production wherein goods could be produced with increased efficiency. While describing the factory system, Max Weber (1961) had explained that when "labor discipline within the shop is combined with technical specialization and co-ordination and the application of non-human sources of power, we are face to face with the modern factory" (p. 133). Hobsbawm (1996) explained that a factory system encouraged production "in such vast quantities and at such rapidly diminishing cost, as to be no longer dependent on existing demand, but to create its own market" (p. 32). The common example provided in this case related to the automobile industry wherein Ford began to manufacture cheap cars which led to post-facto increase in demand for motor cars.

In order that an efficient system of production can be achieved, the available resources had to be optimally managed. Since power and raw material were necessary to drive the factories, they were initially located near sources of power and raw material like coal, water or iron. However, with the advent of railways, factories were increasingly located near the markets where the finished goods could be sold and this led to rapid urbanization wherein the predominantly agrarian English society turned into an urban industrial society. Thus, mines, factories and railroads presented as the main drivers of the new cities of the times (Mumford, 1961). The results of this transformation were not wholly functional and led to certain undesirable outcomes. The urban townships that resulted from the industrial revolution were ghastly, dirty and unhealthy;[3] in the words of Lewis Mumford (1961), "the change from organized urban handicraft to large scale factory production transformed the industrial towns into dark hives, busily puffing, clanking, screeching, smoking for twelve and fourteen hours a day, sometimes going around the clock. The slavish routine of the mines, whose labor was an intentional punishment for criminals, became the normal environment of the new industrial worker" (p. 446). Friedrich Engels spent some years in England as an agent of his father's textile business; he wrote tellingly about the social and physical conditions of the industrial cities of the times: "The streets are generally unpaved, rough, dirty, filled with vegetable and animal refuse, without sewers or gutters, but supplied with foul, stagnant pools instead. Moreover, ventilation is impeded by the bad, confused method of building of the whole quarter, and since many human beings here live crowded into a small space, the atmosphere that prevails in these working-men's quarters may readily be imagined" (Engels, 1987, p. 108). The industrial cities of the times were thus festering hellholes of poverty, grime, disease, crime and rampant exploitation of fellow humans with little or no scope for empathic behaviour. Human activity had a single sole objective: "aggressive desire to increase the wealth of individuals: that was the be-all and the end-all" (Mumford, 1961, p. 448). Engels, too, had elaborated upon this unempathetic society: "Everywhere barbarous indifference, hard egotism on one hand, and nameless misery on the other, everywhere social warfare, every man's house in a state of siege, everywhere reciprocal plundering under the protection of the law, and all so shameless, so openly avowed that one shrinks before the consequences of our social state as they manifest themselves here undisguised, and can only wonder that the whole crazy fabric still hangs together" (Engels, 1987, p. 106).

The industrial revolution led to a rethinking of traditional economic models and ideations. Economists initially recognized land and labour as the two factors of production, subsequently a third factor was recognized in the form of capital which included the physical assets of plants and equipment which were directly used to enhance production capacity.

Richard Cantllion, an Irish economist of French descent, is widely credited with the introduction of a fourth factor of production: entrepreneur. An entrepreneur is a person who 'invests' in goods and services of workers and resells them to consumers. Thus, the workers producing such goods and services are assured of a stable income in the short run while the entrepreneur takes the risk of fluctuating market conditions (Wren & Bedeian, 2006; Casson, 2002). The role and functions as well as the qualities of an entrepreneur were further expanded upon by Jean Baptiste Say who proposed that entrepreneurship "[r]equires a combination of moral qualities that are not often found together. Judgment, perseverance, and a knowledge of the world as well as of business. [The entrepreneur] is called upon to estimate with tolerable accuracy the importance of the specific product, the probable amount of the demand, and the means of its production: at one time he must employ a great number of hands; at another, buy or order the raw material, collect laborers, find consumers, and give at all times a rigid attention to order and economy; in a word, he must possess the art of superintendence and administration" (Say, 1821, p. 72 as cited in Wren & Bedeian, 2006, p. 43). Entrepreneurs were often managers of businesses that they only partly owned. They received an income for their contribution to the capital as well as an additional income for the managerial work that they performed. Moreover, as businesses expanded entrepreneurs employed managers under them who did not own any part of the business (Wren & Bedeian, 2006). Thus, an economic model recognizing the role of professional managers managing businesses evolved.

While large-scale organizations like government departments or the military forces had existed during the pre-industrial revolution era, these organizations were either non-profits which were not under pressure to earn profits (e.g., government departments) or were managed through strict traditional disciplinarian protocols as in the military. The industrial revolution introduced the factory system of production wherein hundreds of workers, mostly from rural agrarian backgrounds, worked. The initial managerial problems in the factories related to recruitment, training and sustained motivation to work. There was a significant shift of rural agrarian workers from farms to factories leading to migration from rural areas to the industrialized zones. However, skilled workers were few in number; thus they were important to the employers who offered additional incentives for their skill and expertise. Since the large part of the labour force of the times was illiterate and unfamiliar to factory and industrial work, training them for the factory environment presented a challenge. A large part of the training was completed on the job through demonstration and trial and error. The most challenging aspect however was to keep the workers motivated to work; since most of the workers had a behavioural history of independent self-sufficient work, the disciplined timings and rules of the factory was difficult for them to adhere to. If four days of work was sufficient to feed the family, the workers would skip the remaining days of work. It was from this practice that certain employers brought forth the theory that workers' wages should be kept at mere subsistence levels so that they are forced to work in order to survive. The Prussian-German philosopher Ferdinand Lassalle had propounded the Iron Law of wages wherein it was proposed that in the long run real wages tend towards the minimum level required for the sustenance of workers. David Ricardo proposed a similar theory of wages wherein he posited, "Labour, like all other things which are purchased and sold, and which may be increased or diminished in quantity, has its natural and its market price. The natural price of labour is that price which is necessary to enable the labourers, one with another, to subsist and to perpetuate their race, without either increase or diminution" (Ricardo, 1821, p. 58). Adam Smith however had disagreed with this line of thought; he had proposed that "The wages of labour are the encouragement of industry, which, like every other human quality, improves in proportion to the encouragement it receives. A plentiful subsistence increases the bodily strength of the labourer, and the comfortable hope of bettering his condition, and of ending his days perhaps in ease and plenty, animates him to exert that strength to the utmost. Where wages are high, accordingly, we shall always find the workmen more active, diligent, and expeditious than where they are low" (Smith, 1776, p. 119).

A close scrutiny of the economic model that was used during the industrial revolution reveals that exploitation formed the basis of the model. The unempathetic and cruel model not only dehumanized fellow humans from Africa and the colonies and allowed them to be traded as cattle but also ensured that the work force from England itself was treated abysmally and condemned to a life of poverty and grime while being dependent on the employers for mere sustenance of life. The exploitative practices of the economic model practiced during the industrial revolution led to a disequilibrium in society which further induced the idea of socialism. As a concept socialism was introduced as utopian socialism which was championed by the Welsh businessman and thinker Robert Cowen who was also a pioneer in the trade union movement. Utopian socialists believed that positive ideals would present as the drivers for society to help it develop.

They believed that all members and classes in the society would voluntarily play their part in society. However, the later socialists like Karl Marx differed from the Utopian socialists and found their ideations to be impractical and unrealistic. The later socialist ideations like Marxism or social democracy involved the concept of class struggle and revolution. In fact, Karl Marx had written a scathing indictment of Ferdinand Lassalle's iron law of wages, wherein he had declared, "Since Lassalle's death, there has asserted itself in our party the scientific understanding that wages are not what they appear to be—namely, the value, or price, of labor—but only a masked form for the value, or price, of labor power" (Marx, 1875).

The upheaval that the industrial revolution caused to societies all over the world and the increased need for professional management in business led to the establishment of certain institutions dedicated to the study of commerce and management. In 1759, the Aula do Comércio was set up in Lisbon and the Ecole Supérieure de Commerce de Paris (ESCP) was set up in 1819. Meanwhile in the United States of America, the Wharton School was established at the University of Pennsylvania in 1881. The recognition of management as a mainstream discipline of study was however catalysed in 1909 when an American mechanical engineer named Frederick Winslow Taylor wrote his famous book *The Principles of Scientific Management*. Taylor's foremost objective was to maximize production and efficiency in factories, and he proposed to do that by methods that he deemed were scientific. Taylor proposed that rule of thumb techniques be replaced with techniques that had scientific basis; prioritize training and development of staff; encourage coordination between workers and management wherein management plan the work through scientific methods and the workers execute it; promote specialization of work by matching people with the correct job meant for them. While Taylor revolutionized the management philosophy of the times by involving the workers in the planning process, his ideas also ensured that the workers were relegated to the status of mechanical units devoid of thinking and merely performing a repetitive task ad infinitum. The process ensured that workers did not learn any additional skills and were de facto left with little autonomy over their task. Edward Cadbury wrote, "any further sub-division of labour in the direction of eliminating any little judgement initiative as to the methods of work, valuable as it might be in its immediate impact on production, would almost certainly in the long run produce effects which would lower the whole capacity of the worker" (Cadbury, 1914, p. 104). Adam Smith had similar thoughts on the division of labour: "The man whose whole life is spent in performing a few simple operations, of which the effects are perhaps always the same, or very nearly the same, has no occasion to exert his understanding or to exercise his invention in finding out expedients for removing difficulties which never occur. He naturally loses, therefore, the habit of such exertion, and generally becomes as stupid and ignorant as it is possible for a human creature to become. The torpor of his mind renders him not only incapable of relishing or bearing a part in any rational conversation, but of conceiving any generous, noble, or tender sentiment, and consequently of forming any just judgment concerning many even of the ordinary duties of private life" (Smith, 1776, p. 1040). Taylor's attempt at division of labour was in fact a clever plan to control workers through deskilling and thus making them easily replaceable. Division of labour limited the knowledge of the production process among the workers thus rendering them virtually ineffective and powerless. Taylor's obsession with control and hierarchical dominance was evident in his concept of shop floor management: "Perhaps the most important part of the gang boss's and foreman's education lies in teaching them to promptly obey orders and instructions received not only from the superintendent or some official high in the company, but from any member of the planning room whose especial function it is to direct the rest of the works in his particular line; and it may be accepted as an unquestioned fact that no gang boss is fit to direct his men until after he has learned to promptly obey instructions received from any proper source, whether he likes his instructions and the instructor or not, and even although he may be convinced that he knows a much better way of doing the work" (Taylor, 1903, p. 139). Thus, within the realms of Taylorism, coordination merely meant seamless acceptance and following of orders without any scope for the workers or even their immediate superiors to voice their opinion, however valuable that opinion might be. Hanlon (2016) was of the opinion that Taylorism singularly provided the managerial elite with an unquestionable right to lead and control. Further Hanlon (2016) commented that Taylor was aware of the superior competencies and intellect of the workers and thus wanted to prevent the workers from controlling the production processes by rendering them dependent on the management. This was shrewdly orchestrated by limiting the knowledge of the production process and deskilling the workers through division of labour. Further the complete avoidance of listening to the workers' points of view on the production process led to compromised confidence and a lowering of the level of competencies among the workers.

While Frederick Winslow Taylor, Henry Fayol[4] and Hugo Münsterberg[5] presented theories and ideas that had efficiency and profit maximization as the sole objectives, a new era of management thought evolved from a set of studies that were conducted at the Hawthorne plant of the Western Electric company in the United States of America. The first phase of the study was conducted between 1924 and 1927; this phase was known as the illumination studies and essentially tested the effects of illumination on productivity. The results however were inconclusive wherein diminished lighting sometimes led to higher productivity and vice versa. The second phase of the Hawthorne studies was conducted between 1927 and 1932; the studies in this phase were called the relay-assembly test room studies. This phase of studies explored the effects of variables like rest-room breaks, mode of payment and free lunch on the productivity of the workers. The results showed that while certain variables like rest room breaks produced no significant change in productivity, others like changes in modes of payment or empathetic supervision led to enhanced productivity. In the latter half of the Hawthorne studies, a Harvard University professor named George Elton Mayo was included in the study. Mayo visited the Hawthorne plant in 1928 and again in 1929, he found significant changes in the behaviour and attitude of the workers; apparently the relay-assembly group of workers had organized themselves into an organized group. Mayo had described the changes as "The most significant change that the Western Electric Company introduced into its 'test room' bore only a casual relation to the experimental changes. What the Company actually did for the group was to reconstruct entirely its whole industrial situation" (Mayo, 1933, p. 70). Elton Mayo was influenced by the Gestalt School of Psychology which believed that the whole was different from the sum of its parts. Mayo thus advocated that the problems of the workers within the scope of the workplace were influenced by a plethora of factors rather than a few seemingly important ones. Mayo applied his philosophy by conducting several in-depth conversational interviews with the workers which led to the recognition of the importance of empathic concern, understanding and listening to the workers in the realm of industrial relations. Mayo is thus often credited with having introduced emotions within the scope of managerial functions. In subsequent years one of Elton Mayo's students Fritz J. Roethlisberger described organizations as social systems which comprised of two components: external balance and internal equilibrium (Roethlisberger & Dickson, 1939). While external balance described the economic activities of the organization, internal equilibrium described "the maintenance of a kind of social organization in which individuals and groups through working together can satisfy their own desires" (Roethlisberger & Dickson, 1939, p. 397). The Hawthorne experiment thus laid the foundations of the human relations movement in management.[6]

The fundamental philosophies of human relations movement had found echoes within the thoughts of numerous experts. Mary Parker Follet, an American philosopher, had a profound impact on the ideations of this nature. Just as Elton Mayo, Follet was influenced by the Gestalts. Wren and Bedeian (2006) explained: "the basis of Follett's thinking was the 'whole man' and, in particular, relations between 'whole men' within groups" (Wren & Bedeian, 2006, p. 311). Her studies thus focussed on groups and the manner in which individual differences could integrate into the whole. Moreover, allied areas related to group dynamics such as leadership and conflict management also formed part of her intellectual exploration. Follett (1918) had explained, "we find the true man only through group organization. The potentialities of the individual remain potentialities until they are released by group life. Man discovers his true nature, gains his true freedom only through the group" (p. 6). Mary Parker Follet emphasized that businesses should approach employees as partners. She explained, "When you have made your employees feel that they are in some sense partners in the business, they do not improve the quality of their work, save waste in time and material, because of the Golden Rule, but because their interests are the same as yours" (Follett, 1926, p. 160). The human relations approach further encouraged studies in human needs and motivation, as the reader would no doubt recall motivating workers presented as a major area of worry for the management during the industrial revolution and had led to cruel and unthinking economic theories based on exploitation and coercion. Gradually however managers came to realize that coercion and exploitative conditions did not serve to sustain human motivation over the long term. Research on motivation brought forth the needs theory of motivation which posited that humans are motivated to fulfil their unmet needs. Henry Murray (1893–1988) was one of pioneers in research on the needs theory. He had identified 23 personality needs which motivated human behaviour (Murray, 1938); three of which (need for power, affiliation and achievement) were further explored in subsequent research on the subject (Wren & Bedeian, 2006). The most popular theory of human motivation was however put forward by the American psychologist Abraham Maslow in

1943. Maslow's thoughts and work is often analysed as a commentary against the Behaviorist School of Psychology. The behaviourist school included stalwarts like Ivan Pavlov, B.F. Skinner and John Watson who essentially claimed that humans were essentially organisms and thus behaved as such; thus human behaviour was a reaction to external stimuli. Essentially behaviourists operated with the fundamental notion that human behaviour was hardwired to attract rewards and avoid punishments. Thus, for behaviourists, psychology was essentially a study of human behaviour which in turn was a result of the external environment (and not internal thoughts and processes). In contrast to the behaviourist assumption, Maslow's theory of needs proposed that human behaviour was motivated by a set of needs which were hierarchical in nature and traversed from lower order needs to higher order needs. According to Maslow the lower order needs had to be satisfied before the next higher order need could act as the motivator for behaviour. At the base of this model was physiological needs followed by safety, love, esteem and self-actualization.[7] Maslow (1943) described the concept of self-actualization in the following words: "A musician must make music, an artist must paint, a poet must write, if he is to be ultimately happy. What a man can be, he must be. This need we may call self-actualization" (p. 382). Maslow has been widely criticized by a section of psychologists especially with regard to the perceived lack of empirical evidence for his model. However, Tay and Diener (2011) conducted a robust study involving 60,865 individuals across 123 countries wherein they reported that "The needs emerged to some degree in an order that would be suggested by Maslow's ordering, especially for individuals who have lower total needs fulfilled" (p. 361). Subsequent to Malow's work, further research relating human needs to workplace motivation ensued, notable among the various need-based theories of motivation was two-factor theory that was proposed by the American psychologist Frederick Herzberg (1923–2000). Herzberg categorized factors related to workplace motivation into motivators or factors, which motivated people to work, and hygiene factors, which included factors that reduced workplace motivation; Herzberg (1959) explained that these factors were called Hygiene factors "for they act in a manner analogous to the principles of medical hygiene. Hygiene operates to remove health hazards from the environment of man. It is not curative: it is, rather, a preventive" (p. 113). If the hygiene factors were removed or reduced to threshold levels of tolerance, it did not enhance motivation but removed dissatisfaction and thus had a neutral effect on the overall motivation of the workers.[8] As research on motivation recognized the importance of human needs and their fulfilment as an inherent part of the motivational process, a paradigm shift took place within the attitude of managers. Motivation through coercion, dependency and subsistence wages were no longer acceptable or desired; workers came to be recognized as fellow humans with needs and aspirations just like their managers.

The advent of humanism in management might have been influenced by existentialist thinkers like Jean Paul Sartre and Ludwig Binswanger. Jean Paul Sartre in particular had introduced the concept of existentialist humanism; he had described the core foundation of humanism as "man is always outside of himself, and it is in projecting and losing himself beyond himself that man is realized" (Sartre, 2007, p. 52). Since existentialists did not believe in the existence of God, their form of humanism included self-regulation. Consequently Sartre (2007) described existentialist humanism as "This is humanism because we remind man that there is no legislator other than himself and that he must, in his abandoned state, make his own choices, and also because we show that it is not by turning inward, but by constantly seeking a goal outside of himself in the form of liberation, or of some special achievement, that man will realize himself as truly human" (p. 53). Melé (2016) had posited that the term humanistic management was arguably first used by David E. Lilienthal (1967) in his book *Management: A Humanistic Art.* The book presented management as an art of understanding individuals and their goals or motivations; this approach was an antithesis of the mechanistic nature of Taylorism and the principles of scientific management. Humanistic management endeavoured to step beyond the mere optimal utilization of workers as a means to maximize profit to ensure that wellbeing and prosperity of workers presented as an objective in itself for the management to fulfil. However, humanistic management included divergent ideations; while some experts like Abraham Maslow and Frederick Herzberg stressed on human needs and its relation to human motivation, others like Mary Parker Follet did not separate the technical and the human aspects of the work (Melé, 2016). Notwithstanding the overtly humane façade presented by the practitioners of humanistic management, the ardent critics of management like Hanlon (2016) describe it as a reactionary process to labour collectivity. The principles of so-called scientific management as espoused through Taylorism was dependent on physical violence (coercion) in order to control workers, humanistic management merely transformed the nature of the instruments of control and adopted a manipulative approach wherein the worker would be controlled through his or her conscience (mental violence) without abandonment of the coercive element (Hanlon, 2016; Mills, 1951; McKinlay & Wilson, 2013).

Rita Gunther McGrath from the Columbia Business School has posited that management thought has evolved over three distinct phases (McGrath, 2014). It may be safely surmised that the formal idea of management did not exist prior to the industrial revolution; subsequently as Taylor, Fayol and the other proponents of the scientific management paradigm emphasized on techniques to maximize efficiency through specialization of labour, assembly line production and standardization of output, a distinct era of management thoughts emerged, McGrath (2014) called it the execution era. Further research and development in management led to the acquisition of a knowledge base which in turn led to institutions disseminating knowledge through formal curriculum; moreover, tools and techniques from different fields of study such as psychology, mathematics and statistics were introduced to enhance the field. This era was termed as the expertise era wherein workers were no longer unthinking robots but active participants in knowledge creation. The current era of management requires an understanding of employees as well as customers and their emotions; thus, the current era has been described as the empathy era (McGrath, 2014).

As the science (and art) of management evolved over the decades, the nature of business and production too changed over time. The early years of the twentieth century had witnessed a system of mass production characterized by standardized low-cost products produced in assembly lines by workers who were paid just enough to be able to afford those products. The resultant economic system and its associated socio-political ecosystem were described as Fordism[9] (after the Ford Motor Car company of Henry Ford which pioneered the assembly line production system). Fordism promoted mass production and its consequent mass consumption; the system is widely believed to have led to economic growth and relative prosperity, particularly in the post-war era. Moreover, the system had a kinder and gentler façade which was starkly different from the brutality and exploitation that the business models of the industrial revolution thrived on. However, Fordism too promoted institutionalized control of workers who had to accede to the management's diktats in lieu of respectable wages. The changes in economic models and business however continued, and Fordism witnessed a decline in the later parts of the twentieth century, this period is thus termed as post-Fordism. The post-Fordist economy thrives on niche products, skilled workforce and increased global competition. Experts like Mead (2004) have termed this phenomenon as millennial capitalism. One of the telling impacts of the changed paradigms of business is the use of technology in production. The advent of technology has led to a fundamental shift in the nature of the human workforce over time. Machines have taken over a large part of the manufacturing process and thus a significant percentage of labour force has shifted from factories into jobs that require empathic disposition such as healthcare (nurses, paramedics, technicians, etc.), teaching and education or service sectors like hospitality and travel. Thus, brute force and strength has yielded to compassion hence bringing about a priority shift from physical prowess to mental ability and the power to understand others. The practice of professional management has undergone a fundamental transformation over the past century to recognize the value of emotions within its nature of operational functioning. Hatcher (2008) has thus opined, "Emotional labor is now a much valued resource in organizations and has become so common in describing what constitutes the ideal corporate manager that to be without passion for one's work and to 'lack' emotional responsiveness is be corporate-character-deficient (CCD). Self-development imperatives in organizations are translated into intensified processes of *emotionalization* and *aestheticization* that have become part of the work of (self-) management and managing others in a performance culture" (p. 154).

It is within the humdrum of recognizing mental capabilities and emotions as important assets that the concept of intelligence was revisited by experts and the idea of emotional intelligence[10] was proposed by Salovey and Mayer (1989). Emotional intelligence was described as "a set of skills hypothesized to contribute to the accurate appraisal and expression of emotion in oneself and in others, the effective regulation of emotion in self and others, and the use of feelings to motivate, plan, and achieve in one's life" (Salovey & Mayer, 1989, p. 185). Ioannidou and Konstantikaki (2008) explained that the concept of emotional intelligence reaches beyond empathy to include within its fold "perception, expression and control of emotions, self-control" (p. 118) as well as communication, approaches to conflict resolution, and individual conscience. However, empathy is considered to be an important constituent of emotional intelligence. The idea that emotional intelligence and its constituent empathy play an important role in managerial efficacy has been widely promoted by the American psychologist and author Daniel Goleman. In this context, Goleman (2017) had observed that "Executives who can effectively focus on others are easy to recognize. They are the ones who find common ground, whose opinions carry the most weight, and with whom other people want to work. They emerge as natural leaders regardless of organizational or social rank" (p. 3). Goleman (2017) had elaborated upon the managerial implications that may be derived from the three aspects of the empathy triad; he had explained that while cognitive empathy may help managers to think from the perspective of their followers and thus help in explaining their points of view of the group, emotional empathy helps in client management, understanding group dynamics and in mentoring members of the organization and compassionate empathy (emotional contagion) helps in understanding what clients, customers and members of the organization need from the management. Similar opinions have been put forward by experts such as Emma Seppala, Science Director of Stanford University's Center for Compassion and Altruism Research and Education (and lecturer at Yale school of management). Seppälä (2015) had dwelled on why compassion presents as better managerial tactic than tough behaviour. She had argued that compassion enhances employee's loyalty and trust in the management. In furtherance of her argument, Seppälä (2015) had advised that while dealing with serious instances of mistakes made by employee, management should avoid knee-jerk reactions which most often are driven by anger or frustration. She proposed that stepping back, putting oneself in the employee's shoes and inculcating a forgiving attitude most often enhances employee trust, creativity and loyalty while decreasing workplace stress. Research over the years have reported that empathic management culture and the consequent empathic behaviour that is encouraged through such culture results in better workplace outcomes. Rego et al. (2007) reported that leaders' empathy was positively related to enhanced creativity among the organizational members. Similarly, several other studies have linked managerial and leadership empathy to better workplace performances (Gentry et al., 2007; Barsade & O'Neill, 2014). In addition, certain studies have reported that empathic behaviour of management and leaders result in positive emotions like warmth, appreciation and affection for the leader or manager in employees; a psychological state which has been termed as elevation (Haidt, 2003; Vianello et al., 2010; Seppälä, 2015). It has been posited that empathic behaviour towards one employee can create feelings of loyalty and trust not only within the particular employee but also among all those who have witnessed the act (Seppälä, 2015).

Notwithstanding the positivity that empathic managerial behaviour might nurture the common workplace reality is however different; the predicament was explained by Goleman (1998), "From the perspective of work, feelings matter to the extent that they facilitate or interfere with the shared goal" (Goleman, 1998, p. 339). Goleman (1998) went to explain, "In too many organizations, the ground rules that marginalize emotional realities guide our attention away from such emotional static as though it did not matter. These blinders propagate endless problems: decisions that demoralize; difficulty managing creativity and making decisions; ignoring the crucial value of social skill; the inability to motivate, let alone inspire; hollow mission statements and empty slogans of the day" (p. 339). The problem of unempathetic management is magnified many folds when managers exhibit a severe lack of empathy and border on psychopathy. This phenomenon unfortunately is not rare and finds widespread prevalence among corporate managers. Such managers are characterized by behavioural traits such as absence of empathy or of guilt, ego-centricity, lack of self-control or of feelings of responsibility (Hare, 1994; Holt & Marques, 2011). However certain researchers like Babiak (1995) who had conducted his study on a group whom he described as 'industrial psychopaths' assert that psychopathic managers do not exhibit overt anti-social behaviour but are rather manipulative and play on divergent views of organizational members to further their cause become successful. The perceived successes of psychopathic leaders might have diluted the perception that empathy is an important managerial quality and should be nurtured and encouraged among managers. Holt and Marques (2011) had thus opined, "there is still a leading paradigm among business corporations that leaders should be narcissistic in order to successfully maneuver through the increasingly competitive corporate waters. As an immediate consequence, this disparaging paradigm still resonates in business schools, where the development of future leaders takes place" (p. 104).

A logical extension of the discussion would lead to an inquiry as to the reasons why certain managers are unempathetic towards the other members of the organization. The reasons would be varied and complex; some managers are inherently unempathetic while others perceive empathy as a barrier to their success and growth within the organization and are motivated to be unempathetic or even psychopathic in disposition. Several researchers however have conducted empirical studies on the effect of power on the empathic disposition of a person. Gerben A. van Kleef and his colleagues studied the effect of power on compassionate behaviour;

the researchers reported "participants with a higher sense of power experienced less distress and less compassion and exhibited greater autonomic emotion regulation when confronted with another participant's suffering" (van Kleef et al., 2008, p. 1315). Galinsky et al. (2006) had reported that "high-power participants were less accurate than control participants in determining other people's emotion expressions; these results suggest a power-induced impediment to experiencing empathy" (p. 1068). In an interesting study on the effect of power on individuals, Hogeveen et al. (2014) reported that individuals with power exhibited reduced mirroring of other people within the areas of the brain which constitute "the human mirror system" (p. 755). Thus, power has the capacity to alter brain function in individuals thus turning them less empathic towards others.

However, power isn't the sole variable that influences managerial empathy; complex and often surprising patterns influence human behaviour. While it is common and rational to assume that individuals who have experienced a painful and upsetting event would be more empathic towards others who are experiencing the same or similar events, Ruttan et al. (2015) in their study reported that the reality is shockingly antithetical to that surmise. The researchers posited, "participants who had previously endured an emotionally distressing event (e.g., bullying) more harshly evaluated another person's failure to endure a similar distressing event compared with participants with no experience enduring the event or those currently enduring the event" (p. 610). Moreover, empathic behaviour comes at a cost of high cognitive and emotional loads, thus it is exhausting and sometimes debilitating. Continuous requirement for workplace empathy leads to a condition known as compassion fatigue. Compassion fatigue is common in the healthcare industry and in schools, it might lead to anxiety disorders, burn outs and high attrition rates (Abendroth & Flannery, 2006; Sung et al., 2012). Empathy is not above the influence of cognitive biases either and one such bias that influences empathic behaviour particularly in the workplace is in-group bias. Waytz (2016) explained: "Empathy toward insiders—say, people on our teams or in our organizations—can limit our capacity to empathize with people outside our immediate circles." Thus, managers might be more empathetic towards the plight of their fellow managers or workers might feel empathetic towards their own rather than towards managers. This aspect of empathic behaviour sometimes leads to dysfunctional situations wherein a section or group feels unwanted or unjustly treated.

While a discussion on the implication of managerial empathy might project an abstract nature with indefinite consequences for organizational productivity, several studies have however helped to present certain definitive outcomes of managerial empathy in quantitative terms with direct implications for organizational productivity. The 2017 Businessolver Workplace Empathy Monitor survey revealed that 77% of the employees surveyed would work for longer hours for an empathetic employer while 60% of the participants revealed that they would work for a lower salary if the employer was empathetic; in addition, more than 80% of the millennials who were surveyed in the study responded that they would leave their current job if the employer would turn less empathetic towards them (Schmotzer, 2017). In 2020 the Businessolver State of Workplace Empathy revealed similar findings; while 74% of employees were willing to work longer hours for an empathetic management, 57% declared that they would be willing to work for lesser pay if the management was empathetic, interestingly around 80% of the respondents were willing to shift to other companies at the same pay if the management there was more empathetic (Businessolver, 2020). The responses evidently have direct consequences on the productivity and profitability of an organization, thus establishing a direct connection between empathic management and organizational productivity and outcome.

Karl Marx had used the term relations of production (German: Produktionsverhältnisse) to describe the relationship between those that own the means of production and those who do not own those means. The former group might include capitalists and bourgeoise while the latter group might include workers and the proletariat (Marx, 1955). The history of a society and its evolution is most often shaped through the relations of production. If changes in the relations follow Darwinian patterns of evolution, then in the long term the relations in production should traverse towards a point that is beneficial to both entities. Marx (1955) had explained, "the mode of production, the relations in which productive forces are developed, are anything but eternal laws, but that they correspond to a definite development of men and of their productive forces, and that a change in men's productive forces necessarily brings about a change in their relations of production" (p. 81). Over the past two centuries business models have witnessed this change; from the oppressive slave driven business models that powered the imperial economies to the efficient but mechanistic and dehumanizing processes of the scientific management era, through Fordism and post Fordism to the increased popularity of humanistic management and subsequently the empathy era.

Over the past several decades business management has gradually integrated empathy within the organizational culture. The knowledge economy of the present times stresses on the value of the minds and the power of emotions over coercion or brute force. The importance that modern business places on empathy can be witnessed from the fact that an organization named "The Empathy Business" has published an annual empathy audit of organizations in the Harvard Business Review wherein it has been claimed that "The top 10 companies in the Global Empathy Index 2015 increased in value more than twice as much as the bottom 10 and generated 50% more earnings" (Parmar, 2015). Thus, empathy is both profitable for business and provides better functional and emotional workplace environment for employees, as Parmar (2015) asserts: "There is a direct link between empathy and commercial success. Businesses are more profitable and productive when they act ethically, treat their staff well."

Notes

1. The population of England grew from a mere 7 million in the 1770s to 19 million in the 1850s. See Clark (2010).
2. The term industrial revolution was first popularized in English by the British economic historian Arnold Toynbee in the title of his book *Lectures on the Industrial Revolution,* which was published posthumously in 1844. See Wilson. (2014).
3. Charles Dickens in his novel *Hard Times* (Dickens, 2006) had described a typical industrial town of the times within his portrayal of the fictional city Coketown. Dickens had further presented the unempathetic treatment of citizens during the times in his various novels like Oliver twist and David Copperfield.
4. Henry Fayol was a French mining engineer who along with F.W. Taylor is regarded as the founder of scientific management. His main contribution was the formulation of five functions of management: planning, organizing, commanding, coordinating and controlling. See*:* Fayol (1917).
5. Hugo Münsterberg was a pioneer in the field of industrial psychology and was one of the first experts to apply the theories and practices of psychology in business and industries. He was also firm believer in Taylorism. His seminal work titled Psychology and Industrial Efficiency (Münsterberg, 2012) was great influencer of management thoughts of the times.

6. The term Hawthorne Effect was coined by Henry A. Landsberger (1958). It refers to the inherent tendency of individuals to work harder and perform better when they are observed. Landsberger (1958) argued that the increase in productivity which was observed during the Hawthorne experiment was a result of the attention that was paid to the employees and not due to the tweaking of variables like illumination or even changes in payment modes. See: Landsberger (1958).
7. Prior to Herzberg, a Belgian psychologist named Hendrik de Man had conducted studies on human motivation and identified a set of factors which he categorized as motivators and inhibitors (those that inhibited motivation). De Man's studies are often presented as precursors to Herzberg's studies (Wren & Bedeian, 2006). For more on De Man's work, see De Man (1977).
8. Ibid.
9. The term Fordism is believed to have been first used in 1934 by Antonio Gramsci in his writing "Americanism and Fordism". See Gramsci (1992).
10. The concept of emotional intelligence echoed the concept of social intelligence that was proposed by the American Psychologist Edward Thorndike in 1920. Thorndike had then described social intelligence as "social intelligence is meant the ability to understand and manage men and women, boys and girls—to act wisely in human relations" (Thorndike, 1920, p. 228). See Thorndike (1920).

References

Abendroth, M., & Flannery, J. (2006). Predicting the risk of compassion fatigue: A study of hospice nurses. *Journal of Hospice and Palliative Nursing, 8*(6), 346–356. https://doi.org/10.1097/00129191-200611000-00007

Babiak, P. (1995). When psychopaths go to work: A case study of an industrial psychopath. *Applied Psychology. An International Review, 44*(2), 171–188. https://doi.org/10.1111/j.1464-0597.1995.tb01073.x

Barsade, S. G., & O'Neill, A. O. (2014). What's love got to do with it? A longitudinal study of the culture of companionate love and employee and client outcomes in a long-term care setting. *Administrative Science Quarterly, XX*(X), 1–48. https://doi.org/10.1177/0001839214538636

Businessolver. (2020). *The state of workplace empathy*. Retrieved March 3, 2020, from https://info.businessolver.com/en-us/empathy-2020-exec-summary-ty?submissionGuid=02e880cd-02cf-4972-8ce9-3fcc12167457

Cadbury, E. (1914). Some principles of industrial organization: The case for and against scientific management. *The Sociological Review, 7*(2), 99–117.

Casson, M. (2002). *Entrepreneurship*. Retrieved February 22, 2021, from https://www.econlib.org/library/Enc1/Entrepreneurship.html

Clark, G. (2010). Industrial revolution. In S. N. Durlauf & L. E. Blume (Eds.), *Economic growth. The new Palgrave economics collection*. Palgrave Macmillan. https://doi.org/10.1057/9780230280823_22
De Man, H. (1977). *Joy in work*. Amo Press.
Dickens, C. (2006). *Hard times*. Icon Classics.
Engels, F. (1987). *The condition of the working class in England*. Penguin.
Farr, R. J. (2003). *World eras. Industrial revolution in Europe. Volume 9. 1750–1914*. Gale.
Fayol, H. (1917). *Administration industrielle et générale; prévoyance, organisation, commandement, coordination, controle*. H. Dunod et E. Pinat.
Follett, M. P. (1918). *The new state: Group organization the solution of popular government*. Longmans, Green.
Follett, M. P. (1926). The psychological foundations: Business as an integrative unity. In H. C. Metcalf (Ed.), *Scientific foundations of business administration*. Williams & Wilkins.
Galinsky, A. D., et al. (2006). Power and perspectives not taken. *Psychological Science, 17*(*12*), 1068–1074. https://doi.org/10.2307/40064508
Gentry, A. W., et al. (2007). Empathy in the workplace. A tool for effective leadership. In *Proceedings from the society of industrial organizational psychology conference*.
Goleman, D. (1998). *Working with emotional intelligence*. Bantam Books.
Goleman, D. (2017). What is empathy? And why it's important. In *Empathy. HBR emotional intelligence series*. Harvard Business Review Press.
Gramsci, A. (1992). Americanism and Fordism. In Q. Hoare & G. N. Smith (Eds.), *Selections from the prison notebooks of Antonio Gramsci*. International Publishers.
Haidt, J. (2003). Elevation and the positive psychology of morality. In C. L. M. Keyes & J. Haidt (Eds.), *Flourishing: Positive psychology and the life well-lived*. https://doi.org/10.1037/10594-012. ISBN 1-55798-930-3.
Hanlon, G. (2016). *The dark side of management*. Routledge.
Hare, R. (1994). Predators: The disturbing world of the psychopaths among us. *Psychology Today, 27*(1), 54–63.
Hatcher, C. (2008). Becoming a successful corporate character and the role of emotional management. In S. Fineman (Ed.), *The emotional organization*. Blackwell Publishing.
Herzberg, F. (1959). *The motivation to work*. Routledge, 2017.
Hobsbawm, E. (1996). *The age of revolution. 1789–1848*. Vintage Books.
Hogeveen, J., et al. (2014). Power changes how the brain responds to others. *Journal of Experimental Psychology: General, 143*(2), 755–762. https://doi.org/10.1037/a0033477

Holt, S., & Marques, J. (2011). Empathy in leadership: Appropriate or misplaced? An empirical study on a topic that is asking for attention. *Journal of Business Ethics, 105*(1), 95–105. https://doi.org/10.1007/s10551-011-0951-5

Ioannidou, F., & Konstantikaki, V. (2008). Empathy and emotional intelligence: What is it really about? *International Journal of Caring Sciences, 1*(3), 118–123. Retrieved March 19, 2021, from http://internationaljournalofcaringsciences.org/docs/Vol1_Issue3_03_Ioannidou.pdf

Johnson, C., et al. (1998). *Africans in America: America's journey through slavery.* Harcourt Brace.

Kumar, P. G. (2017). *The diaspora men.* Retrieved February 4, 2020, from https://www.thehindu.com/society/the-diaspora-men/article19932674.ece

Landsberger, A. H. (1958). *Hawthorne revisited: Management and the worker, its critics, and developments in human relations in industry.* Cornell University.

Lilienthal, D. E. (1967). *Management: A humanist art.* Carnegie Institute of Technology.

Lordshaughn, A. (2020). *How slavery fueled the industrial revolution.* Retrieved February 2, 2021, from https://medium.com/history-of-yesterday/how-slavery-fueled-the-industrial-revolution-a0190a9b48a1

Marx, K. (1875). *Critique of the Gotha Programme. Part II.* Retrieved April 8, 2020, from https://www.marxists.org/archive/marx/works/1875/gotha/ch02.htm

Marx, K. (1955). *Poverty of philosophy.* Progress Publishers.

Maslow, A. (1943). A theory of human motivation. *Psychological Review, 50*(4). https://doi.org/10.1037/h0054346

Mayo, E. (1933). *The human problems of an industrial civilization.* Macmillan.

McGrath, G. R. (2014). *Management's three eras: A brief history.* Retrieved April 15, 2020, from https://hbr.org/2014/07/managements-three-eras-a-brief-history

McKinlay, A., & Wilson, J. (2013). "All They Lose is the Scream": Foucault, Ford and Mass Production. *Management and Organizational History, 7*(1), 45–60.

Mead, W. R. (2004). The decline of Fordism and the challenge to American power. *New Perspectives Quarterly, 21*(3), 53–61. https://doi.org/10.1111/j.1540-5842.2004.00684.x

Melé, D. (2016). Understanding humanistic management. *Humanistic Management Journal, 1*, 33–55. https://doi.org/10.1007/s41463-016-0011-5

Mills, C. W. (1951). *White collar work.* Oxford University Press.

Mokyr, J. (2001). The rise and fall of the factory system: Technology, firms, and households since the industrial revolution. *Carnegie-Rochester Conference Series on Public Policy, 55*(1), 1–45. https://doi.org/10.1016/s0167-2231(01)00050-1

Mumford, L. (1961). *The city in history.* Harcourt Brace.

Münsterberg, H. (2012). *Psychology and industrial efficiency*. Duke Classics.
Murray, A. H. (1938). *Explorations in personality: A clinical and experimental study of fifty men of college age*. Oxford University Press.
Parmar, B. (2015). The most (and least) empathetic companies. *Harvard Business Review*. Retrieved March 23, 2021, from https://hbr.org/2015/11/2015-empathy-index
Rego, A., et al. (2007). Leader self-reported emotional intelligence and perceived employee creativity: An exploratory study. *Creativity and Innovation Management, 16*(3), 250–264. https://doi.org/10.1111/j.1467-8691.2007.00435.x
Ricardo, D. (1821). Principles of political economy and taxation. In P. Sraffa (Ed.), *Vol I of the collected works and correspondence of David Ricardo*. Cambridge University Press, 1951.
Roethlisberger, F. J., & Dickson, W. J. (1939). *Management and the worker*. Routledge, 2003.
Ruttan, R. L., et al. (2015). Having "been there" doesn't mean I care: When prior experience reduces compassion for emotional distress. *Journal of Personality and Social Psychology, 108*(4), 610–622. https://doi.org/10.1037/pspi0000012
Salovey, P., & Mayer, J. D. (1989). Emotional intelligence. *Imagination, Cognition and Personality, 9*(3), 185–211. https://doi.org/10.2190/DUGG-P24E-52WK-6CDG
Sartre, J.-P. (2007). *Existentialism is a humanism*. Yale University Press.
Say, J. B. (1821). *A treatise on political economy, 2 Vols*. (C. R. Princep, Trans.). Wells and Lilly.
Schmotzer, K. (2017). *Businessolver finds workplaces still lack empathy*. Retrieved March 21, 2021, from https://www.businessolver.com/who-we-are/news/businessolver-finds-workplaces-still-lack-empathy#gref
Seppälä, E. (2015). *Why compassion is a better managerial tactic than toughness*. Retrieved March 18, 2021, from https://hbr.org/2015/05/why-compassion-is-a-better-managerial-tactic-than-toughness
Smith, A. (1776). *The wealth of nations. An inquiry into the nature and causes of the wealth of nations*. University of Chicago Press, 1977.
Sung, K., et al. (2012). Relationships between compassion fatigue, burnout, and turnover intention in Korean hospital nurses. *Journal of Korean Academy of Nursing, 42*(7), 1087–1094. https://doi.org/10.4040/jkan.2012.42.7.1087
Tay, L., & Diener, E. (2011). Needs and subjective well-being around the world. *Journal of Personality and Social Psychology, 101*(2), 354–365. https://doi.org/10.1037/a0023779
Taylor, F. W. (1903). Shop management. In *Scientific management*. Greenwood press publishers, 1972.

Thorndike, E. L. (1920). Intelligence and its uses. *Harper's Magazine, 140*, 227–235.
Van Kleef, G. A., et al. (2008). Power, distress, and compassion. *Psychological Science, 19*(12), 1315–1322. https://doi.org/10.1111/j.1467-9280.2008.02241.x
Vianello, M., et al. (2010). Elevation at work: The effects of leaders' moral excellence. *The Journal of Positive Psychology, 5*(5), 390–411. https://doi.org/10.1080/17439760.2010.516764
Walker, T. (2004). *Mothership connections*. State University of New York Press.
Waytz, A. (2016, January–February). The limits of empathy. *Harvard Business Review*.
Weber, M. (1961). *General economic history*. Collier Books. (Translated from German edition, published in 1923).
Williams, E. (1944). *Capitalism and slavery*. The University of North Carolina Press.
Wilson, D. C. S. (2014). Arnold Toynbee and the industrial revolution: The science of history, political economy and the machine past. *History and Memory, 26*(2), 133–161. https://doi.org/10.2979/histmemo.26.2.133
Wren, A. D., & Bedeian, G. A. (2006). *The evolution of management thought*. John Wiley.
Wyatt, T. L. (2009). *The industrial revolution*. Greenwood Press.

CHAPTER 6

Empathy, Welfare and the Welfare State

The word welfare is used within a wide range of contexts and among diverse fields of study. Consequently, the definition, description and usage of the term vary immensely and often leads to confusion and contradictions. In the context of the present discussion however, the economists' view of welfare presents as the most relevant. One of the earliest connections between the field of economics and welfare was presented by the English economist Alfred Marshall (1842–1924) who in his iconic book *Principles of Economics* had defined economics as "a study of mankind in the ordinary business of life; it examines that part of individual and social action which is most closely connected with the attainment and with the use of the material requisites of wellbeing" (Marshall, 2013, p. 1). Marshall's definition, while relating economics to welfare, had introduced an empathic dimension to the study of economics; his concept of economics did not primarily involve a study of money and wealth but instead focused on the study of mankind. The approach prioritized a study of the manner in which humans make a living through the income they earn and the use of that income in their welfare (wellbeing and welfare in this case could be used as synonyms). Thus, Marshall's definition of economics predominantly involved the understanding of common people and their material welfare and is generally referred to as the welfare definition of economics. Marshall's ideations revolved around the philosophy that the only function of wealth should be the benefit of mankind and that the true

D. Roy, *Empathonomics*,
https://doi.org/10.1007/978-981-95-4033-4_6

value of wealth can be judged only by its capacity to improve wellbeing (Nishizawa, 2021). It was in this regard that Marshall's thoughts had a deep empathic connection to people and their plight with a view to improve the quality and standards of human life, thus connecting his concept of welfare closely to empathy.

Alfred Marshall's student Arthur Cecil Pigou (1877–1959) succeeded Marshall as the professor of political economy at Cambridge and carried on the Marshallian ideations albeit in his own way. Marshall and Pigou adhered to the thought that the objective of economic knowledge and activities was to achieve what was good for the individual and the society. Marshall and Pigou based their positions on normative Benthamite traditions of consequentialism and held that actions could be considered to be morally right if the consequences of such actions were favourable and good for the majority (Knight, 2018). Pigou had introduced the concept of total welfare and posited that enhancements in economic welfare lead to enhancement in total welfare (Knight, 2018). Pigou (1920) had clarified the concept of economic welfare as "that part of social welfare that can be brought directly or indirectly into relation with the measuring-rod of money. This part of welfare may be called economic welfare" (p. 11). Pigou (1920) had recognized the fact that economic welfare might not act as an index of total welfare and total welfare might change even if economic welfare remains the same. In this regard Pigou (1920) had explained that while economic welfare cannot be taken as a complete measure of total welfare, it does not however imply that its study is incapable of yielding insight into the latter. Even though a whole is composed of varying and diverse elements, and a change in one part does not measure the alteration of the whole, the variation in one part might nevertheless contribute fully to an alteration of the whole. If this condition holds, the practical significance of economic inquiry stands firmly assured. The concept of methodological individualism also reinforces this view. It insists that collective outcomes must be traced to changes in individual conditions and choices. Consequently, the study of economic welfare, while partial in nature, remains indispensable for understanding the movement of total welfare.

Economists commonly place the concept of welfare within three dimensions: individual welfare, social welfare and the relationship between the two dimensions (Hamlin, 2007). The problem however still lies in the definition of welfare itself and a succinct description of what constitutes welfare is difficult to formulate. Hamlin (2007) argued that at the individual level most economists identify welfare with utility. Even if economists like Broome (1991) and Sen (1991) differ in the usage of the term utility, in a narrow sense individual welfare or utility basically consists of the satisfaction of individual needs and desires whatever they might entail. The transition from individual to social welfare however introduces certain complexities. If individual welfare is described in terms of individual good, then it could be argued that social welfare is a summation of individual good and all that contributes to individual good also contributes to social good. However, this approach is different from the standard economic concept of welfarism which typically equates welfare with utility that is based on actual preferences. Moreover, if social welfare is taken as a summation of individual welfare, then the idea of irreducibly social goods which are goods contributing to collective social welfare but not individual welfare becomes redundant (Hamlin, 2007).

A common and effective approach to define welfare would require the alignment of the concept of welfare to that of utility. Jeremy Bentham had explained the concept of utility as "By utility is meant that property in any object, whereby it tends to produce benefit, advantage, pleasure, good, or happiness, (all this in the present case comes to the same thing) or (what comes again to the same thing) to prevent the happening of mischief, pain, evil, or unhappiness to the party whose interest is considered: if that party be the community in general, then the happiness of the community: if a particular individual, then the happiness of that individual" (Bentham, 2000, pp. 14–15). The concept of utility as espoused by utilitarians however is specific and as Broome (1991) had explained, "Generally, utilitarians refer to those things they believe to constitute good by their specific names: 'pleasure,' 'happiness,' 'satisfaction,' 'wellbeing,' 'welfare,' and so on" (p. 9). Thus, welfare could be explained as form of utility. However, the discussion eventually recirculates on the description of what constitutes welfare. Hamlin (2007) had commented, "On this narrow account individual welfare (or utility) simply consists in the satisfaction of the individual's actual desires – whatever they may be" (p. 2). The idea of individual welfare within this context is dependent on preference satisfaction which in this case is not restricted to preference between commodity bundles but as Hamlin (2007) explained "preferences over alternative social arrangements, over alternative distributions of income; most generally, over alternative states of the world" (pp. 2–3). However, as Hamlin (2007) clarified, there remains a certain level of obscurity between the conceptual usage of the terms preference[1] and choice. Individual choice might be influenced by a number of factors, thus eventually when one chooses ‘a’ over ‘b,’ it does not necessarily mean that one prefers ‘a’ over ‘b’. An important influence for individual choice lies within the freedom to make that choice. Freedom might present simply as the absence of coercion or as the liberty to take voluntary actions towards an end with or without consideration for the consequences of such actions (Hamlin, 2007). Freedom itself could be interpreted through varied theories and ideations. Hamlin (2007) had posited that if the range over which an individual had the liberty to choose was expanded, it would lead to greater good irrespective of the choice that the individual made. Dworkin (1981a, 1981b) had stressed upon the importance of an individual’s control of the resources as an important indicator of freedom, while Sen (1999) had linked freedom with the capability of choose. Such capabilities consist of the intrinsic capabilities of the individual as in skill, talent and physical abilities as well as resources and opportunities that the ambient society around her position in life might provide to her (Hamlin, 2007). Consequently, welfare can be broadly described as that which enhances quality of life or reduces factors that bring about unhappiness and other negativity within individuals or groups. In addition, welfare encompasses two related facilitating factors, namely choice and the freedom to choose.

In this context it is relevant to discuss an important theorem put forward by Kenneth Arrow (1950) which is now known as Arrow’s Theorem, or the Impossibility Theorem. The theorem presents a fundamental posit in social choice theory. Arrow explained that when attempting to combine individual preferences into a single collective decision, no decision-making rule might satisfy all the set of conditions for reasonable fairness at the same time if there are at the least three choices. The conditions that were deemed essential for reasonable fairness were pareto efficiency (unanimity) wherein if every individual prefers option A to option B, then the social preference must also rank A above B; independence of irrelevant alternatives (the ranking between A and B should not depend on the presence of a third option) and absence of dictatorship (no single individual should always determine the outcome). Arrow’s theorem demonstrated the inherent difficulty of designing a perfectly fair and democratic system of social choice.

In the broader sense Arrow’s theorem is intricately connected to the idea of freedom. The theorem posits that when individuals freely express their choices or preferences, it is impossible to aggregate those individual choices or preferences into a form of collective social choice without violating at least one of the conditions that are deemed essential for reasonable fairness. Thus, Arrow's theorem posits that complete freedom of individual choice inevitably creates tensions when those choices are reconciled at the social level. Alternatively, Arrow's theorem might be interpreted to mean that any attempt at a perfectly fair and democratic aggregation of individual choices might lead to an unintentional restriction of freedom. Arrow's theorem dwells upon the fundamental issue of a trade-off between individual freedom of choices or preference and the achievement of a fair, coherent collective social decision.

The importance and necessity of welfare for the needy might be contextualized within a fundamental psychological aspiration of all humans: wellbeing. Eudemonic wellbeing, an ancient concept present within the writings of Greek philosophers like Aristotle, focuses on virtue in individual wellbeing and integrates welfare of others with personal wellbeing and happiness. Ryff (1989) had developed a model of wellbeing wherein one dimension as proposed by the researcher emphasized upon positive relations with others which was explained as "warm, satisfying, trusting relationships with others; is concerned about the welfare of others; capable of strong empathy, affection, and intimacy; understands give and take of human relationships" (p. 1072). Thus, within this framework it was proposed that individual psychological wellbeing and happiness depends on the ability of individuals to be concerned about the welfare of others rather than grudge them the help. The concept of Eudemonic wellbeing finds an echo within the idea of empathy utility that was proposed by Leibenstein (1976) and was defined as "satisfaction received from an income transfer spent on someone else" (Leibenstein, 1976, p. 192 as quoted in Fontaine, 2001, p. 387). Thus, empathy presents as a fundamental requisite for human wellbeing, not only for the empathic targets but also for the empath.

The fundamental nature of benevolent empathic reactions towards those in need of welfare lies within an understanding of the reasons for their plight and a concern for their wellbeing. The welfare measures initiated by governments might present with better outcomes if empathic perspectives are encouraged within the understanding of the reasons for the target groups' plight. Further, an empathic concern for the wellbeing of the targets might lead to better planning of welfare measures. Moreover, an empathic understanding of the reasons for poverty serves to generate public support for welfare measures. Yoo and Jang (2019) had explained "Those who have an empathetic understanding that people suffer from poverty due to structural inequalities tend to have positive and supportive attitudes towards government expenditures of social welfare for the poor" (p. 25). Such an understanding can be augmented through social empathy. Social empathy has been described as "the ability to more deeply understand people by perceiving or experiencing their life situations and as a result gain insight into structural inequalities and disparities" (Segal, 2011, p. 266). Segal (2011) had presented a model of social empathy which comprised of three components: 'individual empathy, contextual understanding, and social responsibility" (p. 266). Individual empathy encourages prosocial behaviour and societal interactions; it helps people to shed inhibitions about the other and reduces stereotyping, racial bias and class divide. Contextual understanding describes the process of a deep understanding of the life experiences of a group of people (Segal, 2011). Contextualization leads to an accurate empathic understanding of the situation. If for example an individual observes a poor person's hut being demolished by an earthmover, the initial empathic reaction is sadness and anger, in fact individuals might even be encouraged to protest against the demolition. However, if it is revealed that the government will build a bigger and better house for the poor man through a social welfare scheme at the same spot, the strong reaction against the demolition is tempered. Contextualization also guards against the problem of excessive empathy (McManaman, 2002). While it is often fashionable to portray the poor and homeless as the oppressed and victims of injustice while denigrating the upper class as the oppressors, it is not always so. Sometimes poverty and despondency are results of bad life choices too. Experts have opined that when an accurate empathic perspective has been obtained through contextualization of the situation, people feel more socially responsible and involved. (Hoffman, 2000; Frank, 2001; Segal, 2011).

Social welfare is most often analysed through the concept of welfarism which posits that social welfare is wholly dependent on individual welfare. Sen(year?) had described welfarism as "the principle that the goodness of a state of affairs depends ultimately on the set of individual utilities in that state, and—more demandingly—can be seen as an increasing function of that set. Welfarism implies that any two states of affairs that are identical in terms of individual utility characteristics must be judged to be equally good no matter how different they are in nonutility respects" (Sen, 1979, p. 464). Even though welfarism is often presented as a normative approach steeped within the ideation of utilitarianism, psychosocial deliberations on the concept lead to some anomalies especially when viewed within the light of empathy. Coons (2012) had distinguished between the act of valuing welfare per se and valuing it for those to whom such welfare accrues. Moreover Coons (2012) had distinguished between acting for someone's sake and promoting his or her welfare. For example, welfarism might dictate that a middle-aged jobless person be provided with a comfortable dole by the government on which he could live the rest of his life. While such action might be viewed as justified in the context of welfarism, it does not address a core question. Is the welfare actually enhancing the person's wellbeing or would assistance to provide him with a job present as a better form of intervention? The answer to the question would be markedly different if the person was elderly. The consequent argument that is put forward by Coons (2012) distinguishes between maximizing a person's wellbeing through unthinking and often standardized acts of welfarism and an empathic approach that understands what is best for a person and acts on that.

Feulner (1999) had explained, "True compassion requires personal involvement with another's misfortune. It requires people to understand suffering before they try to alleviate it. It does not countenance unreflective giving. It requires society to think before it acts. This is why the institutions of civil society 'succeed' at compassion—and why government typically fails."

Empathy predominantly influences the perception, attitude and approach towards different forms of welfare measures. Ryan (1971) had identified two perceptual approaches to social welfare: the exceptionalism approach and the universalism approach. The exceptionalism approach to social welfare posits that problems related to poverty or other unfortunate circumstances are specific and unusual and are thus exceptions to the normal. According to the exceptionalism approach, such problems occur due to the faults or bad choices of the victim, accidents or other unusual circumstances. The universalist approach posits that social problems occur due to the problems of the society or community. Thus, according to the universalist approach, individuals or set of individuals facing problems like poverty are not to be blamed as being at fault as they are not exceptions but their predicament is the natural fallout of an imperfect society or community of which they are a part. The universalist approach is empathic towards the victims and does not attempt to blame or shame them for their predicament; be as it may, the relationship between welfare and empathy is complex and paradoxical. There have been numerous attempts to explain the disparities in income, wealth and standards of living between different sections of society through unempathic and exclusionary theories like social Darwinism which builds upon the idea of Darwinian evolution to posit that a group of people become richer and more powerful than others because they are inherently better than others and thus are the fittest to survive. In fact, Herbert Spencer, a pioneering proponent of the idea of social Darwinism, had coined the term "survival of the fittest" (Spencer, 1864, p. 444). Over time Social Darwinism had been used to justify a wide range of inhuman, immoral and unethical practices like racism, colonialism, slavery and even Nazism and eugenics. However, Social Darwinism was viewed in a different light by a section of liberal thinkers who posited that welfare measures like education, health, nutrition, hygiene and better living conditions could lead to a reduction in poverty, crime or malnutrition and thus help the underdeveloped sections of society to move upwards in the socioeconomic ladder. Andrew Carnegie (1981) had elucidated this line of thought: "the best means of benefiting the community is to place within its reach the ladders upon which the aspiring can rise-parks, and means of recreation, by which men are helped in body and mind; works of art, certain to give pleasure and improve the public taste, and public institutions of various kinds, which will improve the general condition of the people; in this manner returning their surplus wealth to the mass of their fellows in the forms best calculated to do them lasting good" (p. 64).

The fundamental need for welfare predominantly arises from a lack of income, which in turn, very often, finds its roots within the phenomenon of unemployment. The societal perceptions of the reasons for such unemployment might provide a fairly objective idea of the societal perceptions of those who are in need of welfare, especially within the context of empathic understanding of the predicament. Furnham (1982) had studied the perceptions of unemployment through explanations provided by the employed as well as the unemployed in Britain for the reasons of such unemployment. The reasons that were attributed for unemployment were divided into three categories: individualistic (reasons that were internal to an individual viz. ability, intelligence or initiative), societal (external factors like government policies, etc.) and fatalistic (luck and chance). It was reported that individuals who were employed tended to prefer individual factors to explain unemployment in comparison to the unemployed who tended to prefer societal and fatalistic factors to an extent. Furnham (1983) in a subsequent study found that individuals who were employed tended to nurture negative attitudes towards those who were not employed. The commonly held notions were that the unemployed did not try hard enough to seek work; that some of the unemployed were dishonest and misused welfare measures and also that an element of stigma was attached to welfare measures like social security. Furnham (1983) attempted to explain the psychological background to the responses in the light of the phenomenon of Ultimate Attribution Error that was put forward by Pettigrew (1979). Pettigrew (1979) had explained the phenomena as "(1) when prejudiced people perceive what they regard as a negative act by an outgroup member, they will more than others attribute it dispositionally, often as genetically determined in comparison to the same act by an ingroup member: (2) when prejudiced people perceive what they regard as a positive act by an outgroup member, they will more than others attribute it in comparison to the same act by an ingroup member to one or more of the following: (a) 'the exceptional case,' (b) luck or special advantage, (c) high motivation and effort, and (d) manipulable situational context" (p. 461). According to Furnham (1983), Ultimate Attribution Error ensures that at least some of those who are employed harbour untrue beliefs about the unemployed. The disparity in attitudes towards welfare also present as reflections of socio-political affiliations; consequently, it has been observed that the conservative party supporters in Britain (who are traditionally more affluent) are generally more anti-welfare and less pro-welfare as opposed to Labour party supporters who are less affluent and come from working-class background.

While the public attitudes towards welfare could be explained as self-interest, it could alternatively arise from in-group empathy of the vulnerable, for people facing similar problems as them. The question thus would ultimately revolve around the thin line that seemingly demarcates empathy from self-interest. The contrarian viewpoint of welfare is presented within the concept of economic individualism which posits that "each individual is responsible for his or her own welfare and that economic success is a function of hard work and thrift. Poverty is viewed, therefore, as a consequence of personal deficiencies ranging from biological to cultural. These deficiencies result in lack of commitment to the work ethic, which is perceived to be a major determinant of success. Government intervention is perceived to foster dependency and thus as morally corrupting" (Hasenfeld & Rafferty, 1989, p. 1030).

It will however be erroneous to declare that the ensuing predicament is totally bereft of empathy. As explained earlier, the affluent empathize with their own group while the less affluent empathize with theirs; a classic example of in-group empathy at work. It is established from the empirical studies that while the economically insufficient are empathic towards their own kind and prefer welfare, those that are affluent are empathic towards their group who they perceive as hard working or industrious and thus do not support welfare (which is mostly viewed by the affluent as unjust and a deterrent to economic growth). It could be argued that an asymmetrical empathy gap thus exists between the rich and the poor. The asymmetrical nature of the gap might be evidently clear through a rational analysis of the two points of view; while it would be irrational to expect the poor to forego welfare and starve in order to be empathic towards the rich, it would not be similarly irrational to expect the rich (especially those who have had the good fortune to inherit wealth rather than earn it) to be empathic towards the poor and not grudge their welfare. The argument is strengthened by the fact that state welfare while funded out of taxes does not significantly alter the economic status of the wealthy. However, the dynamics of the problem are not so simple and several other factors influence this predicament.

The negative attitude towards those who need welfare is additionally encouraged by the perception of dependency. While dependency in personal relationships is not viewed as taboo, "It is in the public realm that dependence – especially on the state – is seen as shameful, particularly to modern welfare reformers" (Sennett, 2002, p. 127). Consequently, neo-welfare policies stress on temporary relief with a view to promote self-reliance rather than encourage dependency on state welfare. Dependency on state welfare has been analysed through the prism of infantilization: wherein adults are dependent on a paternal authority (in this case the state) for critical decisions with regard to their life and wellbeing, just as infants who are not matured enough to take such decisions. The point of deliberation however is whether infantilism observed in adults (within the context of dependency on welfare) is deliberately incurred by the persons concerned or whether social and political conditions force such dependencies on persons. In either case it could be inferred that it is the duty of a functional state to create empathic enabling conditions for citizens to free themselves from such dependency (Sennett, 2002). Sennett (2002) described the denial of the freedom and opportunity to think like an adult as a fear and posited, "This fear carries a tragic weight: it diminishes the possibility of trust among unequals; it inhibits confidence in or surrender to the judgment of others. Mutual respect requires the maintenance of a certain wary distance. In the workings of the welfare, this liberal formula has an undeniable logic. The patient to whom a doctor explains nothing, the student taught by rote commands, the employee who is ignored – all have become spectators to their own needs, objects worked upon by a superior power" (p. 128). Consequently, individualism and empathy are two seemingly conflicting factors which determine public attitudes to social welfare to an extent. Feldman et al. (2020) had studied the contrarian effects of empathy and individualism within the context of support for social welfare. The researchers had reported that while empathy does increase support for people on welfare as well as social welfare policies, empathy is down-regulated within the perception that government welfare might lead to dependency. Interestingly charitable support is not perceived to be long term in nature and even individualists who are against government welfare measures lend their support to charitable causes, consequently up-regulating their empathy in such cases. The relationship between the support for welfare and empathy is thus mired in complexities, and a direct causal inference is elusive and unsustainable. Bor and Simonovits (2021) had conducted an experiment to test whether empathic perspective taking was a predictor for support of welfare. The researchers reported that "perspective-taking with a poor, deserving individual does not necessarily reduce stereotypes about the poor in general; nor does it change views towards redistributive policies." Thus, according to Bor and Simonovits (2021) empathic perspective taking in itself has no significant causal effect on the attitudes to welfare. Interestingly a contradictory result was reported by Wagaman and Segal (2014) wherein the researchers reported "that increased levels of empathy are associated with more positive attitudes toward government intervention" (p. 91).

Lane (2001) explained that human behaviour is often explained through a reference to circumstances (accidents, persecution or exploitation) or to dispositions (incompetence, greed laziness, etc.). The two categories of reference are not mutually exclusive and circumstances might have causal effects on dispositions; for example, an accident (circumstance) leads to lack of competence in memory functions (disposition). Individual attitude towards social welfare and poverty is also influenced by the belief in a just world (Lane, 2001). The theory of belief in a just world posits that people get what they deserve; if a person is doing well in life, she has earned her good fortune through some actions of hers; conversely if people are going through bad times, they must have done something to deserve such misfortune. Very often such ideations are connected to religious beliefs. People who score high on the belief in a just world scale are less empathic towards those who are poor and thus do not show support for welfare measures or even individual philanthropy. In a related ideation, the theory of deserts posits that people should be treated fairly and justly, thus individuals who work hard deserve better payment or those who break the law deserve punishment. When the theory of deserts is linked to dispositional attribution, people surmise that individuals have the control over their poverty-stricken situations are thus voluntarily poor, hence they don't deserve welfare (Lane, 2001).

Feldman and Steenbergen (2001) argued that the core idea of humanitarian sentiment plays an important role in shaping the societal attitude towards welfare. In this regard Feldman and Steenbergen (2001) defined humanitarianism as "the belief that people have responsibilities toward their fellow human beings and should come to the assistance of others in need" (p. 370). Feldman and Steenbergen (2001) had described humanitarianism as a relational value which is a class of values that "defines a clear relationship between an individual and other member of society" (Feldman & Steenbergen, 2001, p. 372). To illustrate the concept, the researchers had used the example of forgiveness which is a relational value since it creates a relationship between an individual who holds that value and others. In contrast broadmindedness does not create a relationship and is thus a nonrelational value. The researchers emphasized that when people care and help each other, a relationship develops, thus humanitarianism is a relational value while egalitarianism, economic individualism and limited governance are nonrelational values. Feldman and Steenbergen (2001) claimed that egalitarianism and humanitarianism are distinct concepts with no significant connection between them, consequently their effect on public opinion are also divergent. The difference in viewpoints on welfare policies stem from this divergence. While humanitarian values encourage help and support for the underprivileged, the nonrelational egalitarian values support more permanent solutions to the problem of poverty through structural changes rather than temporary assistance which might eventually lead to dependency.

It can be inferred that social welfare is inextricably entwined within the normative concepts of equity and justice. Equity as described by economists is often presented within the dimensions of horizontal and vertical equity. The concept of horizontal equity posits that equals should be treated equally while the concept of vertical equity posits that the unequal should be treated unequally (Lambert & Yitzhaki, 1995). This conceptual framework of equity serves as the guide for numerous important public policy decisions like taxation as well as critical judicial decisions where precedence forms the basis of judgements. There are certain parameters on which it is acceptable for society to distinguish among people especially in the light of social welfare (age, income, need, disability, etc.). However there are also those parameters on which any kind of distinction is not acceptable viz. religion, race, sex, sexual orientation (Lambert & Yitzhaki, 1995). In this respect it is important to understand the difference between distinction and discrimination. While distinctions might be made to help the disadvantaged sections of society, discriminations are essentially negative in nature and seek to deprive sections of the society of their right to better life. In this context Hendriks (1995) had posited: "The principle of equality encompasses the right not to be discriminated against. It is important to distinguish between discrimination and differentiation when seeking to promote and protect the right to equal treatment of disadvantaged or otherwise vulnerable groups. The achievement of equality not only prohibits abstaining from discrimination, but also entails a positive obligation to rectify inequalities. Differentiation may be an adequate means to remedy disadvantages and to enhance the equal rights of vulnerable groups. Discrimination against disabled people may occur as a result of both differentiation and a lack thereof" (p. 152). In this regard, Dworkin (1978) had distinguished between the right to equal treatment and right to treatment as an equal. He had explained the right to equal treatment as "right to an equal distribution of some opportunity or resource or burden" (Dworkin, 1978, p. 227) and the right to treatment as an equal as "the right, not to receive the same distribution of some burden or benefit, but to be treated with the same respect and concern as anyone else" (Dworkin, 1978, p. 227). Dworkin (1978) had described the right to treatment as an equal as fundamental in nature while the right to equal treatment being derivative, thus while at times the right to treatment as an equal might result in equal treatment, at other others it might not. Dworkin (1978) had explained that if equality was recognized as the collective goal of a society, a distribution model could be designed on that parameter. Such a goal of equality could however lead to a redistribution of resources or wealth which in turn could be partial or discriminatory to some sections of the society. This discrimination could then be justified by citing enhanced aggregate collective good leading to better overall welfare.

The phenomena of equality and discrimination are inherently connected to empathy and the lack of it. Schultz (2012) had posited that it is with empathy and not cold reason that humans perceive others as equal. Conversely discrimination might be inferred to be a result of a lack of empathy. The phenomenon of in-group empathy ensures that individuals are empathic towards their own kind or group. Schultz (2012) posited that normative in-group cultural beliefs and habits lead to the development of a collective identity. Oftentimes this leads to a bias against who are not a part of the group and might have different cultural values and norms. The lack of understanding of the 'other' leads to an empathy gap. Thus, the rich and the upper class are empathic towards their own kind while lacking empathy for those who are in need of welfare. On the other hand, the poor or the working class, while being empathic towards their own, view the rich as tormentors.

Consequently, it will be useful to understand if empathy can be used as an interventional tool to reduce discrimination and promote a sense of equality among the population. Guthridge et al. (2023) proposed a model which was based on three components of affective empathy, namely intersubjectivity, multisensory engagement and empathic embodiment. Intersubjectivity had been defined by Cipolletta et al. (2020) as "mutual coordination, incorporation and sharing of meaning and experience between people over time" (p. 1). Sheng and Han (2012) had demonstrated that intersubjectivity reduces bias and enhances empathy. In this regard, intersubjectivity encourages a powerful empathic connection based upon the principle, "I will help you because you are me" (Thomas et al., 2009, p. 321). Multisensory experience, which formed the second element within the model proposed by Guthridge et al. (2023) "is the perception of two or more of the five primary senses of sight, hearing, touch, taste and smell" (Guthridge et al., 2023, p. 443). It was posited that multisensory engagement can encourage prosocial change and motivate actions that reduce discrimination (Guthridge et al., 2023). For example, if an individual or a group of individuals from an affluent managerial background regularly share lunch with workers from the disadvantaged sections of the society, the senses of sight, taste, smell and touch would work and the affluent would develop a better empathic connection with the out-group in contrast to a situation where they are apprised of the workers' lunch only through an office memo. The third element within the model comprised of empathic embodiment which essentially describes a fundamental aspect of empathy, namely mirroring. Embodiment refers to the mirroring of the other whether in postures, facial expressions or even in emotions and mood. (Tanner et al., 2008). Empathic embodiment helps individuals become one with the other by actually showing it overtly (Guthridge et al., 2023, p. 443). For example, if engineers designing hand pumps in an arid area use the hand pumps themselves or walk long distances to reach the hand pumps from far-flung villages mirroring the actions of the villagers who might be the ultimate beneficiary of the hand pumps, they might design a handpump that is easier to handle and in addition construct a shade for the villagers to rest.

Closely linked to equality is the phenomenon of inequality. While numerous forms and types of inequality exist in modern society, in the context of the present analysis, economic inequality could be recognized as the relevant form of inequality to be discussed. Economic inequality has the potential to encourage dissent and rebellion; however, as Foster and Sen (1997) explained such dissent and rebellion is motivated only when the deprived section of populace is empowered enough to rebel. Thus, as Foster and Sen (1997) remarked, the inequal treatment of the slaves did not find a place among the intellectual discourse of the Athenian intellectuals. Consequently, an inequal society might present as being outwardly content if the deprived populace does not have the capacity, power or the intentions to dissent. The freedom and capacity to dissent and rebel is the hallmark of any liberal, free and democratic society; however, when sections of such society are so deprived that they are too weak to rebel, the society does little to diminish the inequality, consequently the gap between the haves and the have-nots widen further. In order that inequalities in society are studied and corrective actions are taken to diminish the gap between the haves and the have-nots, it is imperative to find a logical measure of economic inequality. There are two approaches to measuring inequality, one comprises of an objective attempt through the use of statistics to bring forth such inequality and the other presents as a largely subjective attempt which seeks to measure inequality through some ideas of social welfare wherein lesser levels of social welfare for some given total income is consistent with higher levels of inequality (Foster & Sen, 1997). As was discussed earlier, the utilitarian approach to measuring social welfare consists of a summation of the individual utilities, thus:

$$W = \sum_{i=1}^{n} U_i\left(Y_i\right) \tag{6.1}$$

(Reproduced from Lillelien, 2009).

In Eq. (6.1), W represents the total welfare in a population of n individuals while U_i represents the individual utility of person i and U_i (Y_i)

represents the utility derived by person i from an income of Y_i. The goal of public policy is to maximize W.[2] The problem with measuring social welfare as an aggregate of all the individual utility is that the final outcome does not identify the levels of inequality in society. Foster and Sen (1997) had explained this problem: "maximizing the sum of individual utilities is supremely unconcerned with the interpersonal distribution of that sum. This should make it a particularly unsuitable approach to use for measuring or judging inequality" (p. 16). Moreover, a utilitarian distribution of income would differ from an egalitarian welfare distribution. While a welfare egalitarian would distribute welfare equally among the members of a society, a utilitarian distribution would be different. For example, two individual 'x' and 'y' might have the same utility but 'x' might have a higher income than 'y.' There could be numerous reasons for this predicament; 'x' might have more expensive tastes than 'y' or 'x' could be ill, or handicapped (Lillelien, 2009). Social welfare and resource allocation might be assessed using an analytic tool that was developed by the Italian polymath Vilfredo Pareto (1848–1923). According to this tool of analysis, an allocation can be considered to the pareto optimal if no other allocation could make an individual better off without making someone worse off. Pareto optimality however has its limitations particularly in the identification of inequality. As Foster and Sen (1997) had explained, "A situation is Pareto optimal if there exists no other attainable situation such that a move to it would be a Pareto-improvement. That is, Pareto optimality only guarantees that no change is possible such that someone would become better off without making anyone worse off. If the lot of the poor cannot be made any better without cutting into the affluence of the rich, the situation would be Pareto optimal despite the disparity between the rich and the poor" (p. 7).

Notwithstanding the criticism of Pareto optimality in the analysis of welfarism, several studies have been conducted to explore this area. In this context, Heal (2021) had studied the relationship of pareto optimality with empathy and welfare and had posited, "In an economy where everyone has maximally empathetic preferences, interpersonal externalities in consumption do not cause inefficiency, and public goods are provided at a Pareto efficient level" (p. 19). Further the researcher had proposed that an increase in empathy results in an increase in the provision of public goods, and if such public goods are complimentary to private goods, the result is pareto improving. Heal (2021) had concluded that "[i]n the case of public goods, an increase in empathy leads to a greater level of provision and an approach to the efficient level" (p. 20).

The concept of Pareto Optimality can be placed within the phenomena of partial and complete empathic identification (which were discussed in detail within an earlier chapter): partial empathic identification describes the act of putting oneself in the shoe of the other while keeping one's own identity (and henceforth one's preferences) intact (if I were in her place, I would do that...), complete empathic identification refers to putting oneself in the other's place wholly as the other by adopting the preferences of the other person. These two aspects of empathy have the potential to influence welfare economics significantly and have been discussed in detail by several economists. If the empathizer assumes the complete identity of the other, the personal identity of the empathizer is blurred and the social preference ordering based on individual preferences becomes difficult. If the empathizer keeps his identity intact and indulges in partial empathic identification, then a scope for pareto inferior outcomes exist as also the basic criterion that empathizers should be interested in the feelings of the empathic targets and not their own would be violated (Fontaine, 2001; Kirman & Teschl, 2010). An attempt to overcome the problem of loss of identity in complete empathic identification involves stepping beyond the mere adoption of the others' preferences and attempting to deductively understand the reasons for those preferences (Fontaine, 2001; Kirman & Teschl, 2010).

It is evidently clear that all societies are inherently inequal in most if not all aspects and the fundamental differences in societies often find their source within the differences between individual human beings and their position in life. Among all the different types of inequalities that humans present with, economic inequality is one that can be reduced to an extent or at the least honest attempts can be made to that effect. This effort to create a semblance of an egalitarian society while accepting its inequalities finds an echo within the objectives of the concept of distributive justice. Distributive justice "is justice in the distribution of material or economic advantages only, or that it only concerns the allocation, as opposed to the production, of given goods: others have instead equated the idea of distributive justice with that of social justice, and used it to refer to all the principles regulating the balancing of individuals' claims to all of the possible benefits of social cooperation" (Olsaretti, 2018, p. 2). The complexities and contradictions in the fair and egalitarian distribution of resources were addressed by the American philosophers John Rawls and Ronald Dworkin.

Rawlsian egalitarianism posits that any fair and just distribution of welfare will ensure that the highest benefit of such distribution accrues to the most disadvantaged section of the population among whom the distribution has taken place. Rawls had recognized the part that fate or luck plays in peoples' lives and had put forward the argument that individual talent and capacity to work are "outcome of the natural lottery; and this outcome is arbitrary from a moral perspective" (Rawls, 1971, p. 64).

Rawls' argument was based on the belief that individuals having empathy towards others' interests would judge that the others' interests should be treated equally and any difference was acceptable only when such difference permitted reciprocal advantages to the interests of each of the individuals (Aguayo, 2020). Rawls described that this arrangement "simply invokes the thought that morality, and in particular justice, is imbedded in the act of recognizing persons as persons: justice is the reciprocal recognition of persons as persons" (Rawls as quoted in Aguayo, 2020, p. 195).

Further, the Rawlsian approach to the concept of justice incorporated a very important concept which had the potential to turn it inherently empathic: the veil of ignorance. Rawls had posited that veil of ignorance was essentially a benevolent phenomenon wherein an individual was unaware of his or her position in society and was thus "compelled to imagine what life would be like for all, including, for instance, if you were among the worst off. Therefore, you would not favour, and cannot favour, a high degree of inequality, as you may find yourself among the least advantaged" (Edge, 2016, p. 63). In addition, the veil of ignorance imparts an important characteristic of impartiality to the concept of Rawlsian justice while attempting to involve empathic perspective taking within the process. However, Edge (2016) had argued that the veil of ignorance "deprives people of a vast amount of information which may be key in constructing a theory of justice" (p. 68). It is natural that knowledge and understanding of the other is important for empathic perspective taking. Edge (2016) thus proposed that the veil of ignorance could be replaced by affective and benevolent knowledge and called this process radical concern. The process involves an impartial entity (one who has no prior connection to a society) who empathetically gathers information "about the basic structure of society and the lives of those who live within it" (p. 69).

Ronald Dworkin's approach to egalitarianism (Dworkinian egalitarianism) while recognizing the role of luck in people's lives distinguished between pure bad luck over which individuals could not exercise any control (brute luck) and that luck which was within an individual's control (option luck). Dworkin thus advocated that those individuals who were victims of brute luck over which they had no control should be treated differentially from those who faced an unfortunate situation due to their own actions or behaviour. This line of thought led to the recognition of luck as an influence on socio-economic situations and was known as luck egalitarianism.

Rawlsian as well as Dworkinian egalitarianism was shift from the mindset that judged the poor as lazy or incompetent thus introducing an aspect of empathic understanding of the unfortunate. However, the peoples' perception of a welfare distribution model is subjective. Hoffman (2000) had argued that individuals would be guided by their self-centred biases and would prefer a merit-based system (based on reciprocity) if they were high achievers and a system based on Rawlsian or Dworkinian egalitarianism if they were not well off. If such distribution methods are based on empathy, even high achievers would prefer models that promoted equal distribution or merit regulated distribution (Rawlsian or Dworkinian models) (Roy, 2022).

The concepts of individual and social welfare could be placed within the context of a welfare state. A welfare state might be broadly described as a form of government where the state promotes the social and economic wellbeing of citizens. Such forms of government are fundamentally based upon the tenets of empathy, equality, social security and benevolence. Briggs (1961) described a welfare state as one wherein organized power of the state is used to ensure that families and individuals receive a minimum regular income, reduce insecurities by providing for contingencies such as illness or old age and all citizens without discrimination are provided with the best available standards of social services.

The term welfare state however is used to describe a wide range of governance models. Béland et al. (2021) had explained "the term 'welfare state' itself is radically undetermined. At its narrowest, it may simply describe a given country's arrangements for income maintenance. At its broadest, it is a descriptor for the full range of economic, social, political, and even cultural traits of a given polity" (p. 1). The term welfare state is oftentimes linked to the concept of social democracy. Social democracy has been described as the conscious and deliberate use of political power to balance out the inequalities that are often created by capitalism. However, the purpose of social democracy is not to dismantle or abolish the market altogether but to regulate it. Social democracy in fact seeks to supplement the market with welfare measures, social rights, and collective safeguards against insecurity. It has been posited that social policies under social democracy should address the three central problems of poverty, insecurity and inequality. In attempting to alleviate these conditions, social democracy aims to create a fairer distribution of resources and opportunities while at the same time maintaining democratic freedoms and the vitality of a mixed economy (Burns, 1995).

While some describe welfare states as the "fruits of "social democracy"" (Briggs, 1961, p. 222) and strive to improve upon the current standards that define welfare states others prefer that governments provide a limited number of services to the underprivileged till the poorer section might be able to "rise above the level of a minimum standard of living to reach" freedom "to buy for themselves the services (health, education, etc.) which they want." (Briggs, 1961, p. 222). Most if not all modern governments represent welfare states and they vary only in their degree of interference in the market in order to deliver the services to their citizens (Varghese, 2018). A welfare state is inherently empathic, as Varghese (2018) had explained: "Empathy forms the foundation for welfare state and its liberal social welfare programmes" (p. 122).

The concept of a welfare state is not new. Welfare states were established by rulers at various points of time in history. In India emperor Ashoka, who was a ruler of the Maurya empire from 268 to 232 BC, had set up his own version of the welfare state. Ashoka's philosophy of governance found its source within the concept of 'Dhamma.' Dhamma is the Prakrit[3] word for the Sanskrit word dharma (Agarwal, 2005). Sarkisyanz (1965) had explained the meaning of dhamma as "The term Dhamma has been translated as what has been made intelligible by Buddha to be the law of the world's immanent order, uncreated but eternal. Dhamma thus means the universal causality of rational and at the same time moral norm" (Sarkisyanz, 1965, p. 26). Ashoka's empire was governed, administered and protected according to dhamma. Ashoka's mode of governance was inclusive and sought to include all prevailing faiths, beliefs and practices of the times within the realms of dhamma. Consequently, within Ashoka's state Brahmanical, Jain and Buddhist faiths co-existed and were honoured and cared for by the king. The king sought to uplift those that needed upliftment. Ashoka had undertaken extensive welfare projects for his subjects; he had planted trees to provide shade to humans and other animals, planted fruit trees and dug wells to provide fruit and water to those that were hungry and thirsty. He built rest houses and water tanks for travellers and provided the sick with medicinal plants. Ashoka had appointed special officers known as Dhamma-Mahamattas to oversee and implement the welfare work of the state. An interesting aspect of Ashoka's approach to governance was that he never emphasized (or even mentioned) the duties of his subjects towards the king or the state, but only stressed upon the duties of the king towards the subjects. However, Ashoka's welfare state was based upon very fundamental Buddhist ideals. Ashoka claimed that all the measures were undertaken so that his subjects practiced dhamma or the moral law. Ashoka had ruled over 200 years before the birth of Christ; thus, his welfare state was established in India long before the concept was introduced in the Christian world (Sarkisyanz, 1965). The Han dynasty (206 BC–220 AD) which ruled over China was noted for numerous welfare measures and is often described as a proto welfare state. It was decreed in Han China that the elderly were to be respected and individuals over the age of 70 could not be prosecuted except when they had led actions to kill or wound others. Men and women above 60 years of age who did not have male children were declared to be widowers and widows, they were not to be taxed and were exempted from paying all government duties. Similarly, men and women who had no male children were exempt from paying taxes. Orphans, blind and physically challenged individuals were not to be called for government duties and they were not to be detained. It has been reported that in the summer of 167 BC Emperor Wen, the fifth ruler of the Han dynasty, had gifted cloth, silk and silk floss to widows and orphans, several other distributions have been recorded after that (Hulsewe´, 1987). There were instances of welfare measures from the Roman empire too, Emperor Augustus distributed doles of grain to the poor while Emperor Trajan strived to create an egalitarian and fair state wherein he distributed grains to citizens and introduced welfare measures for poor children.

A formal attempt to introduce welfare for the poor was witnessed in the enactment of the Poor Laws in sixteenth-century England (1587–1601). These laws were promulgated during the reign of Queen Elizabeth I and provided for relief for the poor of the country. If citizens could not afford to pay their property taxes or provide for their family, they were judged as poor or paupers. The local parish had the duty to provide for the paupers settled in the parish, only the poor settled in a parish had the right to poor relief from the parish. The non-settled poor were not entitled to any relief under the law and would only be provided with some temporary relief as official inquiries and proceedings continued with regard to their settlement (Charlesworth, 1999). The paupers were divided into three categories: able-bodied adults, children and non-able-bodied adults. The able-bodied adults were provided with some work to earn an income while children were provided with training and opportunities to learn some skill or trade and the old and infirm were given some money. In 1834 however there was change to the laws with an amendment. The amendments were unempathic to the poor and were based on the premise "that people wilfully chose to be poor and thus needed discouraging from seeking aid" (Charlesworth, 1999, p. 153). Thus, punitive measures like debtor's prisons were introduced which could incarcerate the entire families of debtors. The new amendments ensured that the able-bodied poor would receive aid only if they lived and worked in workhouses. These workhouses were examples of living hell where the residents were degraded, dehumanized and forced to live and work like animals without proper food or clothing. Charles Dickens' epic novel Oliver Twist deals in detail on the horrors of the workhouse system. The underlying cause and rationale of the poor laws of England was summarized succinctly by Charlesworth (1999): "The criminalising of the poor in England is an old tradition. From the fourteenth century onwards the link between the methods used to control vagrancy and the later operation of formal poor relief in England and Wales created an association between the two which influenced both legislation and the treatment of the poor; a connection which continues today" (p. 149). In the late nineteenth century, the German chancellor Otto Eduard Leopold von Bismarck had introduced certain welfare reforms in Germany. He had introduced laws related to health and accident insurance as well as retirement pension for workers in Germany; the scope and reach of the insurance schemes were expanded over a period of time to include disability insurance and unemployment insurance (Boissoneault, 2017). Bismarck was categorical in stating that the state's help of the needy was not an act of pity but a matter of right for the poor. The system was described as Staatssozialismus or state socialism. It is often argued that Bismarck's steps towards creating a welfare state in Germany was motivated by the need to keep radical socialists at bay (Hernandez, 2017). If it was so it had failed in its objective and the socialists rose to become a formidable political force during the times. However, the welfare schemes especially the health insurance schemes proved to be very successful. As researchers, Bauernschuster et al. (2019) reported, "Bismarck's health insurance generated a significant mortality reduction. Despite the absence of antibiotics and most vaccines, we find the results to be largely driven by a decline of deaths from infectious diseases. We present evidence suggesting that the decline is associated with access to health services but not sick pay" (p. 1).

The term welfare state as it is used in its modern connotation was introduced in Britain when the labour party came to power in 1945. The definition and description of welfare state that had emerged during the time was entangled within twin important social demands: abolition of poverty and reduction of unemployment. In 1947 when India gained independence the founding fathers of the nation envisaged a welfare state in India. Article 38[4] of the Constitution of India states:

> 38[(1)] The State shall strive to promote the welfare of the people by securing and protecting as effectively as it may a social order in which justice, social, economic and political, shall inform all the institutions of the national life.
>
> [2] The State shall, in particular, strive to minimize the inequalities in income, and endeavour to eliminate inequalities in status, facilities and opportunities, not only amongst individuals but also amongst groups of people residing in different areas or engaged in different vocations.

(The constitution of India, Part 4, Directive Principles of State Policy, as quoted in https://www.mea.gov.in/Images/pdf1/Part4.pdf).

As agrarian societies transformed definitively into industrial ones, the problems facing societies changed in dimensions. This was clearly witnessed in the problem of mass unemployment. Ironically mass unemployment was a result of industries scaling production methods to a point where opportunity for mass employment was created. In contrast, when the poor laws were implemented in sixteenth-century England, the problem that the laws sought to solve was that of unemployability. The problem of mass unemployment led to different stakeholders attempting in their own way to solve the problem of mass unemployment or at the least mitigate its negative fallout. Since the political consequences of mass unemployment were perceived to be devastating, post war governments all over the world began to explore and augment policies of the welfare state (Briggs, 1961).

The rationale of organized state intervention to provide welfare to needy individuals and groups has often been questioned. It is argued that relief in times of crisis should primarily emanate from society (family and friends), self-help groups, non-governmental organizations, religious organizations, relevant trade unions and professional associations rather than from state power. However, the use of state power to organize and distribute welfare has been encouraged by some owing to the expertise of the state machinery in delivery, distribution, design and control of the welfare machinery as well as in the intricate knowledge of the needs and requirements of the target groups that are earmarked for welfare measures. Moreover, state machinery ensures equality in approach. While it might be impractical and in fact naïve to proclaim that all individuals are completely equal and should have the same levels of lifestyle, it is however necessary to remember all individuals, regardless of their background, belief, class and position in life, are treated equally under the eyes of the law in most democratic countries. The consequent argument that welfare which is distributed through the aegis of legally bound state-controlled institutions will override any unequal and biased nature of distributing welfare is thus not unreasonable. The counterargument that is put forward in many developed countries like the United States of America relates to the often-misplaced notion of equality of opportunity. The concept of equality of opportunity surmises that all individuals in a country are provided with the same opportunity to succeed in life. While it might seem to be a fair proposition prima-facie, the concept of equality of opportunity places the blame squarely on the poor for their poverty. When it is surmised that every individual has the same opportunity to succeed in life, the corollary to the argument essentially posits that anyone who remains poor has not made good use of the opportunities provided to him or her. If the case of the United States of America is analysed, it has been empirically established that "All Americans do not have an equal shot at getting ahead, and one's chances are largely dependent on one's parents' economic position" (Issacs, 2017, p. 5). Moreover, as Issacs (2017) further reported, "Children born to parents in the top quintile have the highest likelihood of attaining the top, and children born to parents in the bottom quintile have the highest likelihood of being in the bottom themselves" (p. 5). In addition, welfare states are also motivated by the need to undo the wrongs of the past. As Briggs (1961) had put forward, welfare states are also based on "the conviction that societies can be shaped by conscious policies *designed to eliminate*" *abuses* "*which in earlier generations had* been accepted as 'inevitable' features of the human condition" (Briggs, 1961, pp. 229–230, emphasis in original).

The concept of welfare states is controversial and prone to criticism. As Garland (2016) had explained, the fundamental objective for the creation of a welfare state is often misunderstood. Welfare states are not created as a cure for the ills of the socio-economic system but rather as an attempt to manage the problems that are inherently associated with those systems. Welfare states do not present a perfect outcome with the complete eradication of poverty or inequality; they attempt to optimally manage them within the constraints that the socio-economic system presents. The constraints on the system are particularly strong in democratic societies where individuals are free to make choices with regard to their life, even if such choices are dysfunctional or suboptimal. Garland (2016) explained that welfare states create new interest groups who are at times in conflict with each other. For example, employers and employees, high earners and those who are low paid, retirees and youngsters all have conflicting interests. Moreover, there are unscrupulous entities both on the supply side and the demand side who tend to game the system to their ends by cheating and malpractice. Further if welfare states try to reduce poverty through the distribution of benefits for the poor, the number of claimants for the benefits will increase due to 'magnet effect' (Garland, 2016, p. 105).

The concept of the Welfare State has evolved over time. Within the context of recent times, Garland (2016) had noted "Some of our misunderstandings about the welfare state flow from the name it has been given. Welfare states are not primarily about 'welfare' and certainly not primarily about welfare for the poor. They are about social insurance, social rights, social provision, and the social regulation of economic action—the chief beneficiaries of which are not the poor but the middle classes and those in employment" (p. 26). Garland (2016) had described welfare states through three conceptual frameworks. The first of these was a simple and fundamental description of the welfare state as one that provides welfare to the poor. The earlier welfare states of the ancient and mediaeval era as well the basic objectives that formed the motivation of the poor laws in England could be described through the prism of this concept. The second approach to the description of a welfare state includes social security measures in the form of formal instruments like insurance and retirement benefits, social rights and the provision of social services like healthcare and education by the state. The third concept of a welfare state is the broadest, most complex and important. It includes the economic management and planning undertaken by government for promoting growth, reducing unemployment and poverty, while ensuring the welfare of citizens as well as business. Garland (2016) had explained that the three conceptual frameworks of a welfare state did not exist in isolation or as competitive concepts. Rather the three frameworks were complimentary to each other and existed as parts of a concentric ring. At the core of this set of concentric rings were the formal institutions that provided social security to the public: insurance schemes, old-age pension schemes, disability benefits and such other instruments of social security. At the next level of the concentric rings were the government economic policies which helped to fund the social security schemes. This included government policies with regard to taxation, promoting economic growth and reducing unemployment, utilization of public resources and other such important areas. The very top of the concentric rings included non-contributory safety nets for those who did not have recourse to other social security instruments and could not afford instruments that required contribution from their parts: in other words, the poor who needed direct welfare benefits.

While state help to the poor and needy might seem to present as a fairly simple, ethical and rational activity conforming to normative moral standards of governmental functioning, the public perception of welfare and the welfare state is complex. The complexity in the public attitude towards social welfare fundamentally relates to the perception of justice and fairness within interest groups. Thus, while the affluent are empathic towards their own ilk and feel that government welfare for the poor is unjust towards those who have worked hard for a better life, the poor feel that they are entitled to government welfare because they have been deprived of opportunities in an unequal and skewed socio-economic system. Interestingly, it is not that the affluent do not empathize with the poor at all, there are significant instances of charitable activities being conducted by affluent sections of societies; the problem that is perceived with state welfare is that long-term welfare measures might lead to potential dependencies on welfare which would be dysfunctional for the economy since it might create a section of 'free-loaders,' thus creating an inefficient economic system wherein a section does not contribute, as also encourage a fundamentally unjust system where a section works hard and earns money while another lives off them. The potential solution lies in the empathic understanding of the situation that is causing the poverty and deprivation, taking measures to remove the causative factors, followed by compassionate action through detailed models to create income generation. Some interventions could involve skill-based training, mapping local resources and encouraging local business models, attitudinal and behavioural training and investment in training and development infrastructure in areas that are economically backward.

Some governments have historically used welfare as a strategic of control to keep the impoverished and needy dependent on the government for survival, while these methods might have ensured the survival of the governments they hardly lead to economic development and the upliftment of the sections that deserve better standards of living through self-sustained economic freedom. The idea of welfare should not be limited to the distribution of free food and necessities but also to the imparting of free quality education, skill and knowledge all of which might be used as assets for upward socio-economic mobility. The ideation is best expressed within the proverb, "you give a man a fish you feed him for a day, you teach a man to fish you feed him for a lifetime."

The relationship between empathy and the concept of a welfare state presents within an important socio-psychological dimension: the attitude of the public towards the concept and the functioning of a welfare state. The attitude of the public towards individual welfare or even group welfare is largely different from their attitude towards a welfare state. This is mainly because the concept of a welfare state leads to the perception of broader dimension of welfare measures which would include those who might not, within some opinions, 'deserve' welfare at the cost of higher taxation of those who work hard for their living. Such board-based welfare measures are often perceived as rewarding laziness and demotivating hard work. This perception of injustice has the potential to turn a large section of the population unempathic towards the underprivileged sections within a welfare state and in fact begin to describe them as the de-facto privileged ones. A welfare state as a basic philosophy for state functioning also leads to the perception of permanence, thus implying that a section will always remain under welfare and will not be able to enjoy the fruits of socioeconomic development. This creates the perception, even among the underprivileged, that the basic principles of a welfare state are sometimes used as convenient tools to ensure that sections of the population permanently survive on welfare and thus remain dependent on and consequently controlled by the state machinery. Nations prioritizing the good of the people often have planned, time-bound measures to wean the underprivileged sections of society from welfare. Consequently, such welfare states work towards ensuring that the welfare state itself withers into a redundancy when no one needs to be on welfare.

The attitude of the public is thus dichotomous in relation to welfare and the welfare state. As Feldman and Steenbergen (2001) had reported within their study conducted in the United States of America, most people support social welfare policies but are against the idea of a welfare state which they view as unjust. Consequently, the recipients of state welfare are perceived as "unduly advantaged at the expense of the middle class" (Feldman & Steenbergen, 2001, p. 367). While it has been popular to attribute this behavioural pattern to the values of egalitarianism, economic individualism and limited government, Feldman and Steenbergen (2001) differed in their viewpoint even while accepting that the popular values of egalitarianism, economic individualism and limited government do form some basis for the public's attitude towards the welfare state. Hasenfeld and Rafferty (1989) had studied the determinants of public attitudes towards state welfare programs. The researchers had reported that the "support of welfare state programs is a function of self-interest and the resultant identification with dominant social ideologies—work ethic and social equality" (p. 1027). The researchers further commented that the social groups which tend to support a welfare state are themselves prone to social and economic vulnerability. Similar social viewpoints on welfare and poverty were reported by Alston and Dean (1972) who studied the perception of poverty and welfare among respondents in the United States of America. The researchers reported that a significant section of the respondents described poverty as the consequence of lack of effort; the younger, male and well educated were particularly harsh in their description. The older respondents were more sympathetic towards the poor but did not approve of increases in the amount of welfare.

Empathy thus contributes significantly to decisions on welfare both in terms of the public perception of the concept and process of social welfare and in the planning and operation of effective welfare measures. The public perception of welfare is mediated through the complexities of individualism, in-group empathy and the idea that people are ultimately responsible for their own fates. It is important thus to note that when governments apply welfare measures in standardized, unthinking manner, the detriments often outweigh the good. Thus, empathic perspectives are important within policy-making processes for effective long-term good. It is within these psychosocial perspectives that the preceding discussion on the relevance of empathy within welfare measures and the broader dimension of the welfare state was placed.

Notes

1. As an alternative to the preference satisfaction theory of individual welfare, some economists prefer the informed preference theory which posits that actual preferences might change when an individual is fully informed. Thus, actual preferences should not form the basis of individual welfare. See Hamlin (2007).
2. The subscript *i* in the individual utility function represents individual preferences according to the preference satisfaction theory of welfare wherein an individual prefers one situation over another. See Lillelien (2009).
3. A Middle Indo-Aryan language spoken between about 500 B.C. and 500 A.D. The term Prakrit meant 'derived.' See https://orinst.web.ox.ac.uk/prakrit.
4. Article 38 that falls under the Directive Principles of State Policy are *non-justiciable* and thus are unenforceable in any court of law.

References

Agarwal, M. (2005). *The philosophy of inspiration*. Dawn Publishers.

Aguayo, P. (2020). John Rawls on redistribution and recognition. *Cinta Moebio, 69*, 192–200. https://doi.org/10.4067/S0717-554X2020000300192

Alston, J. P., & Dean, K. I. (1972). Socioeconomic factors associated with attitudes toward welfare recipients and the causes of poverty. *Social Service Review, 46*(*1*), *13–23*. https://doi.org/10.1086/642795

Arrow, K. J. (1950). A difficulty in the concept of social welfare. *The Journal of Political Economy, 58*(4), 328–346. https://doi.org/10.1086/256963

Bauernschuster, S., et al. (2019). Bismarck's health insurance and the mortality decline. *Journal of the European Economic Association*. https://doi.org/10.1093/jeea/jvz052

Béland, D., et al. (2021). Introduction. In D. Béland, K. J. Morgan, H. Obinger, & C. Pierson (Eds.), *The Oxford handbook of the welfare state* (2nd ed.). Oxford University Press.

Bentham, J. (2000). *An introduction to the principles of morals and legislation*. Batoche Books.

Boissoneault, L. (2017). *Bismarck tried to end socialism's grip—By offering government healthcare*. Retrieved December 12, 2022, from https://www.smithsonianmag.com/history/bismarck-tried-end-socialisms-grip-offering-government-healthcare-180964064/

Bor, A., & Simonovits, G. (2021). Empathy, deservingness, and preferences for welfare assistance: A large-scale online perspective-taking experiment. *Political Behavior, 43*, 1247–1264. https://doi.org/10.1007/s11109-021-09728-4
Briggs, A. (1961). The welfare state in historical perspective. *European Journal of Sociology, 2*(2), 221–258. https://doi.org/10.1017/S0003975600000412
Broome, J. (1991). Utility. *Economics and Philosophy, 7*(1), 1–12. https://doi.org/10.1017/S0266267100000882
Burns, P. (1995). Socialism, social democracy, and markets. *Science & Society, 59*(2), 193–197. https://doi.org/10.2307/40403486
Carnegie, A. (1981). Wealth. *The North American Review, 266*(3), 60–64. https://doi.org/10.2307/25124186
Charlesworth, L. (1999). Why is it a crime to be poor? *Liverpool Law Review, 21*(2–3), 149–167. https://doi.org/10.1023/a:1005686302457
Cipolletta, S., et al. (2020). Intersubjectivity, joint action and sociality. *Journal of Constructivist Psychology, 1–26.* https://doi.org/10.1080/10720537.2020.1805066
Coons, C. (2012). The best expression of welfarism. In M. Timmons (Ed.), *Oxford studies in normative ethics* (Vol. 2). Oxford University Press. https://doi.org/10.1093/acprof:oso/9780199662951.003.0009
Dworkin, R. (1978). *Taking rights seriously.* Harvard University Press.
Dworkin, R. (1981a). What is equality? Part 1: Equality of welfare. *Philosophy and Public Affairs, 10*, 185–246.
Dworkin, R. (1981b). What is equality? Part 2: Equality of resources. *Philosophy and Public Affairs, 10*, 283–345.
Edge, M. (2016). *Political philosophy, empathy and political justice.* Routledge.
Feldman, S., & Steenbergen, M. (2001). Social welfare attitudes and the humanitarian sensibility. In J. H. Kuklinski (Ed.), *Citizens and politics* (pp. 366–400). Cambridge University Press. https://doi.org/10.1017/cbo9780511896941.018
Feldman, S., et al. (2020). The interplay of empathy and individualism in support for social welfare policies. *Political Psychology, 41*(2), 343–362. https://doi.org/10.1111/pops.12620
Feulner, E. J. (1999). *Welfare state turns compassion upside down.* Retrieved September 19, 2024, from https://www.heritage.org/welfare/commentary/welfare-state-turns-compassion-upside-down
Fontaine, P. (2001). The changing place of empathy in welfare economics. *History of Political Economy, 33*(3), 387–409. https://doi.org/10.1215/00182702-33-3-387
Foster, J. E., & Sen, A. (1997). *On economic inequality.* Oxford University Press.
Frank, R. H. (2001). Cooperation through emotional commitment. In R. M. Nesse (Ed.), *Evolution and the capacity for commitment* (pp. 57–76). Russell Sage Foundation.

Furnham, A. (1982). Explanations for unemployment in Britain. *European Journal of Social Psychology, 12*(4), 335–352. https://doi.org/10.1002/ejsp.2420120402

Furnham, A. (1983). Attitudes toward the unemployed receiving social security benefits. *Human Relations, 36*(2), 135–149. https://doi.org/10.1177/001872678303600204

Garland, D. (2016). *The welfare state. A very short introduction.* Oxford University Press.

Guthridge, M., et al. (2023). The role of affective empathy in eliminating discrimination against women: A conceptual proposition. *Human Rights Review, 24*, 433–456. https://doi.org/10.1007/s12142-023-00692-6

Hamlin, A. (2007). *The idea of welfare and the welfare state.* Retrieved January 28, 2023, from https://hummedia.manchester.ac.uk/schools/soss/politics/research/workingpapers/mancept/IdeaofWELFARE2.pdf

Hasenfeld, Y., & Rafferty, J. A. (1989). The determinants of public attitudes toward the welfare state. *Social Forces, 67*(4), 1027–1048. https://doi.org/10.1093/sf/67.4.1027

Heal, G. (2021). Empathy and the efficient provision of public goods. *NBER Working Paper No. 29255.* Retrieved August 29, 2024, from https://www.nber.org/system/files/working_papers/w29255/w29255.pdf

Hendriks, A. (1995). Disabled persons and their right to equal treatment: Allowing differentiation while ending discrimination. *Health and Human Rights, 1*(2), 152–173. https://doi.org/10.2307/4065212

Hernandez, I. (2017). *Bismarck and the welfare state.* Retrieved December 30, 2022, from https://fvinstitute.org/bismarck2017

Hoffman, M. L. (2000). *Empathy and moral development. Implications for caring and justice.* Cambridge University Press.

Hulsewé, A. F. P. (1987). Han China: A proto "Welfare State"? *T'oung Pao, Second Series, 73*(4/5), 265–285. https://doi.org/10.2307/4528391

Issacs, J. B. (2017). *Economic mobility of families across generations.* Retrieved January 9, 2023, from https://www.brookings.edu/wp-content/uploads/2016/06/11_generations_isaacs.pdf

Kirman, A., & Teschl, M. (2010). Selfish or selfless? The role of empathy in economics. *Philosophical Transactions of the Royal Society, 365*, 303–317. https://doi.org/10.1098/rstb.2009.0192

Knight, K. L. (2018). *A.C. Pigou and the 'Marshallian' thought style.* Palgrave Macmillan.

Lambert, P. J., & Yitzhaki, S. (1995). Equity, equality and welfare. *European Economic Review, 39*(3–4), 674–682. https://doi.org/10.1016/0014-2921(94)00074-a

Lane, R. E. (2001). Self-reliance and empathy: The enemies of poverty—And of the poor. *Political Psychology, 22*(3), 473–492. https://doi.org/10.1111/0162-895X.00250

Leibenstein, H. (1976). *Beyond economic man: A new foundation for microeconomics.* Harvard University Press.

Lillelien, S. (2009). *Utilitarianism and other welfarist approaches to distributive justice.* Retrieved January 31, 2023, from https://www.uio.no/studier/emner/sv/oekonomi/ECON4270/h09/sverre_lillelien_4270oblig.pdf

Marshall, A. (2013). *Principles of economics* (8th ed.). Palgrave Macmillan.

McManaman, D. (2002). *Free will and empathy.* Retrieved September 1, 2024, from https://www.lifeissues.net/writers/mcm/mcm_76empathy.html

Nishizawa, T. (2021). Alfred Marshall on progress and human wellbeing. In R. E. Backhouse, A. Baujard, & T. Nishizawa (Eds.), *Welfare theory, public action, and ethical values: Revisiting the history of welfare economics* (pp. 77–96). Cambridge University Press.

Olsaretti, S. (2018). Introduction: The idea of distributive justice. In S. Olsaretti (Ed.), *The Oxford handbook of distributive justice.* Oxford University Press. https://doi.org/10.1093/oxfordhb/9780199645121.013.38

Pettigrew, T. F. (1979). The ultimate attribution error: Extending Allport's cognitive analysis of prejudice. *Personality and Social Psychology Bulletin, 5*(4), 461–476. https://doi.org/10.1177/014616727900500407

Pigou, A. C. (1920). *The economics of welfare.* Macmillan.

Rawls, J. A. (1971). *A theory of justice revised edition 1991.* Belnap Press of Harvard University Press.

Roy, D. (2022). Development and validation of an empirical instrument to assess empathy driven organizational justice systems in schools. *Berkeley Review of Education, 11*(1). https://doi.org/10.5070/B811151325

Ryan, W. (1971). Emotional disorder as a social problem: Implications for mental health programs. *American Journal of Orthopsychiatry, 41*(*4*), 638–645. https://doi.org/10.1111/j.1939-0025.1971.tb03224

Ryff, C. D. (1989). Happiness is everything, or is it? Explorations on the meaning of psychological well-being. *Journal of Personality and Social Psychology, 57*(6), 1069–1081. https://doi.org/10.1037/0022-3514.57.6.1069

Sarkisyanz, E. (1965). *Buddhist backgrounds of the Burmese revolution.* Springer.

Schultz, N. (2012). *Empathy as the key to equality and human rights.* Retrieved September 4, 2024, from https://repository.gchumanrights.org/server/api/core/bitstreams/11b58b8e-9696-4864-b01c-3332f9dcc6db/content

Segal, E. A. (2011). Social empathy: A model built on empathy, contextual understanding, and social responsibility that promotes social justice. *Journal of Social Service Research, 37*(3), 266–277. https://doi.org/10.1080/01488376.2011.564040

Sen, A. (1979). Utilitarianism and welfarism. *The Journal of Philosophy, 76*(*9*), 463–489. https://doi.org/10.2307/2025934

Sen, A. K. (1991). Utility: Ideas and terminology. *Economics and Philosophy, 7*(2), 277–283. https://doi.org/10.1017/S0266267100000l425

Sen, A. (1999). *Commodities and capabilities*. Oxford University Press.

Sennett, R. (2002). On welfare & the psychology of dependence. *Daedalus, 131*(3), 126–131. https://doi.org/10.2307/20027797

Sheng, F., & Han, S. (2012). Manipulations of cognitive strategies and intergroup relationships reduce the racial bias in empathic neural responses. *NeuroImage, 61*(*4*), *786–797*. https://doi.org/10.1016/j.neuroimage.2012.04.028

Spencer, H. (1864). *Principles of biology* (Vol. 1). Williams and Norgate.

Tanner, R. J., et al. (2008). Of chameleons and consumption: The impact of mimicry on choice and preferences. *Journal of Consumer Research, 34*(6), 754–766. https://doi.org/10.1086/522322

The Constitution of India, Part 4, Directive Principles of State Policy. Retrieved January 2, 2022., from https://www.mea.gov.in/Images/pdf1/Part4.pdf

Thomas, E. F., et al. (2009). Transforming "Apathy into Movement": The role of prosocial emotions in motivating action for social change. *Personality and Social Psychology Review, 13*(*4*), *310–333*. https://doi.org/10.1177/1088868309343290

Varghese, N. V. (2018). Criticality, empathy and welfare in educational discourses. *Contemporary Education Dialogue, 15*(2), 122–142. https://doi.org/10.1177/0973184918781209

Wagaman, M. A., & Segal, E. A. (2014). The relationship between empathy and attitudes toward government intervention. *Journal of Sociology & Social Welfare, 41*(4), 91–112. Retrieved February 14, 2022, from https://scholarworks.wmich.edu/cgi/viewcontent.cgi?article=3984&context=jssw&httpsredir=1&referer=

Yoo, C., & Jang, W. (2019). Social empathy for society beyond the social work profession: A contextual understanding of poverty and attitudes towards government interventions. *Sociétés, 3*(145), 25–36. https://doi.org/10.3917/soc.145.0025

CHAPTER 7

Empathy and Education

The term education has been used to describe divergent processes which have often been conflated with schooling and learning. Yet, schooling does not necessarily ensure either learning or education. UNESCO defines education as "the process of facilitating learning or the acquisition of knowledge, skills, values, beliefs and habits" (en.unesco.org, n.d.). This definition of education presents it as a broad psychological and social process, extending beyond knowledge acquisition to inculcating moral principles, faith and social enculturation.

While literacy, which might be described as education's lowest denominator, remains essential for participation in modern society, its role is far from sufficient. Dreze and Sen (1995) describe literacy as "a basic tool of self-defence in a society where social interaction often involves the written media" (p. 164). Illiteracy restricts access to justice, technology, economic opportunities and political life. It is further posited that education has intrinsic value, expands economic freedom, reduces child labour, empowers women and generates positive externalities. Educated individuals often share knowledge or engage in social activism that benefits entire communities (Dreze & Sen, 1995).

Education also plays a crucial role in economic development. Landes (1980) asserted, "The heart of the whole process of industrialization and economic development is intellectual: it consists in the acquisition and application of a corpus of knowledge" (p. 111). Easterlin (1981) similarly

D. Roy, *Empathonomics*,
https://doi.org/10.1007/978-981-95-4033-4_7

emphasized that while modern economic growth spread through the diffusion of knowledge, its adoption depended on populations' motivations and traits which were shaped by formal schooling which was in turn influenced by political and ideological conditions (p. 1). However, this ideation narrows education to institutional settings. In reality, traditional and informal knowledge systems such as crafts passed down generations or a dairy farmer's experiential expertise also embody education; a factor that is often dismissed as mere training. This approach constrains the manner in which education is defined and valued. Consequently, within the paradox that emerges, a farmer with no formal schooling may know more about cattle than a dairy technology graduate, but only the latter is recognized as 'educated.'

Thus modern societies have come to equate education almost exclusively with formal schooling. As Counts (1931) observed: "With the coming of the modern age formal education assumed a significance far in excess of anything that the world had yet seen ... until it took its place along with the state, the church, the family and property as one of society's most powerful institutions" (p. 410).

If, for the sake of argument and simplification, all forms of knowledge acquisition are brought under the broad ambit of education, two rival schools of thought would still emerge: one would view education as a process of personal development, while the other would emphasize on its instrumentality (Oladi, 2013). The instrumentalist view stresses practical knowledge and skills for employment and economic activities, while moving away from the paradigm "education for education's sake." Scholars such as Lubienski (2003), Kuttner (1999) and Oladi (2013) argue that this transforms education into an individualistic, commodified, privatized good purchased for socioeconomic gain.

At first glance, instrumentalism may appear utilitarian and unempathic. However, since education is also a pathway to socioeconomic upliftment, particularly for marginalized groups, instrumentalist approaches can align with empathic objectives. Consequently, it be argued that what matters is not the goal but the process: models of education can be cooperative rather than competitive, inclusive rather than exclusionary, encouraging rather than judgmental—thus creating an empathic instrumentalist framework without altering its core purpose.

The method of knowledge dissemination is therefore central to the empathic quality of education. While education is often treated as a means to an end, it is the empathic (or unempathic) character of this means that shapes motivation, confidence and self-esteem, all of which predict outcomes. Empathy enables teachers to gauge students' knowledge through projection—seeing from the learners' perspective—and sometimes through reverse projection or reflection, where teachers reassess their own knowledge based on student understanding (Nickerson et al., 2009). Though projection may lead to overestimation, empathic projection remains vital for effective learning.

Empathic education systems not only enhance teaching-learning outcomes but also cultivate empathy among students. Extant research has linked student empathy to reductions in prejudice, racism and conflict (Doyle & Aboud, 1995; Feshbach & Feshbach, 2009), as well as to prosocial behaviours like cooperation, sharing and altruism (Feshbach & Feshbach, 2009). Empathy is inversely related to aggression (Feshbach & Feshbach, 1969, 2009) and positively related to achievement. As Feshbach and Feshbach (2009) noted, empathic students learn better, particularly in reading, literature and social studies, because they can more fully place themselves in the role of central characters .

A formalized system of education often raises expectations of higher income and improved social standing. Such expectations are not misplaced, as research consistently shows a positive correlation between education and earnings (Berg, 1970; Blaug, 1972; Wolla & Sullivan, 2017). In the context of India, too, Rani (2014) found that "returns to education increase with the level of education across location, caste-religion and English language ability" (p. 1).

Blaug (1972) had identified three explanations for this correlation: economic, sociological and psychological. Economically, education imparts scarce, high-demand skills that attract higher wages; sociologically, it reinforces social values which are favoured by dominant or ruling classes and psychologically, it signals greater ability among the more educated individuals. The economic explanation is justified to an extent; for example, a neurosurgeon or a rocket scientist does possess skills and acumen that are rare and thus a premium is charged on their services. Yet Blaug cautioned against assuming that education always increases productivity. For example, a highly qualified teacher may not necessarily outperform one with fewer academic credentials, nor does formal education always make farmers or livestock workers more effective in their profession. Productivity, he argued, must be assessed by comparing educated and 'raw' workers under identical conditions of management, capital and resources. Thus, "education makes the marginal worker more productive when he is furnished with the same quantity and quality of management, capital equipment and complement of all other workers as before" (Blaug, 1972, p. 55).

Consequently, higher earnings for educated individuals may stem less from productivity than from scarcity. This is because education is costly, thus formally educated workers are fewer, and labour markets reward them accordingly. Firms prefer candidates with higher qualifications for complex tasks, while others are filtered out through 'skill labelling,' where diplomas and certificates serve as selection tools (Leibenstein, 1969; Blaug, 1972). Yet, it could be argued that these qualifications are often irrelevant to actual job roles. In India, for example, the civil services include a significant number of doctors and engineers whose degrees signal competence but whose talents may be underutilized in bureaucracy.

The difference in earnings among people with differential levels of education is sometimes explained by a concept known as educational wage permia which could be explained as the percentage difference in the mean labour earnings among people with different levels of education (Peracchi, 2006). It has been argued by Peracchi (2006) that the educational wage is the outcome of interactions between market forces like supply and demand of labour (of various kinds) as well as the mediating effect of labour market institutions which influence market forces (viz. statutory wage regulations, labour unions, etc.) to limit its effects. Thus, it is but natural that educational wage permia shows variations among countries and time periods. However, it might be noted that over the past century, there has been a sharp rise in educational attainment and thus the supply of educated individuals in the labour market has increased. If the linear logic of supply and demand is followed, a decrease in the wage of educated labour might be surmised. Peracchi (2006) and Welch (1970) claimed that such a decrease in return to educational attainment has not occurred and the reason attributed to such an outcome is the consequent rise in demand for educated individuals through an increased demand for goods and services as well as a fundamental change in the technology used in the production of goods. The change in demand of skilled workforce caused by the advent of technology is referred to as 'skill-biased technical change' (Peracchi, 2006, p. 215). Notwithstanding this self-balancing model, it might be witnessed, at least within the context of a developing country like India (which has observed a tumultuous rise in the number of graduates and post-graduates from a range of universities), that the premium on educational attainment of graduates and postgraduates (other than those with professional qualifications from premium institutions) have fallen drastically. This is particularly so for management graduates from relatively lesser-known universities and institutions.

While it might be inferred with certain degree of clarity that higher educational attainment is not a guarantee of higher wages (which are most often determined by market forces), individuals often take decisions on education based on expectations of the wage permia. Unfortunately, such expectations are often irrational and overestimated. Several empirical studies conducted in different parts of the world confirm this phenomenon (Betts, 1996; Dominitz & Manski, 1996; Brunello et al., 2001). The fallout of an irrational expectation of the educational wage permia is witnessed among the thousands of middle-class students who are enticed to take substantial student loans to pursue expensive courses with the expectation of high-paying jobs. Accumulated student loans in the United States amount to nearly $1.6 trillion, the amount is more than the accumulated car loans or credit card loans. The amount is projected to reach $3 trillion by the end of the decade (Johnson, 2019). Expensive higher education is leading a section of American youngsters to opt out of college and focus on building competency (Johnson, 2019). Opting out of higher education is not an easy choice in countries like India where education is often viewed as an aspirational exercise which often presents as the only option for upward socio-economic mobility to a substantial segment of the population. When educational attainment presents as the sole agent of socioeconomic upliftment, the situation is sometimes utilized by vested interests to create a vicious and unempathic system of exploitation and worse. Education systems in many parts of the developing world (and also in certain parts of the developed world as witnessed in the USA) thrive on predaceous utilization of the hapless condition of the aspirational middle class. The resultant processes are designed to make the exploitative system necessary for individual survival. This leads to disparity between the demand and supply of seats in educational institutions (demand far exceeding the supply) resulting in high cost of education and the arbitrary framing of rules and regulations to control and exploit the populace that perceives this education as necessary for their future wellbeing. The education ecosystem, especially at the school level, is unforgiving towards those who underperform in standardized examinations (thus leading to a decline in net performance of an institution and consequently its value). The power centric education system commodifies test scores which are exchanged for a seat in a coveted college or university in an attempt to chase the often-elusive dreams of a better tomorrow. In countries like

India this blind objectification of education has led to poor learning outcomes, performance anxiety and rampant exploitation of students by coaching centres who act as dream merchants and prepare students for admission tests to prestigious institutions. Needless to say that such preparations do not prioritize empathy or the wellbeing of the students.

If the relationship between income and education is contextualized within the dimensions of empathic behaviour, the ensuing deliberations invariably lead to the association of power and its mediating role in the relationship. It could be argued that educational attainments and the resultant knowledge accumulation thus leads to the enhancement of power among a set of individuals, consequently, resulting in higher wages being associated with higher levels of education. In other words, the power gained by knowledge is leveraged for economic benefit. While it might seem rational or even just to leverage the gained knowledge for higher income, the problem occurs when such knowledge and its usage have the potential to change or save lives. Professionals like doctors, lawyers, engineers, and those that deal in the direct transfer of knowledge like teachers, professors and other academicians have the power to save or change lives significantly by the usage, transfer or exchange of the knowledge that they have accumulated through education. Thus, such professions are deeply powerful and the consequent power has the potential to encourage two vastly divergent behavioural patterns: altruistic and empathic or ruthless and selfish. While there are examples of empathic altruistic behaviour among such professionals, power oftentimes also encourages unempathic behaviour. Ergo, there are examples of medical professionals providing selfless free service to save lives even in war zones at the risk of their own lives, lawyers fighting pro bono for individuals who cannot afford their service, teachers conducting free classes for underprivileged children and academicians posting their research on the internet as open-source materials for the use of all. There are contrasting examples of expensive doctors who offer only high value medical services for the rich, lawyers who charge fees that are out of reach of the general public, teachers who teach for substantial tuition fees and academic research which is patented or downloadable only after payment of a substantial fee.

Numerous studies have been conducted to study the effect of power on empathy and the results have broadly indicated that being powerful makes people less empathic towards the plight of the others. Keltner et al. (2003) had posited that enhanced power leads to an increased attention to personal rewards (which in the case of highly educated individuals presents as a demand for higher income) and inaccurate or stereotypical reading of others (lower levels of empathy). Contrarily reduced power leads to an enhanced capacity for understanding and prioritizing "others' interests, and those features of the self that are relevant to others' goals" (Keltner et al., 2003, p. 265). It has been posited by some experts that this behavioural phenomenon has physiological causes. Hogeveen et al. (2014) had observed within their study that those with higher power presented with reduced neurological mirroring than those with less power.

Ergo, it could be rationally argued that the higher income which individuals and groups with higher levels of education enjoy might have root causes which are not solely economic in nature. In fact, the eventual economic outcome of higher levels of education may be the result of a power-induced behavioural model which might be fundamentally unempathic. The empathic behaviour that sometimes emerge are just outliers which grab attention and thus remain within public memory for longer periods of time.

The effect of social class on educational achievements (and the consequent higher incomes earned by the educated class) has been the subject of deep introspection by scholars for over a century. Karl Marx and Friedrich Engels had in the opening lines of the Communist Manifesto elaborated on the importance of social classes and the ensuing class struggle in the history of human society: "The history of all hitherto existing society is the history of class struggles. Freeman and slave, patrician and plebeian, lord and serf, guild-master and journeyman, in a word, oppressor and oppressed, stood in constant opposition to one another, carried on an uninterrupted, now hidden, now open fight, a fight that each time ended, either in a revolutionary re-constitution of society at large, or in the common ruin of the contending classes" (Marx & Engels, 1967, p. 79). The Marxist model divided society into two fundamental classes: the Bourgeoisie and Proletariat. While the Bourgeoisie controlled the means of production, the Proletariat consisted of the working class. The Bourgeoisie according to the Marxist model controls the incomes earned by the rest (including the educated members) of the society; according to Marx and Engels, "The bourgeoisie has stripped of its halo every occupation hitherto honoured and looked up to with reverent awe. It has converted the physician, the lawyer, the priest, the poet, the man of science, into its paid wage-labourers" (Marx & Engels, 1967, p. 82). The societal dilemma that Marx had illustrated is all too often experienced in modern society wherein hospitals run by rich investors for profit employ educated professional doctors only as a means to maximize returns on investment, or within schools that might be described as non-profit institutions but are promoted by the rich with a goal to maximize their wealth, some schools too employ educated individuals only as a means to enhance revenue generation. Such profit-driven models within social sectors are inherently unempathic not only towards the society that they pretend to serve but also towards the educated professionals who are employed for their knowledge and skills but are provided little if any say in the formulation of rules and policies of the institutions that they serve.[1,2]

Social classes have an effect on educational attainment. It has been reported within empirical studies that individuals' formal education is correlated to the formal education of the parents (Ferjan & Jereb, 2007). In fact, Ferjan and Jereb (2007) also reported within their study that "there is also a correlation between individuals' formal educational achievement and the social class of the family of origin" (p. 883). Goldthorpe (2010) had specified "children of less advantaged class origins have remained, to much the same extent, more likely than children of more advantaged origins to leave the educational system rather than to continue in it; or, if they do continue, to follow courses that, through the kinds of qualification to which they lead, reduce their chances of continuing further" (p. 318). Curiously such disparities are observed even as countries across the world have made education, especially school education, more accessible to all and in countries like India children have a right to free and compulsory education. Hout (2006) had summarized the predicament: "students whose parents are highly educated and affluent have advantages over students whose parents have less education and other important social resources in virtually every postindustrial society" (p. 237). Hout put forward the same argument for "developing countries too" (p. 237).

Goldthorpe (2010) had explained that the reason for the differential approach to education among classes could be due (at least partly) to the culture that prevails within the classes: "The prevailing culture of more advantaged classes, it is held, leads to parents within these classes setting a higher value on education than parents in other classes and being better equipped to encourage and promote educational success on the part of their children" (p. 318). Goldthorpe (2010) recognized that educational systems are often designed as agents of 'social control' (p. 318), and rather than creating spaces for motivating talented individuals, the pedagogy that is followed in educational institutions (especially in schools) often tend to force socialization into the culture of the dominant and powerful upper class. This phenomenon was described by experts such as the French Sociologist Pierre Bourdieu (2018) as cultural reproduction. Bourdieu (2018) had further explained that "In fact the statistics of theatre, concert, and, above all, museum attendance (since, in the last case, the effect of economic obstacles is more or less nil) are sufficient reminder that the inheritance of cultural wealth which has been accumulated and bequeathed by previous generations only really belongs (although it is theoretically offered to everyone) to those endowed with the means of appropriating it for themselves" (p. 73). Thus, as Goldthorpe (2010) argued, the cultural wealth that children bring to educational institutions differ greatly according to their social class and the institutions do not attempt to minimize the differential but rather utilize it in order to appreciate what is termed as merit. Consequently, children from disadvantaged class backgrounds are often led to either accept their non-performance or rebel against the education system which in either case would mean continuing in their disadvantaged position without scope for upward mobility. The persistent inequality in educational attainment among social classes was explained through two influential hypotheses: Maximally Maintained Inequality (Raftery & Hout, 1993) and Effectively Maintained Inequality (Lucas, 2001). The Maximally Maintained Inequality hypothesis claims that "socioeconomic disparities in educational attainment at the specific level will persist until the given level of education is saturated among individuals from an upper class" (Byun, 2017). The concept of Effectively Maintained Inequality posits that educational achievement depends on the number of years of education as well as the quality of the educational program that was pursued (Lucas & Bryne, 2017). It was argued by Lucas and Bryne (2017) that "EMI contends that socioeconomically well-off children will receive qualitative educational advantage even if quantitative outcomes are equalized or quantitative advantage is impossible. Thus, EMI contends that equalizing quantity is insufficient to undermine inequality, because inequality in the types of education obtained can effectively reproduce patterns of advantage and disadvantage" (p. 3). However, education is often fallaciously measured using years of schooling as the only metric. Freeman and Schettkat (2000) had explained that "Years of education do not provide a particularly good measure of differences in schooling." Thus, a child who has spent 12 years in a rural school in India with the basic minimum facilities cannot be assumed to have had an education which is equivalent to that of students who have spent the same number of years in a privileged urban school with modern facilities, infrastructure and opportunities for additional skill development. Moreover as Peracchi (2006) had explained, “same level of education (either years of schooling or schooling level) may reflect very different levels of literacy in different countries” (p. 194). The difference in educational attainment could be due to various reasons: the socio-economic background of the students, difference in curriculum, the educational objectives, infrastructure and financial status of the schools and many other variables which cannot be effectively controlled for.

It will be pertinent at this point to explore the relationship between social classes and empathic behaviour. The differences in empathic disposition among the various social classes are influenced by divergent norms, cultures and approaches to life. At the fundamental level, while the working class promotes collectivism wherein individuals identify themselves closely with others in the group, the middle class encourages individualism wherein each individual is encouraged to think as a unique being with unique qualities that are different from others (Warren, 2022). It has been posited by experts that individualism decreases empathy and compassion while collectivism increases empathy among individuals (Feldman et al., 2019; Heinke & Louis, 2009). This is further exacerbated by the fact that individuals from higher social classes have a more appreciative view of themselves and their capabilities (Warren, 2022) and such views are often a result of overconfidence (Belmi & Neale, 2020).

Thus, it might be concluded primarily that people from lower socioeconomic backgrounds exhibit more empathic behaviour than the more affluent. While accepting the basic reality of the differentials in empathic disposition among social classes, it should also be noted that education presents an opportunity to inculcate empathy among the students and reduce inter-class bias. As Altavilla et al. (2021) explained, “To help students to develop a greater empathy, stronger relationships and an effective communication, it is useful to induce them to put themselves in the shoes of others, so that they can become aware, for instance, of the suffering that leads children to an exclusive condition. At the teachers is required, always more, a strong educational sensitivity, they can recognize an effective empathic educational approach, which is the pedagogical and educational competence par excellence” (p. 692).

While the reach of educational programs through formal institutions like schools and colleges might be easily measured and evaluated, the quality of the educational programs and consequently the institutions that deliver those programs are difficult to evaluate and measure. The evaluation process is most difficult in the case of schools where the variables for such evaluation are not well defined and oftentimes dichotomous. Roy (2020) had described schools as complex behavioural systems; such systems have no definite equilibrium and are thus difficult to evaluate in terms of educational quality. A cursory study of schools might reveal that the alma maters of Nobel laureates might also present as alma maters of some so-called undesirable elements of society. Roy (2020) had thus posited that the search for the best school is fallacious and all schools are potentially best for some students while being effectively disastrous for some others.

The difficulties in evaluating educational programs (and consequently the institutions that deliver those programs) have encouraged a common cognitive bias: that of substituting a difficult question with an easy one (Kahneman, 2011). The resultant heuristic approach often substitutes the question, 'How well are the students learning' with the question 'How are the students scoring in standardized public examinations.' The easy answer often leads to fallacious judgements, sometimes with bad outcomes. An equally fallacious method would be to attempt an evaluation of the school standards through the salaries that the students earn later in life. Speakman and Welch (2006) had rejected the attempts at projecting correlations between wages earned with perceived indicators of school quality such as school expenditure and teachers' salaries. The researchers had noted, "it is unclear whether the positive correlations between wages and either school expenditures or teachers' wages found in much of this literature is indicative of a causal relationship or whether it captures other economic phenomena that supersede the relationship being suggested" (p. 815). However, at this stage it is prudent to acknowledge that the assessment of educational quality is a difficult exercise. Majumdar and Mooji (2011) had succinctly put forward an approach that could be employed to evaluate school education; they opined: " we regard educational quality not only in terms of academic skills that children may acquire – although these are certainly important – but also in terms of the extent to which schools contribute to the expansion of capabilities and freedoms of all children. This means that quality is fundamentally linked to social justice and equality – and not in opposition to the latter, as it is sometimes conceptualised. Its meaning, hence, extends far beyond the achievement of good exam results or the fulfilment of particular managerial or efficiency targets" (p. 30).

An alternate method of evaluating quality of educational processes and institutions involves evaluating such educational institutions and their processes through the levels of empathy involved within them. The School Empathy Audit Battery or SEAB is an instrument that measures empathy levels of school organizations. The instrument evaluates empathy of school leadership, culture, justice system and the psychological safety of students (Roy, 2022). Psychological safety is a term used to describe a situation where a person is not fearful of making mistakes. In an educational institution, high level of psychological safety promotes risk-taking abilities, confidence and creativity. Psychological safety is an outcome of empathic school systems. The core philosophy of empathic education systems lies within the empowerment of students. Most education systems, especially schools, are hierarchical which are centred asymmetrically away from students. Instruments like SEAB which provide an opportunity for students to evaluate their experience in schools and create benchmarks for performance appraisal of the institution are thus important for quality enhancement of educational institutions.

Macroeconomic analyses of educational policies often use government spending on education as a metric for evaluating government policies on education. More often than not increases in government spending on education overwhelmingly relates to the expansion in educational facilities to include a larger section of the population within the realm of formal education. This is essential for social upliftment, better health and hygiene standards, elimination of superstitions and retrograde social practices as well as general wellbeing. Sen (1999) had emphasized on the intrinsic value that education imparts on human lives: "a person may benefit from education-in reading, communicating, arguing, in being able to choose in a more informed way, in being taken more seriously by others and so on. The benefits of education, thus, exceed its role as human capital in commodity production" (p. 294).[3]

However, the relationship between government spending on education and reduction of poverty is complicated. Stromquist (2001) had thus observed: "In all countries of the world, we are making progress with key social indicators: life expectancy is going up, infant mortality is down, and illiteracy is also down. Yet poverty remains. What does this suggest in terms of the power of education as a tool for change?" (p. 40). Stromquist (2001) had provided a reason for the apparent disconnection between education and poverty alleviation within the context of Latin American economies. He had opined that "poverty is not a question of stubborn pockets of uneducated or untrained people but is rather inherent in the social and economic structure of the region. This structure is both the effect and cause of asymmetrical power relations between urban and rural areas, between indigenous peoples and mestizo subcultures, between men and women" (p. 40). Ahmad and Batul (2013) had studied the long-term relationship between poverty, government expenditure on education and educational status in Pakistan. The researchers concluded that no significant relationship exists between the poverty rate and the expenditure on education. In fact, the researchers argued that "increasing budgetary allocation to funding education sector alone without reducing poverty level, would not be sufficient to improve the education status of the country" (p. 1). While reporting the results of an empirical study on this subject of discussion, Zhu (2020) had contended that while modernization theory argues that an expansion in educational facilities to cover wider section of the population leads to a decrease in social inequality, research from China supports the ideas put forward by the "Maximum Maintained Inequality" (MMI) and "Effectively maintained Inequality" (EMI) hypotheses which fundamentally claim that inequality is embedded within the education system through the inequalities in the social structure. In fact, some scholars question the fundamental nature and intentions of the governments in promoting and spreading education within a nation; as Majumdar and Mooji (2011) had observed, "apparently egalitarian policy rhetoric and actions to spread education for all are usually fraught with contradictory intents, and, even if not, are bound to have outcomes that are basically reproducing the status quo" (p. 29). Stromquist (2001) had observed, "Most nation-states make an effective and yet paradoxical use of education. On the one hand, education is defended in official discourse as a social good open to all. On the other hand, public education is treated with neglect as budgets are held with a tight rein and the children of the poor receive the lowest quality of education" (p. 41). The situation is decidedly worse in the so-called developing world where teacher absenteeism, high drop-out rates, below par performance of students as compared to the formally set learning objectives are common. Moreover, schools in many developing countries suffer from a chronic lack of basic equipment like textbooks, blackboards or benches; at times schools in such countries even lack proper roofs (Glewwe & Kremer, 2006).

Importantly, the role of governments in using a powerful tool like education to promote acculturation of students into a dominant hegemonic narrative is not uncommon. The colonial education system that was promoted by the British was founded on such a principle. Thomas Macaulay had lucidly explained the education policy of the colonizers in his infamous presentation titled Minute on Indian Education (Macaulay, 1835) wherein he had expressed, "We must at present do our best to form a class who may be interpreters between us and the millions whom we govern, – a class of persons Indian in blood and colour, but English in tastes, in opinions, in morals and in intellect. To that class we may leave it to refine the vernacular dialects of the country, to enrich those dialects with terms of science borrowed from the Western nomenclature, and to render them by degrees fit vehicles for conveying knowledge to the great mass of the population."

However, despite certain empirical evidence that points to a relative disconnect between poverty alleviation and educational attainment, it is clear that global literacy rates have increased drastically over the past century. It is often argued that the increase in global literacy is a direct consequence of an increase in the life expectancy of the global human population, especially in the drastic reduction of infant mortality in most parts of the world. Peracchi (2006) had explored this interesting relationship between life expectancy and schooling decisions. The researcher explained that the differentials in life expectancy among the various countries had reduced considerably (this despite the fact that the difference in per-capita GDP among certain countries had increased). However, the relationship between life expectancy and schooling were found to be positive but weak. In a similar vein, Cohen and Soto (2002) had observed "that the reduction of worldwide inequalities regarding life expectancy has not been channelled into a convergence of education patterns across the world" (p. 9). It was proposed that life expectancy and educational attainment have a non-linear relationship; when the life expectancy is below a certain critical value, the increase in life expectancy is directed to work life. However, when the life expectancy crossed the critical value, it was directed to education (Peracchi, 2006). In this regard Cohen and Soto (2002) had presented a model wherein they had posited that schooling begins to rise only when "when life expectancy after 5 is above 55" (p. 17).[4]

An added dimension to the issue of education, especially in the context of developing economies like India, has been introduced by the increasing volume of private investment in education, especially in schools. While private schools have existed for over a century in countries like India and have played a pivotal role in the development of the country, the near sudden spike in the numbers of such institutions has affected the social dynamics of the country leading the creation of a new class elite that has been educated in expensive private institutions which offer facilities far beyond the scope of that which is provided in government institutions. Since the seats in government institutions (especially in institutions of higher and/or professional learning) are limited in number, private educational institutions create a knowledge space which allows for the socioeconomically compromised sections of the society to avail of education in affordable or free government institutions while those who can afford more expensive education might avail of the courses in private institutions. However, this predicament is not wholly functional as Härmä (2010) posited "with the exit of all wealthier families more capable of exercising voice to the private sector, the government sector has become a ghettoised option of last resort for the poorest and most marginalised in society. Those accessing government schools, the choice of last resort, are not achieving meaningful access leading to real learning" (p. 38, emphasis original).

However, in the context of school education, a section of private educational institutions charges affordable (low) fees and caters to the less affluent sections of society. This segment of schools was described by Srivastava (2006) as 'low-fee private' (LFP) schools (p. 497). Several experts have opined that the reasons for the rise of low-fee private schools lie overwhelmingly within the dysfunctionalities and inequalities of the existing government school system (Srivastava, 2006; Govinda, 2002). Härmä (2010) described the phenomenon as "a reflexive reaction to the well-documented failings of the government system" (p. vii). The poor school outcomes in many countries are often caused by substandard and indifferent teaching that is witnessed in many government schools. The deficient teaching often finds roots within multiple causes, chief among them being lack of training and expertise. Glewwe and Kremer (2006) reported that 60% of primary teachers in the rural parts of Northeast Brazil had not completed even primary-level school education, this even in the 1980s. Lack of proper pay, extremely large class sizes and low teacher-student ratios also create barriers to the teaching-learning process, leading to poor school outcomes. The low-fee private schools assist in socioeconomic development in their own way. Srivastava (2006) had judiciously analysed the usefulness of low-fee private schools in India and posited that the sector was important in India for two reasons: "Firstly, because it is uniquely placed as a sector targeted to a clientele traditionally excluded from private education, and secondly, because it refocuses attention on the schooling choices of a group that has otherwise been marginalised in educational research" (p. 497). Importantly, Srivastava (2006) reported that households that chose low-fee private schools for their children "were just as likely to choose LFP schools for their daughters as for their sons" (p. 510). This finding was in stark contrast to the existing mental models that are expected in the scenario. Srivastava (2006) had however explained that the decision to educate girl children in such schools was motivated by considerations of marriageability, employability and self-sufficiency while the patriarchal structures which led to such decision making still existed. However, the low-fee private schools are not affordable for all. Härmä (2010) had studied the affordability of low-fee private schools and concluded that the ability of this segment of schools to substitute for government schools in providing services to the poor was severely limited. The researcher reported that almost 60% of the students within the sample could not access the low-fee private schools. This was because the "proportion of cash income needed to send the average number of children to private schools is simply unmanageable" (Härmä, 2010, p. 38).

An important dimension to the discussion of empathic education systems and their relationship to economics lies in the interpretation and often misrepresentation of the term meritocracy. Littler (2018) described meritocracy as "the idea that whatever your social position at birth, society ought to offer enough opportunity and mobility for 'talent' to combine with 'effort' in order to 'rise to the top'" (p. 1). Mcnamee and Miller (2009) had explained, "While 'merit' is a characteristic of individuals, 'meritocracy' is a characteristic of societies as a whole. Meritocracy refers to a social system as a whole in which individuals get ahead and earn rewards in direct proportion to their individual efforts and abilities" (p. 2). However as Littler (2018) proclaimed, contrary to the ideals propounded by the utopian description, meritocracy in reality is the "key means through which plutocracy – or government by a wealthy elite – perpetuates, reproduces and extends itself" (p. 2). The concept of meritocracy ignores the fundamental differences and constraints that birth endows on individuals; race, socio-economic conditions, opportunities of infrastructure, facilities, health and nourishment, mobility, quality of education and many other such factors that determine outcomes in life. The linear and deliberately oversimplistic model posits that if one works hard while competing with and winning against others, one is bound to succeed. The forced equality places all individuals on the same platform and against the same benchmarks of success without compensating for the inequal positions that individual experience in real life. This model of meritocracy is unforgiving and unempathic in two fundamental ways. For one the model surmises that individuals who do not 'succeed' are not hard working or lack the acumen, and secondly the model encourages individual competition to an extent that it discourages cooperative behaviour among members of the society, thus leading to an unempathic society. The fallout of this approach is the creation of a hierarchical society where the 'winners' form the top bracket while the 'losers' form the lower rung; in a competitive society, only a few will ultimately win. However as is most often the case, the so-called losers who are relegated to the lower echelons of society are not necessarily any less intelligent than the ones at the top; as Mcnamee and Miller (2009) opined, "the simple fact is that there is far more talent, intelligence, hard work, and ability in the population than there are people lucky enough to find themselves in a position to exploit them" (p. 19).

It is thus evident that meritocracy can and does encourage unempathic assumptions on people's situations in life, opportunities and abilities by assuming that stressing on equity. If empathy is explained as understanding the situation of others by putting oneself in others' place, then such an exercise would reinforce the fact that the world is anything but equal. Ergo, the differentials in life situations and opportunities do affect life outcomes and thus measuring merit on certain pre-determined standardized criterion which assume everyone on equal footing is inherently unempathic. However, meritocratic systems can be tempered to become empathic through some fundamental structural changes. Singapore presents a relevant case that could be studied to understand this point. Singapore encouraged a strictly meritocratic outcome-oriented system of education which had little place for egalitarian ideas. However, such an approach established limits on socio-economic mobility and created an unempathic power hungry elite. Thus, the country decided to redesign their system on egalitarian and empathic values. Liberal cross-disciplinary courses were introduced in Singaporean universities on the lines of American Universities; the tuition fees at Singaporean universities were kept at reasonable and affordable levels, even the elite Singaporean schools have reasonable tuition fees. Grants are readily available for meritorious students who cannot afford the fees, the problem of socio-economic barrier to education was solved. Moreover, the Singapore government has ensured that all schools in Singapore are of a good standard, thus providing all students with quality education (Tan, 2016).

It is evident therefore that most meritocratic education systems are fundamentally exclusionary in nature, especially when such systems ignore the importance of social equity and inclusiveness. On the contrary, empathic education systems seek to prioritize egalitarianism and inclusivity. The World Bank describes social inclusion as "the process of improving the terms on which individuals and groups take part in society—improving the ability, opportunity, and dignity of those disadvantaged on the basis of their identity" (https://www.worldbank.org/en/topic/social-inclusion). It is clear that when certain groups of the population are excluded from participating in the normal socioeconomic processes of a country, it acts as a major source of impediment for sustainable socio-economic growth and upliftment. Thus, while social exclusion is unethical and immoral, it also makes for poor economic policy. The World Bank thus posits, "Social inclusion is the right thing to do, and it also makes good economic sense. Left unaddressed, the exclusion of disadvantaged groups can be costly. At the individual level, the most commonly measured impacts include the loss of wages, lifetime earnings, poor education, and employment outcomes. Racism and discrimination also have physical and mental health costs. At the national level, the economic cost of social exclusion can be captured by foregone gross domestic product (GDP) and human capital wealth" (https://www.worldbank.org/en/topic/social-inclusion). Dua et al. (2021) had reported "wealth and income disparities drive stark divides in mental and physical health outcomes, among other outcomes, with low-income individuals reporting sadness, worthlessness, or hopelessness six to ten times more often than high-income individuals and dying six years earlier than high-income individuals, on average" (p. 6).

Exclusionary educational policies might present with differential reasons for such exclusion as well as multiple dimensions and degrees of exclusion. A common reason for exclusionary schools lies within the divisions in society. Societies in many parts of the world are divided on the basis of race, culture, language or even on economic criterion. Borooah and Knox (2015) had described divided societies as "societies which are partitioned – or which partition themselves – into distinct and identifiable groups such that persons from these groups lead 'separate' lives – that is, lives that do not involve association with persons from other groups – with respect to a number of areas" (p. 1). There are examples of divided societies all over the world: Northern Ireland which is divided among the Roman Catholics and Protestants (Borooah & Knox, 2015), parts of India which witness a divide between the Hindus and Muslims (Field et al., 2008) or within the system of apartheid that was practised in South Africa. Borooah and Knox (2015) present the argument that divided societies lead to divided schooling systems wherein children of particular homogenic groups go to schools which seemingly cater only to their own social groups. This division is most often caused by the creation of group centred neighbourhoods that house people from a particular community. One overt form of exclusion would involve formulation of laws, rules and regulations in such a way that one or more social groups are excluded from the benefits of such education. In such cases, the divisive or segregated schooling systems might be created by law as in South Africa during the apartheid regime or in parts of the United States through the infamous Jim Crow laws.[5] The ban on education of women in some countries could also be presented as an example of this method. Most countries however practice exclusion in subtle ways by creating a barrier which some groups of potential students would find difficult to cross. The most common of such barriers is that of expense: often educational systems and institutions keep the cost of education high to make it exclusively available only to a certain section of the society. Other forms of barriers include setting high benchmarks or standards for entry-level requirements which could include high test scores, or high entry-level qualifications. Sometimes support system barriers are used to keep a certain category of people out of some educational courses; for example, if ramps and other supports are not present in an institution, it will be difficult for a person using a wheelchair to access the classrooms and other facilities. Similarly, if schools do not employ special education teachers, the learning environment will be hostile for children with learning disabilities. Exclusion within education systems might thus take many forms and the excluded might encompass a diverse range of groups who are inconvenient to the objectives or ideologies of the educational system or institution. It is often witnessed that the support for exclusionary educational practices come from within the stakeholders in the education system; such support could be a result of biases and prejudices, convenience, status quo bias or even an attempt to benefit from such exclusionary systems. Göransson et al. (2020) had studied the opinion of teachers from segregated schools in Sweden on inclusive education. The researchers reported that the teachers were very strong proponents of segregated schooling and were of the "view that schooling and teaching are not quite compatible with the idea of inclusive education" (p. 1).[6]

However, a lack of segregation does not necessarily translate into inclusive and egalitarian education. This is clearly witnessed in India where marginalized sections like Dalits are sometimes subject to discriminatory treatment. It has been observed by experts that during the late nineteenth and early twentieth century, the privileged upper-class gentry in India were not enthusiastic about the attempt at primary education of the masses. However, notwithstanding the deeply exclusionary nature of education in India at the time, education was also viewed as a means for social upliftment by the Dalits (Majumdar & Mooji, 2011). The exclusionary nature of the Indian education system has however continued to influence educational outcomes and attainments even after more than seven decades of independence. It was in this context that Nambissan (2010) had reported, "social relations and pedagogic processes fail to ensure full participation of Dalit children, and they are in fact subject to discriminatory and unequal treatment in relation to their peers. While on the one hand these experiences are detrimental to children's self-esteem and self-worth, on the other hand they are likely to have serious implications for their interest and motivation in studies. It is not surprising that the majority of Dalit children who enter and are formally 'included' in schools often fail/perform poorly and discontinue their studies" (p. 282). Such discriminatory treatment has been reported by many other researchers including Desai et al. (2010) who had reported: "There are reported instances of Dalit children suffering from discrimination by teachers and other students. Eighty per cent of the Dalit students at a college in Aurangabad said that they were made to sit outside the classroom in primary school" (p. 233). Further the researchers cited a study from The Probe Team (1999) wherein it was reported that a Dalit school teacher had recalled that they were asked to sit separately and their slates or copies were not touched by teachers. Desai et al. (2010) reported that as an outcome of social discrimination, the marginalized sections of Indian society lag behind others in educational attainments and significant disparities exist between them and others. The researchers posited "substantial differences in reading and arithmetic skills between children from different caste, ethnic, and religious backgrounds in India. These differences persist even after controlling for current school enrolment, grade completion, and parental socio-economic status" (p. 250). An interesting proposition put forward by the researchers was that if the children from the marginalized groups could "complete primary school, their likelihood of completing middle school is much closer to that of the other groups" (p. 232). Thus, according to Desai et al. (2010), equal opportunities and inclusive schooling at the primary school level led to better educational outcomes for the children of the marginalized sections of society in India. This is significant because as Nambissan (2010) reported while citing data as recent as the end of the last century (1999–2000), only 48% Dalit children had completed primary school education and that "Even today, the vast majority of Dalit children 'dropout' from school well before they complete eight years of education" (p. 253). In a study conducted among the tribal students of the tea estates of West Bengal, Roy (2021) found an interesting behavioural pattern among the students of the area. Roy (2021) found that "some children who had opted for higher studies and secured government jobs had in turn inadvertently managed to motivate some peers, cousins or siblings to follow their route. The pattern iteratively continued apparently resulting in clusters of such students who have decided to take the proverbial leap towards a life outside the tea estates. Similarly, a contra cluster also seemed to emerge where students who have decided to opt out of formal schooling have indirectly led their friends and others in their contact to drop out of school too. Moreover, a family which has one member completing his or her high school graduation generally led others down the generation to follow their path" (Roy, 2021). This phenomenon was explained by Roy (2021) through the concept of swarm intelligence. Swarm intelligence is a form of collective intelligence which emerges within groups from iterative interactions that occur between the members of the group (Roy, 2021; Bonabeau et al., 1999). In describing the phenomenon of swarm intelligence within the context of the lives of the tea estate workers, Roy (2021) had commented: "Tea Garden workers have been living as groups in tightly knit colonies for generations; consequently, they seem to be thinking as a collective on decisions with regards to education and future plans. Swarm intelligence protects the workers against social isolation during adversities but most importantly provides an evidence based 'pheromone laden' path to follow towards an alternate future goal."

The relationship between education and social inclusion in India might be contextualized within an important case study: that of the Right of Children to Free and Compulsory Education Act (RTE), 2009, which was promulgated in India. As discussed earlier, education in India has been traditionally viewed as a privilege of the upper strata of the society. Even after independence, education in India was largely confined to the upper or middle classes while the masses seemed to be forgotten as the nation focused on capacity building and human resource enhancement for growth and development. However, as the country neared the end of the last millennia, it dawned on the ruling government that universal primary education should be regarded as a right of all citizens and not merely a privilege of the few. As a consequence, The Right of Children to Free and Compulsory Education Act (RTE), 2009, a potentially pathbreaking legislation, was promulgated. The Right of Children to Free and Compulsory Education Act (RTE), 2009 recognized the right to free and compulsory education for all children of India between the age of 6 and 14 as a fundamental right. This in itself was a significant step for the education of children in a country where child labour was still very prevalent. The RTE Act (2009) included various rules and regulations that strived to make school education more empathic and children-oriented. These included prohibition of physical and mental harassment of children (Section 17) as well as prohibition on holding back children in the same class and expulsion of children from school (section 16). The act sought to make school education more inclusive and section 12 (c) of the Act directed schools to admit at least 25% of the strength of class 1 from among the weaker and disadvantaged group in the neighbourhood and provide education to these children for free. The government would in turn reimburse the educational expenses of these children. Not surprisingly several private schools found Section 12 of the Act unacceptable on one pretext or the other. The constitutional validity of the Act was challenged; however, the Supreme Court of India upheld the constitutional validity of the act and in a majority judgement said, "We hold that the Right of Children to Free and Compulsory Education Act, 2009 is constitutionally valid and shall apply to a school established, owned or controlled by the appropriate Government or a local authority; an aided school including aided minority school(s) receiving aid or grants to meet whole or part of its expenses from the appropriate Government or the local authority; a school belonging to specified category; and an unaided non-minority school not receiving any kind of aid or grants to meet its expenses from the appropriate Government or the local authority" (as quoted in Venkatesan, 2012). The opposition to the pathbreaking act thoroughly exposed the fractured, exclusionary nature of education in Indian society and reluctance of the elites to send their wards to schools with the masses. As Majumdar and Mooji (2011) correctly commented: "For a right to education to be effectively enforced, it is therefore necessary that such inequalities are addressed. In fact, the rights debate itself has to engage with cultural notions and practices that define and justify the various hierarchies that exist in such unequal and divided societies as the Indian one" (p. 281). The researchers however opine that if the main objective of the right to education is an acculturation into the dominant mainstream, then it seriously undermines the differences and diversities within the Indian society in an attempt to create an 'equal' and homogenous whole. Consequently, Majumdar and Mooji (2011) query whether a tribal child who is forced to study in a language that is not her own in the name of compulsory universal education might have the right to refuse such education.

A discussion that attempts to unite the fields of economics and education to empathy invariably steps into interesting but diverse complexities. While on one hand the importance of education on individual and societal wellbeing is well documented, the models for the delivery of such education need revisitation as does the current method of analysing individual educational attainments. The attempt to connect education solely with the objective of economic development has rendered most education systems unempathic and unforgiving. The popular narrative that projects meritocracy as an egalitarian concept while conveniently ignoring the inequalities that exist in society just creates and sustains a hierarchical system of haves and have-nots. The prevalent popular model objectifies education as a means to an end and denies knowledge the space to be an end in itself. It is however dangerous to ignore the intrinsic value of education and knowledge, a value which has no conceivable short-term economic benefit but which has been the motivator of the growth and development of the human civilization. Hardly any Nobel Laureate had conducted her research with direct economic benefit in mind; such research was motivated from an inherent fascination with the subject of research. Such excellence can only be achieved and sustained when the education system becomes forgiving, empathic, inclusive and truly egalitarian.

Notes

1. A fairly detailed and comprehensive model of social classes was later developed by the English sociologist John Goldthorpe. The original model that Goldthorpe had proposed consisted of 11 classes. At one end of the model were classes 1 and 2 which comprised of service occupations of higher order (class 1) and lower order (class 2) while the other extreme end of the model consisted of skilled (class 6) and semi or unskilled (class 7) manual workers. A condensed form of this model, known as the CASMIN (Comparative Study of Social Mobility in Industrial Nations) model, was later developed. It consisted of seven classes divided on the same fundamental criteria (Goldthorpe, 1980; Erikson, & Goldthorpe, 1992; Ferjan & Jereb, 2007).

2. While classifying the different levels of education is a complex and difficult exercise especially among cross-cultural international education systems, UNESCO had developed a model of classification known as International Standard Classification of Education (ISCED) to help in the analysis of educational statistics across countries. ISCED 2011 has nine levels of educational attainments which are described from level 0 (Early childhood education below primary levels) to level 8 (doctoral or equivalent). The nine levels are further aggregated into three levels: 0–2 as low level of education, 3–4 as medium levels of education and 5–8 as high levels of education (UNESCO Institute for Statistics, 2012).
3. An important outcome of education presents within the relation of educational attainment with crime. Lochner and Moretti (2004) within their study had reported that "schooling significantly reduces the probability of incarceration and arrest" (p. 155). Several experts propose the human capital approach while analysing the relationship between crime and education. Lochner (2004) explained the role of the human capital approach in such analyses: "The human capital approach, in its simplest form, stresses the role of wages and opportunity costs in determining criminal activity, arguing that older, more intelligent, and more educated individuals commit less crime because they have more human capital and can earn higher wages" (p. 812). The results are however complex when the impact of school quality on crime and other variables are studied. While Deming (2011) posited that going to a better school "greatly reduces crime, and the impact is concentrated among the highest risk youth in the sample" (p. 2111), Cullen et al. (2006) declared that there was little evidence that going to a better school "provides any systematic benefit across a wide variety of traditional academic measures" (p. 1191). In this context Lochner (2011) posited "sizeable improvements in school quality produce minor (at best) improvements in student achievement and educational attainment, while they appear to substantially reduce crime during late adolescence and early adulthood" (p. 185).
4. Several researchers have studied the influence of education on decisions and behaviour related to health. The relation between educational attainment and health is well established. Grossman (2008) had posited, "Many studies suggest that years of formal schooling completed is the most important correlate of good health" (p. 281). Meara et al. (2008) reported, "In 2000, life expectancy for a twenty-five-year-old with a high school diploma or less was fifty years. For a person with some college, life expectancy was nearly fifty-seven years" (p. 253). However, while the reports do posit that health and life expectancy was positively correlated to educational attainment, the

direction of the causality was not well established. Thus, as Grossman (2008) opined, "There is much less consensus as to whether this correlation reflects causality from more schooling to better health. The relationship may be traced in part to reverse causality and may also reflect 'omitted third variables' that cause health and schooling to vary in the same direction" (p. 281). Lochner (2011) analysed the reasons for the relationship between education and health. The researcher opined, "To the extent that education does have small to modest effects on health and mortality, what are the key operating channels or mediating factors? Education may improve decision-making abilities, which may lead to better health decisions and more efficient use of health inputs (productive efficiency). More educated individuals may also be better at acquiring or interpreting information from doctors, other individuals, or the press/internet" (p. 247).

5. Jim Crow laws are a term used to describe laws that enforced racial segregation in the United States of America, specifically the Southern part of the United States. The laws were promulgated in the late 1800s and were repelled by the Civil Rights Act of 1964. However, the laws lost their legal sanction in 1954 when the United States Supreme Court (Brown Vs Board of Education) ruled that segregated schools were illegal (Borooah & Knox, 2015). The term 'Jim Crow' originated from a song-and-dance caricature of the African American people named "Jump Jim Crow" and was derogatory term to describe African Americans. See https://www.britannica.com/event/Jim-Crow-law. While it has sometimes been argued that segregated schools in reality do not lead to significant differences in quality of the education imparted since the investment in all categories of schools are almost the same, Chief Justice Warren had, in his judgement on Brown Vs Board of Education in 1954, very clearly explained the basic psychological problem with segregate schooling: "To separate them from others of similar age and qualifications solely because of their race generates a feeling of inferiority as to their status in the community that may affect their hearts and minds in a way unlikely ever to be undone" (Warren, C.J., 1954).
6. Conversely there have also been conscious attempts to create inclusionary environments in schools for sections of students. An interesting attempt was made by a German paediatrician Dr. Theodor Hellbrügge (1919–2014) to create an inclusive Montessori 'school' for children with special needs. The project was termed "Aktion Sonnenschein" (The Sunshine Project). Dr. Hellbrügge collaborated with Maria Montessori's son Mario Montessori to present a unique approach wherein special children would be imparted Montessori education together with other children. See Dattke (2014).

References

Ahmad, Z., & Batul, T. (2013, July 3–5). Relationship among poverty, education expenditure, and education status: Empirical evidence from Pakistan. In *Proceedings of the world congress on engineering 2013 Vol I, WCE 2013.*

Altavilla, G., et al. (2021). Relevance of empathy in educational relationships and learning processes. *Journal of Physical Education and Sport, 21*(1), 692–695. https://doi.org/10.7752/jpes.2021.s1084

Belmi, P., & Neale, M. A. (2020). The social advantage of miscalibrated individuals: The relationship between social class and overconfidence and its implications for class-based inequality. *Journal of Personality and Social Psychology: Interpersonal Relations and Group Processes, 118*(2), 254–282. https://doi.org/10.1037/pspi0000187

Berg, I. (1970). *Education and jobs: The great training robbery.* Praeger.

Betts, J. R. (1996). What do students know about wages? Evidence from a survey of undergraduates. *Journal of Human Resources, 31*(*1*), 27–56. https://doi.org/10.2307/146042

Blaug, M. (1972). The correlation between education and earnings: What does it signify? *Higher Education, 1*(1), 53–76. https://doi.org/10.1007/bf01956881

Bonabeau, E., et al. (1999). *Swarm intelligence: From natural to artificial systems.* Oxford University Press.

Borooah, V. K., & Knox, C. (2015). *The economics of schooling in a divided society.* Palgrave Macmillan.

Bourdieu, P. (2018). Cultural reproduction and social reproduction. In R. Brown (Ed.), *Knowledge, education, and cultural change.* Routledge.

Brunello, G., et al. (2001). The wage expectations of European college students. *SSRN Electronic Journal.* https://doi.org/10.2139/ssrn.270792

Byun, S.-Y. (2017). *When different types of education matter: Effectively maintained inequality of educational opportunity in Korea.* Retrieved June 12, 2022, from https://ptb2015.wordpress.com/2017/02/01/when-different-types-of-education-matter/

Cohen, D., & Soto, M. (2002). Why are some countries poor? Another look at the evidence and a message of hope. *OECD Development Centre, Technical Paper No. 197.* Retrieved July 24, 2022, from https://www.oecd-ilibrary.org/development/why-are-some-countries-so-poor_205835882383

Counts, G. S. (1931). *Encyclopaedia of the social sciences* (Vol. 5). The Macmillan Company.

Cullen, J. B., et al. (2006). The effect of school choice on participants: Evidence from randomized lotteries. *Econometrica, 74*(5), 1191–1230. https://doi.org/10.1111/j.1468-0262.2006.00702.x

Dattke, J. (2014). A montessori model for inclusion. *The NAMTA Journal, 39*(3), 107–119. Retrieved August 2, 2022, from https://files.eric.ed.gov/fulltext/EJ1183188.pdf

Deming, D. J. (2011). Better schools, less crime? *The Quarterly Journal of Economics, 126*(4), 2063–2115. https://doi.org/10.1093/qje/qjr036

Desai, S., et al. (2010). Segmented schooling: Inequalities in primary education. In S. Thorat & K. S. Newman (Eds.), *Economic discrimination in modern India* (pp. 230–252). Oxford University Press.

Dominitz, J., & Manski, C. F. (1996). Eliciting student expectations of the returns to schooling. *Journal of Human Resources, 31*(1), 1–26. https://doi.org/10.2307/146041

Doyle, A. B., & Aboud, F. E. (1995). A longitudinal study of White children's racial prejudice as a social cognitive development. *Merrill-Palmer Quarterly, 1*(2), 209–228. https://doi.org/10.2307/23090532

Dreze, J., & Sen, A. (1995). *India: Economic development and social opportunity.* Clarendon Press.

Dua, A., et al. (2021). *A case for inclusive growth.* Retrieved August 1, 2022, from https://www.mckinsey.com/industries/public-and-social-sector/our-insights/the-case-for-inclusive-growth

Easterlin, R. A. (1981). Why isn't the whole world developed? *The Journal of Economic History, 41*(1). https://doi.org/10.1017/S0022050700042674

en.unesco.org. (n.d.). *SDG resources for educators – Quality education.* Retrieved February 24, 2022, from https://en.unesco.org/themes/education/sdgs/material/04

Erikson, R., & Goldthorpe, J. (1992). *The constant flux: A study of class mobility in industrial societies.* Oxford University Press.

Feldman, S., et al. (2019). The interplay of empathy and individualism in support for social welfare policies. *Political Psychology.* https://doi.org/10.1111/pops.1262

Ferjan, M., & Jereb, E. (2007). Social class position as a determinant of educational achievement. *Drustvena istrazivanja: Journal for General Social Issues, 17*(4).

Feshbach, S., & Feshbach, N. D. (1969). The relationship between empathy and aggression in two age groups. *Developmental Psychology, 1*, 102–107. https://doi.org/10.1037/h0027016

Feshbach, N. D., & Feshbach, S. (2009). Empathy and education. In J. Decety, J. In Decety, & W. Ickes (Eds.), *The social neuroscience of empathy.* MIT Press.

Field, E., et al. (2008). Segregation, rent control, and riots: The economics of religious conflict in an Indian city. *American Economic Review: Papers and Proceedings, 98*(2), 505–510. https://doi.org/10.1257/aer.98.2.505

Freeman, R. B., & Schettkat, R. (2000). The role of wage and skill differences in US-German employment differences. *Working paper 7474, National Bureau of*

Economic research. Retrieved July 15, 2022, from https://www.nber.org/system/files/working_papers/w7474/w7474.pdf
Glewwe, P., & Kremer, M. (2006). Schools, teachers, and education outcomes in developing countries. In E. Hanushek & F. Welch (Eds.), *Handbook of the economics of education* (Vol. 2). North Holland Publishing Co.
Goldthorpe, J. H. (1980). *Social mobility and class structure in modern Britain*. Clarendon Press.
Goldthorpe, J. H. (2010). Class analysis and the reorientation of class theory: The case of persisting differentials in educational attainment. *The British Journal of Sociology, 61, 311–335*. https://doi.org/10.1111/j.1468-4446.2009.0
Göransson, K., et al. (2020). Segregated education as a challenge to inclusive processes: A total population study of Swedish teachers' views on education for pupils with intellectual disability. *International Journal of Inclusive Education*, 1–16. https://doi.org/10.1080/13603116.2020.1810789
Govinda, R. (2002). Providing education for all in India: An overview. In R. Govinda (Ed.), *India education report: A profile of basic education* (pp. 1–20). Oxford University Press.
Grossman, M. (2008). The relationship between health and schooling. *Eastern Economic Journal, 34*(3), 281–292. https://doi.org/10.1057/eej.2008.13
Härmä, J. (2010). School choice for the poor? The limits of marketisation of primary education in rural India. *CREATE PATHWAYS TO ACCESS Research Monograph No. 23*. Retrieved August 25, 2020, from https://files.eric.ed.gov/fulltext/ED508748.pdf
Heinke, M. S., & Louis, W. R. (2009). Cultural background and individualistic–collectivistic values in relation to similarity, perspective taking, and empathy. *Journal of Applied Social Psychology, 39*(11), 2570–2590. https://doi.org/10.1111/j.1559-1816.2009.00538.x
Hogeveen, J., et al. (2014). Power changes how the brain responds to others. *Journal of Experimental Psychology: General, 143*(2), 755–762. https://doi.org/10.1037/a0033477
Hout, M. (2006). Maximally maintained inequality and essentially maintained inequality: Crossnational comparisons. *Sociological Theory and Methods, 21*(2), 237–252. https://doi.org/10.11218/ojjams.21.237
Johnson, D. M. (2019). *What will it take to solve the student loan crisis?* Retrieved July 26, 2022, from https://hbr.org/2019/09/what-will-it-take-to-solve-the-student-loan-crisis
Kahneman, D. (2011). *Thinking fast and slow*. Penguin Books.
Keltner, D., et al. (2003). Power, approach, and inhibition. *Psychological Review, 110*(2), 265–284. https://doi.org/10.1037/0033-295X.110.2.265
Kuttner, R. (1999). *Everything for sale: The virtues and limits of markets*. University of Chicago Press.

Landes, D. (1980). The creation of knowledge and technique: Today's task and yesterday's experience. *Daedalus, 109*(1), 111–120. https://doi.org/10.2307/20024651

Leibenstein, H. (1969). Economics of skill labelling. In J. A. Lauwerys & D. G. Scanlon (Eds.), *World year book of education 1969. Examinations.* Evans Brothers.

Littler, J. (2018). *Against meritocracy: Culture, power and myths of mobility.* Routledge.

Lochner, L. (2004). Education, work, and crime: A human capital approach. *International Economic Review, 45*(3), 811–843. https://doi.org/10.1111/j.0020-6598.2004.00288.x

Lochner, L. (2011). Nonproduction benefits of education: Crime, health, and good citizenship. In E. Hanushek & F. Welch (Eds.), *Handbook of the economics of education* (Vol. 4). North Holland Publishing Co.

Lochner, L., & Moretti, E. (2004). The effect of education on crime: Evidence from prison inmates, arrests, and self-reports. *American Economic Review, 94*(1), 155–189. https://doi.org/10.2307/3592774

Lubienski, C. (2003). Instrumentalist perspectives on the 'public' in public education: Incentives and purposes. *Educational Policy, 17*(4), *478–502.* https://doi.org/10.1177/0895904803254964

Lucas, S. R. (2001). Effectively maintained inequality: Education transitions, track mobility, and social background effects. *American Journal of Sociology, 106*(6), 1642–1690. https://doi.org/10.1086/321300

Lucas, S. R., & Bryne, D. (2017). Effectively maintained inequality in education: An introduction. *American Behavioral Scientist, 61*(1), 3–7. https://doi.org/10.1177/0002764216682992

Macaulay, T. B. (1835). *Minute on Indian education.* Retrieved August 18, 2022, from http://www.columbia.edu/itc/mealac/pritchett/00generallinks/macaulay/txt_minute_education_1835.html

Majumdar, M., & Mooji, J. (2011). *Education and inequality in India.* Routledge.

Marx, K., & Engels, F. (1967). *The communist manifesto.* Penguin Books.

McNamee, S. J., & Miller, R. K., Jr. (2009). *The meritocracy myth* (2nd ed.). Rowman & Littlefield Publishers.

Meara, E. R., et al. (2008). *Health Affairs, 27*(2), 350–360. https://doi.org/10.1377/hlthaff.27.2.350

Nambissan, G. B. (2010). Exclusion and discrimination in schools. In S. Thorat & K. S. Newman (Eds.), *Economic discrimination in modern India* (pp. 253–286). Oxford University Press.

Nickerson, et al. (2009). Empathy and knowledge projection. In J. Decety & W. Ickes (Eds.), *The social neuroscience of empathy.* MIT Press.

Oladi, S. (2013). The instrumentaliziation of education. *The Atlantic Journal of Graduate Studies in Education: Special Edition.* Retrieved September 27,

2024, from https://www.academia.edu/9494191/The_Instrumentalization_of_Education
Peracchi, F. (2006). Educational wage premia and the distribution of earnings: An international perspective. In E. Hanushek & F. Welch (Eds.), *Handbook of the economics of education* (Vol. 1). North Holland Publishing Co.
Raftery, A. E., & Hout, M. (1993). Maximally maintained inequality: Expansion, reform, and opportunity in Irish education, 1921–1975. *Sociology of Education, 66*(1), 41–62. https://doi.org/10.2307/2112784
Rani, G. (2014). Disparities in earnings and education in India. *Cogent Economics & Finance, 2*(1). https://doi.org/10.1080/23322039.2014.941510
Roy, D. (2020). *Skinned knees and ABCs – The complex world of Schools*. Routledge.
Roy, D. (2021). The role of swarm intelligence in school dropouts among tribal students in the tea estates of West Bengal, India. *Think Pieces Series No. 22. Education. SouthAsia*. Retrieved September, 3, 2022, from https://educationsouthasia.web.ox.ac.uk/
Roy, D. (2022). Auditing for empathy – The new trend in Indian schools. *Think Pieces Series No. 30. Education.SouthAsia*. Retrieved October 11, 2024, from https://educationsouthasia.web.ox.ac.uk/article/thinkpiece30
Sen, A. (1999). *Development as freedom*. Alfred A Knopf.
Speakman, R., & Welch, F. (2006). Using wages to infer school quality. In E. A. Hanushek & F. Welch (Eds.), *Handbook of the economics of education* (Vol. 2). North Holland Publishing Co.
Srivastava, P. (2006). Private schooling and mental models about girls' schooling in India. *Compare: A Journal of Comparative and International Education, 36*(4), 497–514. https://doi.org/10.1080/03057920601024958
Stromquist, N. P. (2001). What poverty does to girls' education: The intersection of class, gender and policy in Latin America. *Compare: A Journal of Comparative and International Education, 31*(1), 39–56. https://doi.org/10.1080/03057920020030153
Tan, K. P. (2016). *How Singapore is fixing its meritocracy*. Retrieved October 11, 2024, from https://www.washingtonpost.com/news/in-theory/wp/2016/04/16/how-singapore-is-fixing-its-meritocracy/
The Probe Team. (1999). *Public report on basic education in India*. Oxford University Press.
UNESCO Institute for Statistics.(2012). *International Standard Classification of Education - ISCED 2011*. Retrieved August 1, 2022 from https://unesdoc.unesco.org/ark:/48223/pf0000219109
Venkatesan, J. (2012). *The supreme court upholds RTE act*. Retrieved September 6, 2022, from https://www.thehindu.com/news/national/Supreme-Court-upholds-RTE-Act/article12960710.ece

Warren, C. J. (1954). *Brown v. board of education – Decision.* Retrieved September 3, 2022, from https://www.law.cornell.edu/supremecourt/text/347/483%26gt

Warren, M. (2022). *How social class is reflected in our Psychology.* Retrieved October 3, 2024, from https://www.bps.org.uk/psychologist/how-social-class-reflected-our-psychology

Welch, F. (1970). Education in production. *Journal of Political Economy, 78*, 312–327. https://doi.org/10.1086/259599

Wolla, S. A., & Sullivan, J. (2017). *Education, income, and wealth.* Retrieved February 26, 2022, from https://research.stlouisfed.org/publications/page1-econ/2017/01/03/education-income-and-wealth/

Worldbank.org. *Social inclusion.* Retrieved August 1, 2022., from https://www.worldbank.org/en/topic/social-inclusion

Zhu, B. (2020). Cultural reproduction or cultural mobility? Unequal education achievement among Chinese college student. *The Journal of Chinese Sociology, 7*(6). https://doi.org/10.1186/s40711-020-00119-6

CHAPTER 8

Empathy and Health

The relationship between healthcare, economics and empathy is complex and multidimensional. At the most perceptible level, it shapes interactions between patients, physicians and healthcare workers. However, these interactions are embedded in broader structural factors such as macroeconomic healthcare policies, health insurance regulations, the scope of public healthcare systems, availability of trained professionals and the economic conditions influencing the lifestyle of the population. Additionally, the business dynamics of pharmaceutical and allied industries which consequently affect the cost and accessibility of medicines, vaccines and equipment directly determine the quality of empathic patient care. However, an important distinction must be made between *healthcare* (medical care) and *health* itself, as Arrow (1963) had noted, health outcomes are driven by numerous factors, with medical care representing only one among many. This chapter explores these multiple dimensions of health and healthcare through the lenses of empathy and economics.

The association between physicians and empathy has deep cultural roots. In Greek mythology, the centaur Chiron was wounded by Hercules' poisoned arrow and had endured unhealed suffering that ultimately made him a legendary healer.[1] Inspired by the myth of Chiron, Carl Jung developed the concept of the *wounded healer*, observing that "a good halt of every treatment that probes at all deeply consists in the doctor's examining himself, for only what he can put right in himself can he hope to put right

D. Roy, *Empathonomics*,
https://doi.org/10.1007/978-981-95-4033-4_8

in the patient. It is no loss, either, if he feels that the patient is hitting him, or even scoring off him: it is his own hurt that gives the measure of his power to heal. This, and nothing else, is the meaning of the Greek myth of the wounded physician" (Jung, 1985, p. 139).

Subsequent empirical research has served to reinforce and validate the wounded healer archetype within healthcare professions. In this regard, Barr (2006) found that 73.9% of therapists disclosed at least some personal experiences that could be described as wounding. Similarly, Straussner et al. (2018) reported that 40.2% of licensed social workers recounted some pre-existing mental health challenges prior to entering the profession. While it would be hasty to derive a definitive causal relationship between the choice of profession and a previous negative experience, it would not be too injudicious to recognize that a correlation might exist between the career choice and the experience. Beyond pre-career experiences, professional wounds also influence workplace behaviour. Piredda et al. (2022), while studying nurses who contracted Covid-19, reported that they returned to their work as "wounded healers," carrying scars of their own illness but with "increased compassion and attention to basic needs" (p. 1). Likewise, Missouridou et al. (2021), while studying Greek nurses during the pandemic, found that while 23% experienced compassion fatigue, 77% reported moderate to high levels of *compassion satisfaction*. The researchers opined "Adequate preparation/education, clear and accountable leadership, and team sharing of feelings, experiences, and responsibilities during the transition in the COVID-19 unit helped participants to deal with overwhelming anxiety which if unattended could bring about frustration and long-lasting feelings of powerlessness" (p. 1).[2]

While the mythological archetypes of Chiron and Aesculapius formed the basis of the wounded healer archetype, modern healthcare has introduced newer and complex dimensions to professional behaviour. Over the last several decades, the science (and art) of medical practice has undergone profound transformation. Historically, medicine was a paternalistic profession wherein doctors were revered as demi-gods or father figures whose authority was unquestionable. Their advice, prescriptions and treatments were rarely challenged or disobeyed and failure in treatment or death was most often attributed to fate, bad luck or divine will rather than on professional error. Medical knowledge was intentionally obscured from common people and non-medicos. Medical information was conveyed through technical jargon and esoteric codes. Alvin Toffler (1991) had aptly described this "choke-hold on medical knowledge" (p. 5): prescriptions written in Latin, journals restricted to professionals, conferences closed to the public and curricula tightly controlled by physicians

Over the years the situation has shifted significantly. The spread of education and relatively easy access to information has ensured that patients and families now have access to extensive knowledge on illnesses, prognosis, treatments, medicines, side-effects, costs and alternatives. As a consequent to this, there is greater demand for transparency from healthcare providers. Furthermore, medical practice has also been introduced to legislative control. Patient autonomy and informed consent are now presented as crucial and compulsory within extant ethical standards. For example, Article 8 of the Model Professional Code for Physicians in Germany (2018) requires informed consent for all treatments and mandates that physicians provide comprehensive, comprehensible information on the nature, risks and alternatives of procedures, with adequate time for patient reflection especially when interventions are elective or high-risk (Model Professional Code for Physicians in Germany, 2018).

The subtle yet observable shift in power has led physicians to discard, at least in part, their historically domineering attitude and become more specialized, while regarding patients and their families as partners in resolving medical problems. However, the asymmetric power equation still persists and is unlikely to be completely discarded given that one party must still entrust her life to the other. As Breyer and Storms (2021) note, "a particular asymmetry characterizes the relationship between doctors and patients, since the latter are usually in a vulnerable, existential situation, i.e., a crisis, in which they experience themselves as helpless and turn to health care professionals with the assumption that those can help them on the basis of their expertise" (p. 363).

Emanuel and Emanuel (1992) examined this complex relationship and proposed four models. The models are determined by the goals of care, the physician's professional obligations, the role of patient values and the scope of autonomy. The paternalistic model presents the physician as a guardian who selectively shares information and limits patient participation, while always prioritizing the patient's wellbeing above personal interest. The informative model prioritizes full disclosure, and the physician provides all relevant and truthful information. This enables the patient to make an informed decision, which the physician then follows. The interpretive model also ensures transparency but goes a step further. The physician within this model acts as counsellor and helps the patient clarify her values and align choices accordingly. Finally, the deliberative model positions the physician as teacher or friend who presents clinical options while highlighting the values they embody, and recommending which values might best be pursued but all without coercion.[3]

The models that have been presented herein do not necessarily presuppose an empathic disposition within the physicians' interactions with patients. The paternalistic model leaves little room for empathic perspectives, while the informative model reduces physician-patient interaction to a cold, factual and emotionless exchange of information. In contrast, the interpretive and deliberative models do provide space for empathic engagement and perspective. This aspect turns most effective when the physician actively connects with and understands the patient's values and perspectives. Breyer and Storms (2021) considered the deliberative model as the most empathic and observed that empathy here is not a one-sided act of "putting oneself in the other's shoes," (p. 366) but an interpersonal process where both physician and patient contribute as partners in a discussion while trying to understand each other. Breyer and Storms (2021) argued that the resultant reciprocity preserves alterity and strengthens the therapeutic bond. Nevertheless, the dynamics of physician-patient interactions remain complex. Patients who present in vulnerable or life-threatening situations often revert to the paternalistic model and entrust decisions to physicians (Breyer & Storms, 2021).

An increasing number of physicians have begun to view patients and their kin as partners thus recognizing the role of empathy in clinical relationships. This shift in attitude has the potential to improve health outcomes by shaping patients' attitudes and resilience in facing illness. Lelorain et al. (2012) found that "clinician's empathy is associated with higher patient satisfaction, better psychosocial adjustment, lesser psychological distress and need for information" (p. 1257). Breyer and Storms (2021) further emphasized on the role of empathy in resilience and noted that empathic perspectives allow patients to reframe crises and embed their struggles within broader personal narratives. The researchers commented "the resilience potential of empathy lies primarily in the additional mental perspectives on a situation of crisis offered by empathizing others" (Breyer & Storms, 2021, p. 362).

It is important to note that the benefits of empathic care extend beyond mental wellbeing. Yang et al. (2018) had studied patients with advanced prostate cancer. The researchers reported an inverse correlation between physician's empathy with patient's feelings of stigma and anxiety. In addition, importantly it was reported that the empathic nature of the physicians had measurable physiological effects on the patients. Patients who were treated by more empathic doctors showed significant improvements in their immune function, particularly in Natural Killer (NK) cells, which play a vital role in destroying tumour cells.

In an attempt to analyse the causes for the positive health outcomes resulting from empathic disposition of physicians, Decety and Fotopoulou (2015) had proposed two neurobiological models which sought to explain the effect of physicians' empathy on health outcomes. The researchers had specified that the two models were not mutually exclusive implying that they could be connected or correlated. The first model was the social-baseline theory (SBT) which posited that "the presence of other people helps individuals to conserve metabolically costly somatic and neural resources through the social regulation of emotion" (Decety & Fotopoulou, 2015, p. 1). The researchers explained that organisms are hard wired to be present among their own kinds. Consequently, the human brain, by default, assumes the social presence of other individuals who might be familiar to or interdependent on each other and have shared goals. The activation of neural pathways and stress hormones are far less when an individual receives social support during stress rather than when she is facing the situation alone and is forced to self-regulate her emotions (Decety & Fotopoulou, 2015). Empirical studies have thus found that the presence of another individual significantly reduces the suffering from pain. This is as true for animals like mice (Langford et al., 2010) as well as for humans (Montoya et al., 2004). Emotions provide information which aid in decision making. In the context of healthcare, relationships with friends or relatives and physicians act as buffer against stress and provide resources for information leading individuals to conserve and optimize precious metabolic energy (Decety & Fotopoulou, 2015).

The second model that Decety and Fotopoulou (2015) had proposed attempted to explain the effect of physicians' empathy on the physical and mental health of patients through the free energy principle,[4] which is a theory in cognitive science that attempts to analyse brain functioning. The human brain seeks to minimize surprises (Friston, 2010; Gershman, 2019) and thus it unconsciously constructs inferential hypotheses on the hidden causes of the various sensory inputs that it receives. Humans, as biological beings, need to maintain homeostasis in order to survive within the environment that they live in. The homeostasis is maintained through the use of the environment; however, the environment is dynamic and constantly changing and herein the inferential models help to predict the world

(Decety & Fotopoulou, 2015). Consequently, it could be argued that the inferential models also help the human brain in the instinctive deciphering of emotions that guide human behaviour, values and reactions. Decety and Fotopoulou (2015) explained that "under the free energy framework, the perceptual and motivational aspects of empathy on health can be unified under the same optimization principle. Specifically, during stressful situations individuals are motivated to act in order to avoid danger. In the FEP, such motivational aspects can be conceptualized as a process of active inference, where actions are performed to change sensory signals related to homeostasis and thus reduce prediction errors. In a social context, such actions may be directed towards the environment with the goal of eliciting help from others and changing sensations via this indirect social channel" (p. 7).

While recognizing the need for empathic understanding in healthcare, it must be contemporaneously acknowledged that healthcare workers often operate in unforgiving professional environments that foster burnout and psychological strain. High-stakes settings, where saving lives and preventing death are of supreme importance, naturally generate stress. Patients and their families are often overwhelmed by fear and anxiety. Consequently, they frequently develop unreasonable expectations of physicians, thus making it difficult to empathize with doctors' limitations. For medical professionals, these challenges are compounded by long work hours with heavy workloads, the constant demand to stay updated with evolving medical knowledge and the pressure to deliver efficient patient care within limited resources.

These factors expose many healthcare workers globally to secondary stress. Secondary stress was defined by Wicks and Donnelly (2021) as "the pressure that results from reaching out to others in need" (p. 19, emphasis original). This condition can result in severe psychological repercussions which might range from emotional numbing to hyper-affectivity (Wicks & Donnelly, 2021). Curiously, however, although patient-physician models such as the deliberative model might be considered to worsen professional stress through an emphasis on empathic engagement, the evidence suggests otherwise. Empathic engagement not only benefits patients but also enhances physicians' psychological wellbeing by strengthening self-efficacy (Breyer & Storms, 2021). Conversely, Huang et al. (2019) found that "self-esteem is one of many factors which contribute to medical students' empathy" (p. 1). Since the connection between self-esteem and self-efficacy is close and intricate, it is reasonable to conclude that empathy correlates with both, regardless of the causal direction of the relationship. This offers a compelling argument for promoting empathic patient-caregiver relationships.

Within the bounds of healthcare, empathy can be conceived in two ways. One perspective perceives it as an intrinsic professional disposition which enables physicians to understand the situations of the patients and initiate treatment which is aligned with their needs. The other contrasting view perceives empathy as an added virtue which is external to medical practice but is nevertheless deeply rooted in ethical traditions (Breyer & Storms, 2021). Pellegrino and Thomasma (1993) had explained that "the ancient codes of medical ethics—Greek, Indian, and Chinese—were virtue-based. Their prescriptions and proscriptions looked to the character of the physician as the final guarantee of the well-being of the patient and as the basis of professional standards and practices. The same can be said of the ethics of Thomas Percival and his eighteenth-century colleagues, James and John Gregory, who so heavily influenced the first ethical code of the American Medical Association" (p. xi).

An empathy-driven physician–patient relationship prioritizes patient wellbeing above all other considerations. However, the introduction of economic dimensions to this relationship complicates the situation. Modern medicine is quite unlike the practices of Chiron, Aesculapius or even Carl Jung and operates within a multibillion-dollar industry which is influenced and controlled by diverse stakeholders and efficiency imperatives. While scientific advances have transformed healthcare into a powerful system for prolonging and enhancing life, they have also introduced economic and ethical constraints, often leaving limited space for empathy.

Doctors are human and while most doctors might not concede that money is the prime motivation for their professional life, it is increasingly evident that in the modern times economics plays an important role in patient care. Weinberg (2012) explained that doctors sometimes diverted patients towards unnecessary medical procedures because in purely economic terms, the doctors get paid more for performing the procedure than for withholding it. Weinberg (2012) called this practice rain making where rain is the metaphor for money. The situation has changed further since the late twentieth century onwards, and the medical profession has witnessed a paradigm shift in many countries including in India. Resnick (2007) explained, "During the last 2 decades in an attempt to either maintain or increase income, physicians looked at other avenues to expand their services, which included not only profits made from sale of specific pharmaceutical products and performance of laboratory services in their offices, but also investment in imaging centers, ambulatory surgical centers and companies providing technological services for patient care such as lithotripsy." (p. 1143). Adashi (2015) described this new role of doctors as that of "physician-entrepreneur" (p. 781). As Adashi (2015) explained, if medical businesses are owned by non-physicians, it might not be a cause for concern, because the primary decisions on treatment procedures would still be taken by physicians who would have no conflicts of interest and would not directly benefit from higher patient bills. However, if physicians owned medical businesses like hospitals, pharmacies or diagnostic clinics, then it could lead to serious cases of conflict of interest eventually creating opportunities for undue profit at the cost of the patients. Moreover, the connection between big pharma and doctors is well known. Mitchell and Korenstein (2020) reported that money and other gifts that are presented to American doctors by pharmaceutical and medical device companies amount to over two billion dollars annually. It goes without saying that such astronomical sums of money cannot be spent without the prospect of a quid pro quo and the resultant conflict of interest. A study that was conducted with the support of the Memorial Sloan Kettering Cancer Center to explore the relationship between financial payments from the pharmaceutical industry and physicians' prescriptions reported that "[t]he association between industry payments and physician prescribing was consistent across all studies that have evaluated this association. Findings regarding a temporal association and dose-response suggest a causal relationship" (Mitchell et al., 2020, p. 1).

The fundamental change that has seeped into medical science and healthcare systems has had an overarching influence on all aspects of the healthcare 'industry.' This might be explained with clarity through a comparative case study involving the discovery and delivery of two entirely different but at the same time epochal vaccines, which, it could be argued, saved the human race from calamity. Polio or Poliomyelitis is a life-threatening viral disease caused by the poliovirus. In 1952, the United States of America had recorded 58,000 cases of polio, the majority of the affected being children: over 3000 individuals died and thousands were forced to a life in iron lung machines (Pizzigati, 2016). Poliomyelitis was effectively controlled and almost eradicated through vaccinations, and at this point of time, wild poliovirus is found only in two countries in the world (Afghanistan and Pakistan). Dr. Jonas Salk, who had developed the first inactivated Polio Vaccine (IPV) in 1955, had refused to patent his work. In a television talk show when Dr Salk was asked about the ownership of the patent for his polio vaccine, he had famously replied, "Well, the people, I would say. There is no patent. Could you patent the sun?" (Oshinsky, 2005, p. 211). It has been reported that Dr Salk would have been richer by several billion dollars if his vaccine had been patented[5] (Prabhu, 2012). Around five decades later when the world faced a terrible crisis during the Covid-19 pandemic, the only conceivable way to combat the crisis was to develop vaccines at an incredibly fast pace. The supply of vaccines during this crisis was limited by constraints in the available production process as well as the complications that arose through patents that had been granted for the vaccines to some companies.[6] Many developing countries including India and South Africa as well as international organizations and agencies like the WHO wanted a waiver of the Intellectual property protection for Covid-19 vaccines; however, the pharmaceutical industry and some of the rich developed nations were initially against such waiver. United States, Russia and China did support the waiver at a later stage; however, the European Union, UK, Japan and South Korea were adamant on keeping the Intellectual property protections. The countries that kept opposing the waiver cited a complex, convoluted and time-consuming World Trade Organization procedure involving compulsory licensing. These countries conveniently ignored the fact that time was a crucial factor in tackling the Covid-19 crisis. Moreover, the Covid-19 vaccines were mostly manufactured by companies in countries which were relatively prosperous. The vaccines were then sold to the respective governments or to richer countries. At one point, out of 8.6 billion doses of confirmed purchases of the vaccine, 6 billion had been pre-ordered by countries that were comparatively prosperous. Consequently, African countries which imported almost 99% of their vaccines were left in a lurch. They did not have the economic capacity to pre-order vaccines, consequently at one of point of time only around 2% of Africa's 1.2 billion people had at least one dose of the vaccine (Editorial, *Nature*, 2021).

While Dr Jonas Salk had chosen not to patent his vaccine, five decades later medical science had evolved enough to view life and death as cold unempathic business decisions involving profit where the haves get a chance to be vaccinated while the have-nots are stuck in a quagmire of legalities while trying to crawl through patent protections to save human lives. The irony of the situation was emotionally presented by Benjamin Davis (The Rosalind Franklin Institute and Department of Chemistry,

University of Oxford): "Why do Salk's words still rattle? Well, my nagging seed of doubt may be one that his question should raise in us all perhaps? The vaccine that has now spread from my upper arm is, unlike his gift to the world (his 'sun'), still managed 'intellectual property' (IP). In this, perhaps the most testing (and perhaps triumphant) moment for medicine in mankind's history, we have continued to adopt an approach that might have left him somewhat incredulous" (Davis, 2021, p. 508).

Davis (2021) subsequently explained the reasons for the deviations from Salk's approach to scientific discovery: "Unlike Salk, the current academic generation appears to accept this. We are all rightly encouraged to consider 'impact', but perhaps too often that impact is viewed only through the lens of commercial translation/spin-out, etc.; impact means of course so much more" (pp. 508–509). Davis (2021) further argued that the proposition which claims that Intellectual Property right incentivizes scientific research is limited and mostly puerile because IP rights might in fact lead to disincentivizing scientific research. Davis (2021) argued, "Many systems are simply not pursued nor developed nor used if there is no so-called 'freedom to operate', even if they might have potentially led to real translational benefit—this can therefore curtail the development of certain discoveries" (p. 509). The pertinent question at this stage would be: How would scientific research be funded without post-development monetization? As Davis (2021) claims in nearly all cases scientific research is paid for by the society and in an overwhelmingly large number of cases through tax payer's money by public funding or charitable donations. In fact, not only were much of the fundamental pioneering work on the mRNA vaccines conducted through public (government) funding,[7] several companies received substantial government funding for their research and development involving the Covid-19 vaccine.[8]

The discussion involving vaccines and patents could be placed within the context of a wider discussion involving the relationship between ethical and empathic medical practices and patents. The ethical dilemma presented in the patent system that governs medical care in the modern world was explained by Reisman (1995): "While physicians' principal concerns must be to provide the best possible care currently available for their patients, the patent system encourages future innovation by granting inventors the right to exclude others from practicing, their innovations for a limited time. For patents containing claims for medical products (e.g., pharmaceuticals and medical devices) or medical processes (e.g., new therapeutic or surgical techniques), the operation of the patent system often means that physicians will either be barred from taking advantage of recent technological advances or, at the very least, be forced to license these advances from inventors for a fee ultimately charged to the patient" (pp. 356–357).

The argument that patents drive innovation is somewhat valid especially when money is recognized as the prime motivator for scientific research. However, the ethical dilemma of the argument for patenting medical products, therapies and procedures presents as a contradiction to the basic purpose of medical science itself; the objective which is envisioned in the Hippocratic Oath, that of preserving human lives. It was this point that Pellegrino and Thomasma (1993) had sought to emphasize upon when they posited that "Medicine is a moral community because it is at heart a moral enterprise and its members are bound together by a common moral purpose" (p. 3). The ethical dilemma and the overreaching unfair and tragic consequences of patenting medical procedures and therapies has been recognized in many forums, consequently more than 80 countries have banned the patenting of medical procedures either expressly within legislations or through case laws. For example, Section 3(i) of the Indian Patents Act 1970 prohibits the patenting of "any process for the medicinal, surgical, curative, prophylactic diagnostic, therapeutic or other treatment of human beings or any process for a similar treatment of animals to render them free of disease or to increase their economic value or that of their products" (Indian Patents Act, 1970). The Agreement on Trade Related Aspects of Intellectual Property Rights (TRIPS) expressly allows members to exclude from patents "diagnostic, therapeutic and surgical methods for the treatment of humans or animals" (Agreement on Trade-Related Aspects of Intellectual Property Rights as Amended by the 2005 Protocol Amending the TRIPS Agreement, Article, 27, paragraph 3, a). The United States of America allows the patenting of medical methods; however, it denies enforceability in case of infringement.[9]

Empathy is connected to healthcare through multiple dimensions, all with differential levels of impact on the wellbeing of patients. The research and development stage in medical science comprises of the discovery, formulation and design of medicines, vaccines, equipment and even treatment procedures that form the fundamental base of the modern healthcare system. Since research and development entail significant costs and years of painstaking study, the outcome of such research is often priced extremely high. Moreover, the inherent system of rewards often recognizes monetary benefits as the highest form of motivation, prioritizing over the intrinsic as well as social value of such research-oriented discovery. The ethical dilemma consists of balancing the rewards and accounting for the research costs while ensuring that the final market price of the products is limited so as to keep them within the reach of the common individual. Expensive medicines lead to calamitous consequences; the effect is pronounced in developing countries like India where it has been reported that more than 55 million people are forced into poverty every year due to exorbitant healthcare expenses. Moreover, of the 55 million who slip below the poverty line, 38 million do so on account of medicinal expenses alone (Khan, 2019). The problem however is not restricted to developing countries like India. Wagstaff et al. (2018) had studied affordable healthcare across 133 countries. The researchers had described catastrophic spending on healthcare as spending that was above 10–25% of household spending. They reported that globally 808 million people had to incur catastrophic spending on healthcare. The global incidence of such spending increased steadily over the years and at the threshold level of 10%, catastrophic spending was estimated at 9.7% in 2000, 11.4% in 2005 and increased to 11.7% in 2010.

As a specific case in point, the National Health Service in the UK had refused to pay over £105,0000 annually per patient to the drug manufacturer Vertex (an American company based in Boston, USA) for an important drug named Orkambi which is used to treat cystic fibrosis. The stalemate which continued for around four years had resulted in serious difficulties for patients who were mostly children. The situation had led to calls for the patent on the medicine to be revoked, before a settlement was reached in 2019 (Boseley, 2019a, 2019b). Similarly in the United States, a crisis related to unaffordable Insulin has led to numerous avoidable deaths. Rajkumar (2020) reported that "[t]he most commonly used forms of analog insulin cost 10 times more in the United States than in any other developed country" (p. 22). McConnell (2022) reported that a single vial of the most commonly prescribed form of insulin can cost an uninsured American patient more than $300. Rajkumar (2020) opined that the main reason for the high cost of insulin in the United States of America was the presence of a vulnerable section of the population whose life depended on the medicine and who thus would pay any amount to survive. Ironically when insulin was discovered by Frederick Banting, J.J.R. Macleod, James Collip and Charles Best in 1923, the discoverers had refused to commercialize their discovery and had sold the patent to the University of Toronto for a sum of $1. The idea was to ensure that everyone who needed the medicine could afford it (Belluz, 2019).

If healthcare is contextualized within the field of economics, it will become apparent that medical care and services present with some unique characteristics. The nature of the demand for medical services is not regular or predictable. While the demand for commodities like clothes or daily consumables can be predicted, it is near impossible to know when people might fall sick and might require medical care (Arrow, 1963). Healthcare services might be broadly categorized into three groups: preventive, curative and palliative, of these preventive healthcare services constitute the most predicable and regular category of healthcare services. Moreover, the demand for healthcare services is sometimes associated with impairment or death. This leads to secondary costs in the way of loss of income which in addition to the cost of medical care enhances the total cost of illness on the patient and her family. On the supply side, the entry to medical profession all over world is restricted in order to ensure the quality of service. The cost of medical education is high; however, in most cases the education is subsidized for the students by government funding so that the students have to bear only a minimal part of the cost; ironically however medical professionals constitute one of the highest earning professional groups in the world. The behavioural expectations from healthcare professionals are however different from other services. Healthcare professionals are expected to be ethical and empathic and the association of profit with the medical profession coupled with the general ignorance and the consequent fear of medical conditions lead to suspicion and antagonism in patients and kins. This predicament is worsened by the fact that the outcome of any medical treatment is uncertain and the consequent perception of the healthcare provider (and products) is not definite and varies according to experience. The uncertainty about the outcome is asymmetric and the physicians are less uncertain about the procedures and outcomes than the patients (Arrow, 1963).

While discussing the macroeconomic aspect healthcare services, especially with relation to public healthcare, it should be emphasized that the demand for healthcare services in most parts of the world far exceeds the supply. Wiseman (2011) had attributed the cause of the higher levels of demand for healthcare services to an increase in the aging population (probably due to higher life expectancies) and higher expectations resulting from sophisticated technology that is now available for treatment of diseases. However, while that causal explanation might hold true for developed countries, the developing world presents with different causes for the inadequacy of healthcare services; lack of adequate fund allocation for the healthcare sector, lack of trained personnel, logistical and infrastructural constraints that prevent the supply and storage of medicines and equipment, social unrest, war and violence are some of the reasons that lead to inadequate healthcare facilities in many developing countries. Peters et al. (2008) had reported that low- and middle-income countries "account for 90% of the global burden of disease but for only 12% of global spending on health" (p. 163). Even when healthcare facilities are available in developing countries, they are often deficient in quality. Peabody et al. (2006) had explained, "ample evidence suggests that quality of care (or the lack of it) must be at the center of every discussion about better health" (p. 1293). Numerous studies have reported on the lack of quality healthcare in developing countries like Papua New Guinea (Beracochea et al., 1995), Bangladesh (Forsberg et al., 1992), Africa (Bryce et al., 1992), Pakistan (Thaver et al., 1998). However, the deficient quality of treatment that is observed in developing countries does not necessarily relate to poor training and lack of knowledge. As Beracochea et al. (1995) had observed, "Not all of the observed poor performance can be related to training and supervision. Shortages of essential drugs and other supplies were common. A lack of essential drugs, clinical aids and equipment will have a direct impact on PHW performance, patient care and the outcome of illness" (p. 73). It is evident that people residing in the poorer countries do not have access to adequate healthcare facilities both in terms of quantity and quality. In fact, even among the richer nations, the poor have lesser access to quality healthcare than the more affluent sections of the society. The often-interrelated dimensions of poverty, ignorance, compromised hygiene and lack of education create barriers to accessing proper healthcare facilities. Moreover, as Peters et al. (2008) had observed, "the causal relationship between access to health services and poverty also runs in the other direction" (p. 161). Poverty and ill health often present as a cyclical relationship wherein "poverty leads to ill health and ill health maintains poverty" (Peters et al., 2008, p. 161).

Since illness and poverty present as a cyclical loop wherein poverty leads to illness and the illness leads to more poverty, the vicious trap results in a significant section of the populace remaining in poverty. Such a situation results in high socio-economic costs, especially since governments have to bear the cost of healthcare in such cases while the economy loses out on the services of individuals who could have contributed positively to the economy through productive effort. In an attempt to study the relationship between health and economics, the World Health Organization had set up the Commission on Macroeconomics and Health (CMH) in 2000. The CMH estimated that an increase in annual health investment of $66 billion would result in annual revenue generation of $360 billion in terms of direct and indirect benefits (WHO, 2013).

The availability of quality healthcare has been posited to be governed by the Inverse Care Law (Hart, 1971). The law states: "The availability of good medical care tends to vary inversely with the need for it in the population served" (Hart, 1971, p. 405). Hart (1971) had explained that the law is most effective when medical care is influenced by market forces and least effective when market forces do not influence medical care. Hart (2001) in a letter to the *British Journal of Medicine* had opined, "No market will ever shift corporate investment from where it is most profitable to where it is most needed" (p. 1363). In creating his case for the law, Hart (1971) had quoted the famous British social scientist Richard Titmuss: "We have learnt from 15 years' experience of the Health Service that the higher income groups know how to make better use of the service; they tend to receive more specialist attention; occupy more of the beds in better equipped and staffed hospitals; receive more elective surgery; have better maternal care, and are more likely to get psychiatric help and psychotherapy than low-income groups particularly the unskilled" (Richard Titmuss, 1968 as quoted in Hart, 1971, p. 405). It is worth noting that Hart as well as Titmuss had commented on the state of healthcare in the British context, in developing countries where the socio-economic gap among the rich and the poor is significantly high and the range of public healthcare services are limited the inverse care law is widely applicable. Watt (2002) had succinctly contextualized Hart's approach to medical practice within the law that he had proposed, in doing so he had suggested a solution to the problem of deprivation in socio-economically challenged areas: "Julian Tudor Hart was not only the epidemiologist who did not go away; he was also the personal doctor who knew his patients well, could see problems in their family and community context, and worked with patients over many years to reverse risks and prevent complications. Could it be that the answer to comorbidity in deprived areas is a personal doctor?" (Watt, 2002, p. 253). The personal doctor that Watt (2002) had proposed would in all probability introduce a certain element of empathy while dealing with patients, since the patients she would be treating would be known to her personally and not present merely as faces of unknown strangers. The family physician of the yesteryears who treated generations of particular families brought similar levels of empathy to the profession.

However, the deprivation of the socio-economically challenged is not restricted to the clinical dimensions of healthcare alone. Since treatment procedures and medical interventions are overwhelmingly based on research outcomes, an important source of deprivation arises when socio-economically challenged sections of the population are not well represented in the various types of medical research studies. In epidemiological studies it has been reported that while an active response rate of 80% is judged to be good in case of affluent areas, a response rate of 60% is considered good for areas that are socio-economically deprived (Watt, 2002). In this context Watt (2002) had opined "the availability of research evidence is socially patterned and tends to exclude populations with the greatest degree of health need" (p. 252).

Equitable healthcare systems are founded on the principles of universality, accessibility and affordability (White, 2015). It has been widely recognized that augmentation of primary healthcare facilities is key to the delivery of equitable healthcare. The important role of primary healthcare in public health was first recognized by the world health organization in 1978 within the Alma Ata declaration that aimed to attain the objective of health for all. The Alma Ata declaration explained: "Primary health care is essential health care based on practical, scientifically sound and socially acceptable methods and technology made universally accessible to individual and families in the community through their full participation and at a cost that the community and country can afford to maintain at every stage of their development in the spirit of self-reliance and self-determination. It forms an integral part both of the country's health system, of which it is the central function and main focus, and of the overall social and economic development of the community. It is the first level of contact of individuals, the family and community with the national health system bringing health care as close as possible to where people live and work, and constitutes the first element of a continuing health care process" (Alma-Ata 1978, Report of the International Conference on Primary Health Care, pp. 3–4).

An empathic public health system could involve steps to address and eliminate barriers that limit access to such health systems. These barriers could be:

Geographical: wherein the health centres are far away from rural areas without adequate means of transportation, roads or other means of access;

Availability: wherein adequate facilities of treatment for diseases wherein equipment, medicines, trained professionals are not available;

Financial and economic: wherein the treatment that is available is too costly for the patients and/or their kins to bear. Many a times while the treatment is free in government healthcare centres some expensive medicines that are prescribed have to be purchased by the patients

Social and cultural acceptability: The design of an empathic public healthcare system has to take into consideration the social and cultural norms of the populace that it intends to serve. Local healthcare professionals who are conversant with such norms might be employed in such centres and the delivery mechanism could be designed keeping in mind such norms.

(Peters et al., 2008)

An important approach to make expensive healthcare affordable to the common public is that of promoting health insurance. However private health insurance companies often come across as overwhelmingly profit oriented and thus unempathic. Basler (2019) had reported that in the United States of America, the experience of consumers with health insurance companies ranks among the lowest in the insurance industry; the cause which was put forward for the predicament was that the insurers do not involve emotion in their dealings and are unempathetic. Several categories of illnesses are often not covered by health insurance policies; congenital ailments, pregnancy, self-inflicted ailments like cirrhosis which is deemed to be caused by alcoholism are some such diseases. Sometimes hospitals charge more from patients who are insured leading to complications in disbursements of the insured amount. Moreover, the premium for private health insurance policies is high especially for those with pre-existing conditions. Expensive private health insurance leads to the exclusion of the very section of people who such insurance policies would benefit the most. In the context of Brazil, Diaz et al. (2020) reported that "less than 6% of the individuals in the poorest income quintile having private health insurance cover in 2013 compared to around 65% of individuals in the richest quintile" (p. 74). In the Indian context the Pradhan Mantri Jan Arogya Yojana of the Central government and state government health insurance schemes like Swastha Sathi Scheme of the government of West Bengal are helping to take health insurance schemes to the common public who might now have a chance to avail of advanced and expensive treatment for their ailments.

While much of the discussion in this chapter has focussed on healthcare, it is prudent at this stage to dwell upon the importance of health itself. As White (2015) had explained, "Most health systems around the world remain heavily focused on illness and do relatively little to optimize health and thereby minimize the burden of illness, especially for vulnerable groups" (p. 104). While empathy within the perspectives of medical care has been the focus of numerous discourses, the empathic dimensions of individual and group behaviour towards health presents as an interesting and important area of introspection. This aspect of human behaviour is significantly mediated by the fact that neither individuals nor groups of individuals are required to pay the costs for actions that might endanger their health or that of others around them unless such actions are illegal and lead to prosecution by law enforcement. Thus, potentially reckless behaviour towards personal or community health is common even among those who are from the educated sections of society. Refusal to be immunized, avoidance of exercise, fatty and unhealthy food, stressed lifestyle, alcohol abuse, smoking, not only extract a direct cost from the immediate patients but also result in enormous social healthcare costs which is ultimately borne directly or indirectly through public money.

While the design and implementation of healthcare systems are expensive to set up and maintain, complicated and time-consuming systems that prioritize good health among the population with a view to prevent illness are relatively far simpler and economical. An empathic approach to public health involves focussed and planned government efforts towards providing the socio-economically deficient sections of the society with proper food and nutrition, clean drinking water, proper sanitation facilities, inputs on personal and social hygiene, as well as knowledge on prevention, management and treatment of common ailments that are not serious in nature (in order to reduce burden on healthcare centres). Further interventions in this regard might involve awareness campaigns for diagnosis and treatment of communicable diseases like tuberculosis, ante-natal care, effective and efficient vaccination and mass inoculation programs in addition to reducing and eliminating superstitions and psychological barriers which prevent individuals and families from seeking medical help. Alcohol and substance abuse extract a great cost on society both in terms of health and as catalysts of undesired social behaviour, interventions to prevent and control such addictive behaviour without stigmatization is an important step towards the creation of an empathic healthcare system. Health-related interventions include community-level interventions to promote healthy lifestyle and behaviour among the citizens. Campaigns to promote physical exercise, anti-smoking campaigns, blood pressure and blood sugar monitoring could help to prevent illness and reduce the burden on the healthcare system (White, 2015).

Health is arguably the most important asset that an individual might possess. A healthy nation or society might be viewed as an aggregation of healthy individuals. The economy of a country is significantly influenced by the portion of the population that is healthy enough to contribute to the economic activities of the country. Thus, government expenditure on public health and healthcare could be viewed as an investment which would ultimately result in incremental returns. Empathic healthcare systems that understand, feel and act with compassion present as the most effective healthcare systems. Such systems are based on a bottom-up approach, emanating from individual physicians who are familiar with the patients and understand their problems and needs, primary healthcare centres employing staff who present with empathic understanding of the community that they serve followed in the hierarchy by advanced specialized healthcare units. Moreover, an empathic healthcare system would prioritize health over healthcare and seek to prevent illness wherever possible. Such systems can be effective only with an empathic understanding of the individuals within a community and society. The rationale proposed herein posits that countries promoting empathic healthcare might present as healthier and thus economically stronger, which in itself presents as a strong argument in favour of empathic healthcare systems.

Notes

1. Aesculapius the Greco-Roman God of medicine had been taught the art of healing and medicine by Chiron.
2. The concept of the wounded healer however is not limited to medical science. Henderson (2019) had reported on the idea of the wounded healer as an archetypal concept which transcended beyond the realms of medicine and physicians to include wounds that were psychological or spiritual in nature and even included those wounds that had been inflicted on countries, institutions, cultures or even to the earth.

3. Emanuel and Emanuel (1992) had clarified that these four models are not exhaustive and more models could exist. They mentioned a fifth model called the instrumental model where the patient and his or her values are considered irrelevant and some goal that is independent of the patient such as scientific discovery or good society is pursued.
4. The free energy principle finds its roots within the works of the German Physicist Hermann von Helmholtz (1948) who had suggested that the brain unconsciously executes inferences. The consequent model of the brain is that of a statistical machine. See von Helmholtz (1948), Demekas et al., 2020.
5. There are a group of scientists who contend that Dr Salk did not patent the vaccine because it might not have been granted a patent due to the prevailing standards of the time. However, the deliberation on whether the patent might or might not have been granted is one of conjecture and is not based on a certain indisputable fact. See https://www.bio.org/blogs/real-reason-why-salk-refused-patent-polio-vaccine.
6. The pathbreaking new type of vaccines used to combat the Covid-19 pandemic was the mRNA vaccines. The foundations of the mRNA vaccine were developed in 1987 by Robert Malone, a student at the Salk Institute. The Salk institute which opened in 1963 was the brainchild of Jonas Salk. See Storz (2022).
7. The vaccines that were developed by Pfizer and Moderna were based on two very important discoveries (both of which were public funded): the viral protein that was designed by virologist Dr. Barney Graham (at Vanderbilt University) through a federally funded project and the fundamental concept of RNA modification which was developed by Drew Weissman and Katalin Karikó at the University of Pennsylvania. In fact, the name Moderna is based on the term Modified -RNA. See Allen (2020).
8. McCarthy (2021) reported that Pfizer and BioNTech received around $800 million in research and development funding for Covid-19 vaccine. Frank et al. (2021) reported that Biomedical Research and Development Authority (BARDA), which is an agency under the United States department of health and Human Services on its own, had spent $19.3 billion on the development of the Covid-19 vaccine. The authors cited several government reports to estimate the US government funding for Covid-19 vaccines at between 18 and 23 billion USD.
9. The approach of the United States towards patents of medical procedures underwent a shift in the 1990s after a court case wherein a surgeon had sued his colleagues for infringement of his patent (The relevant case is Pallin v. Singer, 36 U.S.P.Q. 2d 1050 (D.Vt. 1995)).

References

Adashi, E. Y. (2015). Money and medicine: Indivisible and irreconcilable. *American Medical Association Journal of Ethics, 17*(8), 780–786. https://doi.org/10.1001/journalofethics.2015.17.8.msoc1-1508

Agreement on Trade-Related Aspects of Intellectual Property Rights as Amended by the 2005 Protocol Amending the TRIPS Agreement. (2005). Retrieved September 15, 2022, from https://www.wto.org/english/docs_e/legal_e/trips_e.htm#art27

Allen, A. (2020). *For billion-dollar COVID vaccines, basic government-funded science laid the groundwork.* Retrieved September 9, 2022, from https://www.scientificamerican.com/article/for-billion-dollar-covid-vaccines-basic-government-funded-science-laid-the-groundwork/

Alma-Ata. (1978). *Primary health care. Report of the international conference on primary health care.* World Health Organization.

Arrow, K. J. (1963). Uncertainty and the welfare economics of medical care. *The American Economic Review, 53*(5), 941–973. https://doi.org/10.2307/1812044

Barr, A. (2006). An investigation into the extent to which psychological wounds inspire counsellors and psychotherapists to become wounded healers, the significance of these wounds on their career choice, the causes of these wounds and the overall significance of demographic factors. *The Green Rooms.* Retrieved September 8, 2022, from http://www.thegreenrooms.net/wounded-healer/

Basler, R. (2019). *Empathy transforms health insurance.* Retrieved October 27, 2022, from https://www.insurancethoughtleadership.com/life-health/empathy-transforms-health-insurance

Belluz, J. (2019). *The absurdly high cost of insulin, explained.* Retrieved September 17, 2022, from https://www.vox.com/2019/4/3/18293950/why-is-insulin-so-expensive

Beracochea, E., et al. (1995). Case management quality assessment in rural areas of Papua New Guinea. *Tropical Doctor, 25*(2), *69–74.* https://doi.org/10.1177/004947559502500207

Boseley, S. (2019a). *Calls for action on patients denied £100,000 cystic fibrosis drug.* Retrieved September 17, 2019, from https://www.theguardian.com/science/2019/feb/03/nhs-cystic-fibrosis-drug-orkambi-vertex

Boseley, S. (2019b). *NHS England agrees price for 'unaffordable' cystic fibrosis drug.* Retrieved September 17, 2019, from https://www.theguardian.com/society/2019/oct/24/nhs-england-vertex-agrees-price-for-orkambi-unaffordable-cystic-fibrosis-drug

Breyer, T., & Storms, A. (2021). Empathy as a desideratum in health care – Normative claim or professional competence? *Interdisciplinary Journal for Religion and Transformation in Contemporary Society, 7*, 359–375. https://doi.org/10.30965/23642807-bja10028

Bryce, J., et al. (1992). Assessing the quality of facility-based child survival services. *Health Policy and Planning, 7*(*2*), *155–163*. https://doi.org/10.1093/heapol/7.2.155

Davis, B. G. (2021). Could you patent the sun? *ACS Central Science, 7*(*4*), 508–509. https://doi.org/10.1021/acscentsci.1c00377

Decety, J., & Fotopoulou, A. (2015). Why empathy has a beneficial impact on others in medicine: Unifying theories. *Frontiers in Behavioural Neuroscience, 8*, 457. https://doi.org/10.3389/fnbeh.2014.00457

Demekas, D., et al. (2020). An investigation of the free energy principle for emotion recognition. *Frontiers in Computational Neuroscience, 14*. https://doi.org/10.3389/fncom.2020.00030

Diaz, M. D. M., et al. (2020). Private health insurance in Brazil, Egypt and India. In S. Thomson, A. Sagan, & E. Mossialos (Eds.), *Private health insurance history, politics and performance*. Cambridge University Press. https://doi.org/10.1017/9781139026468

Editorial. (2021). A patent waiver on COVID vaccines is right and fair. *Nature, 593*(478) Retrieved September 11, 2021, from https://www.nature.com/articles/d41586-021-01242-1. https://doi.org/10.1038/d41586-021-01242-1

Emanuel, E. J., & Emanuel, L. L. (1992). Four models of the physician-patient relationship. *Journal of the American Medical Association, 267*(16), 2221–2226. https://doi.org/10.1001/jama.1992.03480160079038

Forsberg, B. C., et al. (1992). Developing countries need more quality assurance: How health facility surveys can contribute. *Health Policy and Planning, 7*(*2*), *193–196*. https://doi.org/10.1093/heapol/7.2.193

Frank, R. G., et al. (2021). *It was the government that produced COVID-19 vaccine success*. Retrieved September 12, 2021, from https://www.healthaffairs.org/do/10.1377/forefront.20210512.191448/

Friston, K. (2010). The free-energy principle: A unified brain theory? *Nature Reviews Neuroscience, 11*, 127–138. https://doi.org/10.1038/nrn2787

Gershman, S. J. (2019). *What does the free energy principle tell us about the brain?* arXiv:1901.07945v5. https://doi.org/10.48550/arXiv.1901.07945

Hart, J. T. (1971). The inverse care law. *The Lancet, 297*(*7696*), *405–412*. https://doi.org/10.1016/s0140-6736(71)92410-X

Hart, J. T. (2001). Unhappiness will be defeated when doctors accept full social responsibility. *British Journal of Medicine, 322*, 1363–1364.

Helmholtz, H. v. (1948). Concerning the perceptions in general, 1867. In W. Dennis (Ed.), *Readings in the history of psychology* (pp. 214–230). Appleton-Century-Crofts. https://doi.org/10.1037/11304-027

Henderson, R. (2019). The wounded healer. *Jung Journal, 13*(2), 115–127. https://doi.org/10.1080/19342039.2019.1600977

Huang, L., et al. (2019). The positive association between empathy and self-esteem in Chinese medical students: A multi-institutional study. *Frontiers in Psychology, 10*(1921). https://doi.org/10.3389/fpsyg.2019.01921
Indian Patents Act. (1970). Retrieved September 15, 2022, from https://ipindia.gov.in/writereaddata/Portal/ev/sections/ps3.html
Jung, C. G. (1985). Fundamental questions of psychotherapy. In H. Read, M. Fordham, G. Adler, & W. Mcguire (Eds.), *The collected works of C. G. Jung* (Vol. 16, 2nd ed.). Princeton University Press.
Khan, A. U. (2019). *India's drug price fix is hurting healthcare.* Retrieved September 17, 2019, from https://www.livemint.com/politics/policy/india-s-drug-price-fix-is-hurting-healthcare-11572334594083.html
Langford, D. J., et al. (2010). Social approach to pain in laboratory mice. *Social Neuroscience, 5*(2), 163–170. https://doi.org/10.1080/17470910903216609
Lelorain, S., et al. (2012). A systematic review of the associations between empathy measures and patient outcomes in cancer care. *Psycho-Oncology, 21*(*12*), *1255–1264.* https://doi.org/10.1002/pon.2115
McCarthy, N. (2021). *Which companies received the most Covid-19 vaccine R&D funding? [Infographic].* Retrieved September 9, 2022, from https://www.forbes.com/sites/niallmccarthy/2021/05/06/which-companies-received-the-most-covid-19-vaccine-rd-funding-infographic/?sh=4ce576044333
McConnell, M. (2022). *US Congress falls short in plan to cut insulin costs.* Retrieved September 17, 2022, from https://www.hrw.org/news/2022/02/23/us-congress-falls-short-plan-cut-insulin-costs
Missouridou, E., et al. (2021). Wounded healers during the COVID-19 syndemic: Compassion fatigue and compassion satisfaction among nursing care providers in Greece. *Perspectives in Psychiatric Care*, 1–12. https://doi.org/10.1111/ppc.12946
Mitchell, A., & Korenstein, D. (2020). *Drug companies' payments and gifts affect physicians' prescribing. It's time to turn off the spigot.* Retrieved September 29, 2020, from https://www.statnews.com/2020/12/04/drug-companies-payments-gifts-affect-physician-prescribing/
Mitchell, A. P., et al. (2020). Are financial payments from the pharmaceutical industry associated with physician prescribing? *Annals of Internal Medicine.* https://doi.org/10.7326/m20-5665
Model Professional code for Physicians in Germany. *The resolutions of the 121st German medical assembly 2018 in Erfurt as amended by a resolution of the executive board of the German medical association on 14/12/2018.* Retrieved September 19, 2022., from https://www.bundesaerztekammer.de/fileadmin/user_upload/_old-files/downloads/pdf-Ordner/MBO/MBO-AE_EN_2018.pdf

Montoya, P., et al. (2004). Influence of social support and emotional context on pain processing and magnetic brain responses in fibromyalgia. *Arthritis & Rheumatism, 50*(12), 4035–4044. https://doi.org/10.1002/art.20660
Oshinsky, D. M. (2005). *Polio: An American story*. Oxford University Press.
Peabody, et al. (2006). Improving the quality of care in developing countries. In *Disease control priorities in developing countries* (2nd ed.). The International Bank for Reconstruction and Development. The World Bank.
Pellegrino, E. D., & Thomasma, D. C. (1993). *The virtues in medical practice*. Oxford University Press.
Peters, D. H., et al. (2008). Poverty and access to health care in developing countries. *Annals of the New York Academy of Sciences, 1136*(*1*), *161–171*. https://doi.org/10.1196/annals.1425.011
Piredda, M., et al. (2022). The wounded healer: A phenomenological study on hospital nurses who contracted COVID-19. *Frontiers in Public Health, 10*, 867826. https://doi.org/10.3389/fpubh.2022.867826
Pizzigati, S. (2016). *Dr. Billionaire, Meet Dr. Salk*. Retrieved September 15, 2022, from https://inequality.org/great-divide/dr-billionaire-meet-dr-salk/
Prabhu, A. (2012). *How much money did Jonas Salk potentially forfeit by not patenting the polio vaccine?* Retrieved September 11, 2022, from https://www.forbes.com/sites/quora/2012/08/09/how-much-money-did-jonas-salk-potentially-forfeit-by-not-patenting-the-polio-vaccine/?sh=7bcb624d69b8
Rajkumar, S. V. (2020). The high cost of insulin in the United States: An urgent call to action. *Mayo Clinic Proceedings, 95*(1), 22–28. https://doi.org/10.1016/j.mayocp.2019.11.013
Reisman, J. M. (1995). Physicians and surgeons as inventors: Reconciling medical process patents and medical ethics. *High Technology Law Journal, 10*(2), 355–403. Retrieved September 12, 2022, from https://lawcat.berkeley.edu/record/1115285/files/fulltext.pdf
Resnick, M. I. (2007). The practice of medicine—A business or a profession? *The Journal of Urology, 178*(4), 1143. https://doi.org/10.1016/j.juro.2007.06.052
Storz, U. (2022). The COVID-19 vaccine patent race. *Nature Biotechnology, 40*, 1001–1004. https://doi.org/10.1038/s41587-022-01376-1
Straussner, S. L. A., et al. (2018). Wounded healers: A multistate study of licensed social workers' behavioral health problems. *Social Work, 63*(2), 125–133. https://doi.org/10.1093/sw/swy012
Thaver, I. H., et al. (1998). Private practitioners in the slums of Karachi: What quality of care do they offer? *Social Science & Medicine, 46*(*11*), *1441–1449*. https://doi.org/10.1016/s0277-9536(97)10134-4
Titmuss, R. (1968). *Commitment to welfare*. George Allen & Unwin Ltd.
Toffler, A. (1991). *Power shift*. Bantam Books.

Wagstaff, A., et al. (2018). Progress on catastrophic health spending in 133 countries: A retrospective observational study. *The Lancet Global Health, 6*(2), e169–e179. https://doi.org/10.1016/s2214-109x(17)30429-1

Watt, G. (2002). The inverse care law today. *The Lancet, 360*(*9328*), *252–254.* https://doi.org/10.1016/s0140-6736(02)09466-7

Weinberg, I. (2012). *How money influences our decisions as doctors.* Retrieved September 29, 2022, from https://www.kevinmd.com/2012/04/money-influences-decisions-doctors.html

White, F. (2015). Primary health care and public health: Foundations of universal health systems. *Medical Principles and Practice, 24*(2), 103–116. https://doi.org/10.1159/000370197

WHO. (2013). *The economics of social determinants of health and health inequalities: A resource book.* World Health Organization.

Wicks, R. J., & Donnelly, G. F. (2021). *Overcoming secondary stress in medical and nursing practice* (2nd ed.). Oxford University Press.

Wiseman, V. (2011). Key concepts in health economics. In L. Guinness & V. Wiseman (Eds.), *Introduction to health economics.* McGraw-Hill.

Yang, N., et al. (2018). Effects of doctors' empathy abilities on the cellular immunity of patients with advanced prostate cancer treated by orchiectomy: the mediating role of patients' stigma, self-efficacy, and anxiety. *Patient Preference and Adherence, 12, 1305–1314.* https://doi.org/10.2147/ppa.s166460

CHAPTER 9

Empathy and the Economics of Migration

The story of human civilization is virtually inseparable from the enduring aspect of human behaviour marked by the movement and settlement of people across geographies: migration. Migration, originally a biological term to describe animal movement, has been for long, central to human history. As Valsiner (2022) noted, "Historically speaking—we as the species of Homo sapiens are all migrants—only at differing times and circumstances" (p. 1). The earliest instances of migration can be traced back to the Rift Valley in Africa, from where the *Homo erectus* and *Homo sapiens* migrated and spread to Europe and beyond (Koser, 2007). Ancient civilizations like the Greek, Roman, Mesopotamian and Indus Valley were also shaped by migratory flows (Koser, 2007).

In the eighteenth and nineteenth centuries, the colonial powers orchestrated forced mass migrations: Africans were enslaved and transported to the America, while indentured labour from India and elsewhere were shipped to work in colonial plantations. Alongside this coercive forced migration, many Europeans voluntarily migrated to colonies, often returning only after decolonization. Between 1850 and 1930, millions of Europeans fled to the United States to escape poverty, oppression and disasters such as the Irish famine (Koser, 2007).

Post-1945, an economic boom in Europe and America drew migrants from Turkey and North Africa into countries like Germany and France (Koser, 2007). Meanwhile, Australia and New Zealand encouraged British

D. Roy, *Empathonomics*,
https://doi.org/10.1007/978-981-95-4033-4_9

migration under the Assisted Passage Migration Scheme, where adults paid only ten pounds for passage while children travelled for free. This earned the participants the nickname "ten-pound poms." Such movements of people significantly boosted global economic growth, as Johnson (1965) argued: "The geographical rearrangement of people over the course of time is a necessary part of the process of increasing economic efficiency, i.e., the efficiency of resource allocation" (p. 300).

However, migration has also been fraught with tragedy. The Partition of India in 1947 triggered violent riots and mass migration. Similar migrations were also witnessed during the time in Palestine. More recently, conflicts in the Middle East have displaced millions, especially from Syria, Iraq and Yemen. As Koser (2007) emphasized, "migration is associated with significant global events – revolutions, wars, and the rise and fall of empires ... significant change – economic expansion, nation-building, and political transformations ... [and] significant problems – conflict, persecution, and dispossession" (p. 4).

Migration however is a complex term to define. Charles Tilly (1976) highlighted the difficulty of distinguishing 'definitive' movements, stressing on the fact that vagrants and nomadic groups like gypsies challenge conventional definitions of migration. He linked clear definitions of migration to the duties of state bureaucracies concerned with taxation, registration and control of migrants.

Lässig and Steinberg (2017) similarly cautioned against narrow definitions of migration and argued that "From a history of knowledge perspective, it is necessary, second, not to limit migration by distance. Moving from the countryside to the nearest town or city can be just as much an occasion of knowledge creation as the relocation from one continent to another or an extended period of transit (and perhaps uncertainty) between home country and eventual land of settlement" (p. 316). To impose objectivity, the United Nations (2012) has defined a migrant as the following: "An international migrant who changes his or her place of usual residence for at least one year is defined as a long-term migrant, while a person who changes his or her place of usual residence for more than three months but less than one year is defined as a short-term migrant" (United Nations, 2012, p. 2).

While the reasons for early human migration involved search for food, inhospitable climatic conditions or even peopling areas where humans did not live, as human civilization developed into formal, structured societies the reasons for migration included economic gains, colonialization and territorial annexation. In the present times human migration is predominantly motivated by the search for jobs and livelihood, though war and human conflict also presents as a significant cause for human migratory behaviour. However as was explained earlier, migratory behaviour is not necessarily voluntary or benevolent and forced coercive migrations like those that were witnessed during the Atlantic slave trade have led to movements of large sections of population from one place to the other. Lüthi (2018) had explained, "modern migration at least since the Atlantic slave trade and the industrialization in England and other parts of Europe have been dominated by the state, empire, and capital" (p. 2).[1] For the sake of a coherent and logical analysis, migrants can be categorized according to three criteria: (1) forced and unforced migrants, while forced migrants can sometimes fall into the category of refugees too; (2) legal and illegal migrants; (3) political migrants, who migrate out of a country or region seeking asylum elsewhere to protect oneself from political oppression, and economic migrants, who migrate for better economic opportunities elsewhere. The categories presented are not watertight and overlaps do occur among the different categories; for example, voluntary migrants are most often economic migrants (Koser, 2007).

One of the earliest studies on the fundamental aspects of migration was conducted by Ernst Georg Ravenstein, a German-English geographer.[2] Ravenstein studied the characteristics of human migration of the time and formulated a set of 'laws' that he claimed influenced human migratory behaviour even as he conceded that "laws of population, and economic laws generally, have not the rigidity of physical laws, as they are continually being interfered with by human agency" (Ravenstein, 1889, p. 241). Ravenstein (1889) had succinctly enumerated the fundamental reasons for human migration; he had written, "Bad or oppressive laws, heavy taxation, an unattractive climate, uncongenial social surroundings, and even compulsion (slave trade, transportation), all have produced and are still producing currents of migration, but none of these currents can compare in volume with that which arises from the desire inherent in most men to 'better' themselves in material respects" (p. 286).

Ravenstein (1885) claimed that the bulk of migrants travelled shorts distances and those that travelled long distances were "exception, not the rule, and do not probably constitute 25 per cent. of all migrants." (p. 183). In this context, Ravenstein (1885) had also posited that "Migrants proceeding long distances generally go by preference to one of the great centres of commerce or industry" (p. 199). The preference for migrating to short distances could be deemed natural given the limitations of transportation facilities at the time. Ravenstein (1885) had introduced an interesting aspect of migration which he termed "migration by stages" (Ravenstein, 1885, p. 183) wherein migrants move from place to place in search of adequate work and finally reach a place which is quite far from the original place from where the person began the journey. Further, Ravenstein (1885) had classified areas as those that witnessed excessive migration to other parts (counties of dispersion) and others that witnessed excessive migration from other parts (counties of absorption). This aspect is very relevant within studies of migration even in the modern times especially in the context of migration within a country. The fundamental reason for the differentials in migration in this context would be socioeconomic backwardness, lack of employment opportunities in an area, lopsided growth coupled with the effects of Myrdal's circular cumulative causation that was explained in an earlier chapter in this book. However, migration away from an area could have natural causes like climate change, natural disasters like earthquakes, landslides, floods or even human causes like ethnic violence, faltering government systems, failed nation states and overall administrative chaos. Ravenstein (1885) proclaimed that "side by side with each main stream or current of migrants there runs a counter-current, which more or less compensates for the losses sustained by emigration" (p. 187). This countercurrent he claimed was not merely caused by the migrants from an area returning back home but by "persons whom business interests take away from their homes" (Ravenstein, 1885, p. 187). The rationale that Ravenstein had presented can be articulated with the help of an example; if artisans from an area send local agents to cities in order to establish contacts and business links, business organizations from the cities too send their representatives to the areas where such artisans work in order to establish and sustain business operations and thus a counter current is established. In modern days with the advent of technology while the specific cause of this counter current might have changed, the broad rationale of a to-and-fro exchange of representatives within economic activities still holds true. If people from small towns migrate to cities to work in large corporations, a counter-current is established when large corporations send their representatives to work and facilitate business operations in small towns. Further Ravenstein (1885) posited that "The inhabitants of the country immediately surrounding a town of rapid growth, flock into it; the gaps thus left in the rural" (p. 199).

Lee (1966) had proposed a simple but effective model of migration where he proposed that essentially migration consisted of factors at the point of origin of the migration (factors which would motivate migration), a set of obstacles to the migratory behaviour (these obstacles could be physical obstacles like oceans, mountains or even man-made walls; legal obstacles or even psychological obstacles) and a set of factors at the destination of the migration. Lee (1966) however was very categorical in stating that a decision to migrate "is never completely rational, and for some persons the rational component is much less than the irrational" (p. 51). An important reason for such irrationality lies within the fact "that it is not so much the actual factors at origin and destination as the perception of these factors which results in migration" (p. 51). Further Lee (1966) recognized that different people have different approaches to tackle situations and thus the negative factors at the origin that might motivate migration to another destination for one set of people might be tackled differentially by a different set of people; thus "migrants are not a random sample of the population at origin" (Lee, 1966, p. 56). They are a selective group of people who chose to overcome the obstacles and migrate to another place.

Ravenstein (1889) and Lee (1966) both recognized that economics was an important (if not the most important) reason for human migration. Free movement of labour from one area to another is analogous to the concept of free trade; such migratory practices recognize and encourage high levels of specialization, thus augmenting the principle of comparative advantage and ultimately leading to higher levels of efficiency (Portes, 2019). If economic migration may be viewed from a strategic perspective, it is evident that the migrants stand out as the obvious beneficiary of such action. Portes (2019) explained the reasons, "The main beneficiaries of immigration are likely to be the immigrants—since, by definition, they are taking advantage of the opportunity to move believing that they will be better off (economically or more broadly) in a different country and by a sufficient amount to justify the costs (again, economic or broader) of moving. While individuals may be wrong about this (as with anyone who makes a decision when there is uncertainty about the future), in general the majority of gains from immigration can be expected to accrue to those who take up the opportunities it presents" (p. 13).

Haaland and Roth (2017) had reported that "In the United States, for instance, 57 percent of those in favor of reducing immigration say that immigrants take jobs away from Americans compared to only 23 percent of those not in favor of reducing immigration" (p. 1). While it is often claimed that migrants take away the jobs of the locals, a converse argument proposes that migrants create more jobs; the converse argument is based on the premise that migrants spend the money they earn, thus in turn creating jobs and leading to an expansion of the economy.

The fallacy behind the argument that migrants take away jobs of the local populace is termed as the "lump of labour" fallacy. The fallacy assumes that the amount of work in the economy is fixed, thus migrants take away jobs that were meant for locals. The argument is termed as a fallacy because the amount of work is not fixed; this was first recognized by an economist named D. F. Schloss (1891) who had described the theory of lump of labour as a "noteworthy fallacy" (p. 324). David Card (1990), Professor of Economics at Princeton University, had studied the effect of migration on existing wages and rates of unemployment in the labour market within the context of the Mariel Boatlift of 1980. The boatlift had led to a 7% increase in the labour force of Miami, Florida; however, the increase in labour force did not cause any significant change in the wages or the rate of unemployment among unskilled workers in the area. David Card's findings have been disputed by a section of economists; however, as Kerr and Kerr (2011) explained, "The likelihood and magnitude of adverse labor market effects for natives from immigration are substantially weaker than often perceived. Within the large empirical literature looking at the effects of immigration on native employment and wages, most studies find only minor displacement effects even after very large immigrant flows" (p. 24).

Discussions on migration popularly revolve around its impact on jobs, wages and the economic issues faced by the area where the migration has taken place (destination). Conversely, however, economists also recognize that the outflow of workers, especially skilled professionals, can have detrimental effects on the development of the regions that they leave behind. This concern is particularly severe when doctors from poorer regions or countries migrate to wealthier areas in search of better opportunities and way of life. Mills et al. (2008) had strongly criticized the recruitment of doctors from sub-Saharan Africa, where number of physicians are already at a critically low level. They observed, "The insufficiency of health staff to provide even basic services is one of the most pressing impediments to health-care delivery in resource-poor settings. The consequences are clearly shown by the inverse relation that exists between health-care worker density and mortality" (p. 685). Consequently, Mills et al. (2008)

proposed stringent regulations to curb such recruitment by developed countries, even suggesting that such recruitments should be treated as a criminal practice.

While regulatory restrictions might present as convenient solutions to the problem, they ignore the complex motivations which drive healthcare professionals to migrate. An empathic understanding of the migratory behaviour reveals that the innate human desire to improve one's circumstances in life cannot be deemed inherently immoral, especially when many poorer regions are also sites of conflict and instability. However, it should also be recognized that people in those regions definitely deserve access to quality healthcare, decent living standards and opportunities for better life.

The challenge, therefore, lies in balancing the competing needs through an empathic framework that addresses the perspectives of all stakeholders. Instead of focusing inordinately on restricting migration, efforts should be made to create conditions that will motivate professionals to remain and thrive in the poorer regions of the world. This solution lies in providing tangible reinforcements such as improved infrastructure, professional development opportunities, study tours and other measures that will serve to reduce the sense of alienation, hopelessness and injustice which is often felt by those serving in remote or resource-constrained settings. Such motivational systems can be effective only when they are empathic and the designers of such systems have complete empathic identification with the professionals; thus, motivational systems to motivate doctors in poorer areas might be most effectively designed by a set of doctors belonging to the specific region and not bureaucrats who essentially belong to areas far removed from the backward areas.

While the effect of migration of professionals from areas of extreme poverty and conflict might present at the extreme limits of a hypothetical scale of such migrational behaviour, developing countries like India have seen talented professionals and academicians leave the parent country for lucrative offers elsewhere. This phenomenon is termed as 'brain drain,'[3] and some experts believe that it extracts a substantial cost on the developing country. The term 'Brain Drain' itself implies a sense of loss (as explicit in the usage of the word drain); as Johnson (1965) explained the word drain cannot relate to the migrants since they are taking a conscious voluntary decision to migrate for better opportunities elsewhere. Thus, as Johnson (1965) explained, the term brain drain describes "a social loss in the mere fact of a privately gainful move outward across the national boundary" (p. 299).

There are two contradictory approaches to the analysis of brain drain. Experts like Johnson (1965, 1966) were opposed to the implied assumption within the concept of brain drain "that what counts is not the welfare of individuals born and brought up in a particular country but only the welfare of those who continue to reside in that country" (p. 300). Further Johnson (1965) challenged the notion that educated individuals can contribute to the welfare and development of their country only if they reside within the country and claimed that migration results in experiencing changed societal norms and culture, thus leading to sense of freedom and enhancing creativity; thus, brain drain ultimately leads to better standards of living all over the world. Johnson (1965) further clarified that continuous migration from an area occurs due to poverty and lack of opportunities for the residents; education was often perceived to provide an opportunity for such migration from poverty-stricken areas. Since the services of these trained or educated individuals are just relocated from one area to another, they cannot be deemed to be redundant; it is only that the beneficiaries of their services change. The obvious argument at this stage would involve the loss that the poor residents of the area incur due to such brain drain. This loss would be greater when the education that is received by individuals is partly or wholly funded by the government from the tax payer's money (as is the case in countries like India where education in government institutions are heavily subsidized). In order to circumvent this loss, Johnson (1965) proposed "providing education free only when the individual so educated will remain in the region, by requiring that individuals oblige themselves to repay their education costs to the community out of future income, or by obliging the migrating individual, or the country or region to which he emigrates, to pay over to the region of origin a capital sum or income stream equal to the cost of his education or the loss of tax revenue his emigration occasions" (pp. 302–303). However, the economic loss to a country through the provision of free or subsidized education to individuals who migrate to other countries is often offset by remittances that are sent by the individuals to their parent country; in fact, such remittances form a significant part of the GDP especially in the developing world.[4] The argument that brain drain denies the parent country or region of migration the services of the professionals and highly educated individuals was countered by Johnson (1965) who claimed that such services were most often still available to the people of the region and at a lesser cost than what could be provided if the professionals were residing permanently in the area. Renowned economists, medical professionals and social scientists from third world countries are known to have provided significant services (often free of cost) to their parent countries even if they did not reside there. Moreover, professionals who have migrated to developed countries can involve their enhanced expertise within their services to their parent countries, thus improving quality of the offered services. Further it has also been suggested by exerts such as Piore (1979) that migration acts as a safety valve in developing countries which have high levels of population wherein the aspirations of a section of the population cannot be fulfilled within their native country.

Certain other experts like Charles Kidd (1965) had disagreed with the view that brain drain has no significant negative effect on developing economies. In fact Kidd (1965) had written a scathing letter criticizing the arguments put forward by Johnson (1965) in which he had enumerated the reasons for his convictions as "(a) science and technology must be adapted for, and in, less developed countries if they are to be useful for economic development; (b) scientists and engineers in less developed countries are much more than producers of science and technology; (c) the movement of scientists and engineers from less developed countries can cripple or destroy a field; (d) the classical doctrines of free trade and the free market cannot be validly applied to developing countries" (p. 105).

The recent years have witnessed significant outflows of skilled labour (particularly among the young and highly educated) from Central, Eastern, and South-eastern Europe (CESEE). Such migration has often benefited both the migrants and the European Union as their primary destination; however, it has had negative consequences for the economies of the sending countries. A study by the International Monetary Fund (Atoyan et al., 2016) estimated that "in 2012, cumulative real GDP growth would have been 7 percentage points higher on average in CESEE in the absence of emigration during 1995–2012, with skilled emigration playing a key contributing factor" (p. 22).

The phenomenon of labour migration requires special attention while exploring the relationship between empathy and migration. While highly skilled professionals do encounter challenges when relocating, their overall experiences are generally better as compared to those of unskilled and semi-skilled workers who migrate in search of basic employment opportunities. However, the economic contribution of the migratory labour force is often underestimated and they are often stigmatized as causes of law-and-order problems, poor hygiene and job displacement. In contrast, professionals such as doctors are readily welcomed as migrants as their contributions to the wellbeing of the community are more socially appreciable and valued.

This perception, however, ignores the indispensable role of the migrant labour force in the sustenance of modern economies. As Bauder (2006) aptly noted, if cleaners, security guards, shop attendants, household help, nannies, delivery staff, construction workers, taxi drivers, and maintenance staff in hotels and public spaces stopped working, "many sectors of the economy in industrialized countries would come to an immediate standstill. The rest of the economy would follow within days, if not hours." (p. 3)

The pattern of labour migration however does not follow the conventional economic wisdom of demand and supply; Bauder (2006) explained that "the stream of migration to the industrialized world is relatively unaffected by cyclical fluctuations in national labor markets" (p. 3). This point was also emphasized by Camarota (2003) who had observed the same phenomenon in the USA and commented, "immigration is not very sensitive to changes in demand for labor. For example, Texas saw a large increase in new immigration, but the rise in the unemployment rate among adults in that state is not that different from California's" (p. 2). Piore (1979) explained that "income is not the critical analytical variable, but rather that it is the attempt to view income as such that leads to the paradoxes" (p. 8). He further expands on the reason for his posit, "One can better understand migration by ignoring income differences and recognizing instead that people are rooted in a social context in ways that other commodities are not; migrant behavior can be better understood in terms of the specific attributes of the jobs available to migrants and the meaning attached to those attributes in the social context in which work is performed" (Piore, 1979, p. 8). Piore's posit might be contextualized within an analysis by Castles and Kosack (1973) who had commented on the nature of work that immigrant workers were forced to perform in industrialized economies: "Immigrant workers have not been recruited throughout the economy, but mainly in the low-paid job sectors which could not attract or retain indigenous workers. Once the immigrants were in these sectors, lack of qualifications and education, discrimination in employment and promotion, and regulations restricting occupational mobility have tended to keep them there" (p. 379). In an interesting argument, Castells (1975) had put forward a contrarian view of the dynamics of demand and supply within the context of immigrant workers; he had posited, "*immigrant workers do not exist because there are 'arduous and badly paid' jobs to be done, but, rather. arduous and badly paid jobs exist because immigrant workers are present or can be sent for to do them*" (p. 54. Original emphasis). Piore (1979) argued that arguments which posit that migrants just take up jobs that the natives do not want to take up place migrants as being complimentary to the native workers and the migratory process "thus works to preserve native jobs and sustain native consumption patterns" (p. 86).

An extension to the discussion of labour migration is that of peasant labour migration. Peasant migration involves peasants who migrate to cities and urban areas as migratory labour to supplement their income from the lands (Piore, 1979). Such activity is mostly seasonal and the peasants perceive industrial work in the urban areas as temporary. Such seasonal migration presents with the prospect of additional income at relatively low risk. However, peasant migration is not an entirely benign and risk-free activity which solely promotes economic wellbeing but is fraught with risks, as Yang (1979) posited: "Although migration is often a response to economic factors, it cannot be assumed that peasants 'investing' in it would not only recover the costs of moving but also derive additional material benefit. On the contrary, peasants as migrants inevitably faced and generated risks by leaving behind established patterns of life for an uncertain future" (p. 38). In his study on peasant migration within the context of India, Yang (1979) found that "migrants will be disproportionately drawn from among the segments of the rural population which occupy the least favored structural positions" (p. 46). Thus, it is the weaker and poorer peasants that present with migratory behaviour. The differential motivations of the different classes of peasants within migratory decisions were brought forth in a study by Wilkie (1973) who had studied the migratory behaviour of peasants from a behavioural sciences perspective. The researcher explored the complex motivational models of the different classes of peasants which led them to migrate or avoid migration. The researcher had prima facie posited that "Perhaps the rational decision relating to internal self-survival of a peasant who misunderstands and fears the outside world is to remain in his traditional surroundings. Though it seems that the so-called rational" economic man "hardly exists, the economic component does seem to be a prime motivating factor in the lower class" (p. 110). Wilkie (1973) further reported that middle-class peasants were posited to be motivated by personal, psychological or social factors while the peasants belonging to the higher class were motivated by the influence of family, peers as well as other external authorities. Thus, according to Wilkie (1973), the lower-class peasants were tradition-directed, while the higher-class peasants were other-directed (externally influenced) and middle-class peasants were inner-directed in their migratory decisions.

Migration is not an easy choice for most people, and a large percentage of people migrate because they are forced to migrate and have no alternate option for survival. The journey to the destination itself is sometimes fraught with life threatening danger and hundreds of people have died while trying to cross international borders through desperately dangerous methods. Even when they manage to reach their destination, poor migrants are exploited, abused and often trafficked into sex trade. Migrants who end up performing unskilled work (and even some of those who are educated professionals) are often mistreated and are frequently victims of discrimination, racial profiling and abuse even after generations of having living in their new place of work. While an overwhelming proportion of studies have attempted to explore and analyse the reasons, motivation and the consequent effects of human migration, it would be interesting to explore the reasons for some humans to be immobile and remain in one place even when there are ample opportunities to migrate to places which will provide better economic opportunities and standard of life. Fischer et al. (2000) within their study in Sweden had proposed that some people accumulate location specific advantages for work as well as leisure and are thus averse (and rationally so) to migrate unless certain events in life require such migration. The researchers termed their theory as the "insider advantage theory of immobility" (p. 8). Mærsk et al. (2021) had conducted a study to explore reasons of immobility among certain students in Denmark and concluded, "immobile students are more likely to have a connection to, and experience with, the local labour market, to be satisfied with their social life, and to live with their parents compared with their geographically mobile peers" (p. 1). While developed economies like Sweden or Denmark might provide ample opportunities for individuals to live a comfortable life without the need to migrate, Chatterji (2017) studied the phenomena among a section of the poor and impoverished in Bengal who had seemingly been immobile not only in face of extreme poverty but as the researcher described "despite violence, impoverishment, and social boycott, which had left them culturally and politically marginalized. They had stayed on while most others around them had fled, in contexts of mass migration, when the 'push factors' could hardly have been more compelling" (p. 512). This behavioural pattern is often described as the 'immobility paradox'. Chatterji (2017) had enumerated the reasons for this immobility wherein she explained, "Physical frailty and obligations of care, it shows, were crucial factors in shaping immobility. Relations of gender and generation, and the inequalities embedded in these relations, produced 'overabundances'—of obligations to people and places—that tied certain people down. Finally, it hints at the reasons why, and the ways in which, stayers-on have grown poorer" (p. 511). In stark contrast to situations that are described by the immobility paradox are predicaments wherein individuals who wish to migrate are not able to do so. Carling (2002) described such situations as 'involuntary immobility' (p. 5). Obstacles to migration might present in many forms such as family obligations, severe economic crisis, restrictive immigration practices, lack of required skill or education, compromised health or psychological barriers like learned helplessness and risk aversion. In the backdrop of this predicament, Carling (2002) had presented the 'aspiration/ability model' (p. 5) which involved an analysis of "a wish to migrate, and second, the realisation of this wish" (p. 5).

It might be argued that empathic governmental and public behaviour towards migrants in the host/destination country or area is most often influenced by a combination of several factors, the prime amongst them being the economic conditions of the host area and the resultant economic situation arising out of migratory activities, the opportunities as well as the obstacles in the process of acculturation of the migrants and the members of the host community towards each other's traditions and cultures, inherent prejudices and the political narrative as well as media representation of the migrants. Emotional acculturation presents as an important factor that influences the process of assimilation of migrants and natives. Emotional acculturation refers to the phenomenon of experiencing and exhibiting emotions in a manner that is similar to the culture of the people that one lives with or interacts with over time even if such culture and the resultant behaviour are different from one's native culture. Leersnyder et al. (2011) studied the effect of emotional acculturation among migrants; in one study among Korean migrants living in the USA, the researchers reported that a consonance between the emotional patterns of the Korean immigrants and the Americans was dependent on the portion of life that the Korean immigrant had spent in the USA. Thus, second generation immigrants presented with higher levels of emotional acculturation. A similar result was obtained from another study by the researchers that was conducted in Belgium. However emotional acculturation is not a passive outcome of iterative interactions but as Jasini et al. (2018) reported, "emotional acculturation is not just a 'skill' that minority individuals acquire, but also a response to the ways in which interactions with majority others develop. Inclusive interactions, especially when they are positive, appear to align immigrant minority individuals with the majority norm" (p. 1). In this context one might argue that such emotional acculturation is possible only when an empathic identification with the other takes places.

It is thus evident that migration presents as a very complex behavioural pattern with multiple and often contradictory perceptions and viewpoints. While the act of migration is often beneficial to the migrants (except in cases of forced migration), migratory behaviour is often perceived as a loss to the poor and backward regions who might have benefited from the expertise of the migrants, similarly migratory behaviour is often perceived negatively in the destination of the migrants where migrants are considered to be outsiders who are usurping the jobs of the locals. On the other hand, remittances from migrations help enhance the standard of living of the families of the migrants who have stayed behind thus leading to economic development; moreover, migrants spend a significant part of their income in the area where they have migrated, thus leading to economic growth in that area too. Thus, migratory behaviour is complex, and a thorough objective analysis of the perceptions and behaviour of the different stakeholders involved in the migratory process requires an empathic understanding of the position of those stakeholders. While discussing migration, de Haas (2011) had opined that it was unrealistic to assume "that people are free from constraints, enjoy full access to information, and make migration decisions with the aim of maximizing their utility" (p. 20). Thus, while migration policies are frequently framed on the assumption that migrants are rational *Homo economicus* and whether they "are entrepreneurs, workers or students, more or less skilled or affluent, they will identify and assess which locations will provide the greatest benefit for them and their families" (Carling & Collins, 2017, p. 3), these assumptions are very often flawed. Klimecki et al. (2020) had succinctly explained, "In many societies, immigration is a conflictual topic, leading to heated exchanges between proponents and opponents of immigration. Such debates on immigration might benefit from the engagement of the discussants in empathy and perspective taking" (p. 1).

Empathic understanding of the migrants however is a complex phenomenon by itself and the ultimate viewpoints are further shaped by several factors, many of which are psychological and influenced by cognitive biases. Klimecki et al. (2020) posited that empathic perspective taking with regard to migratory behaviour might present with differentials within groups presenting with divergent political ideologies (left and right wing). This aspect was further accentuated when the researchers within their study found that while individuals who were pro-migration took an even more positive view of migration after empathic perspective taking however those that were anti-migration hardened their views even further after empathic perspective taking. Berndsen et al. (2018) had similarly reported that the right-wing nationalists perceived asylum seekers as threats to their national interests and "when instructed to take the perspective of an asylum seeker, reactance led glorifiers to respond from their own perspective" (p. 126). Similarly, Vorauer and Sasaki (2009) had reported "among higher-prejudice individuals, toward whom interventions are often targeted, empathy induced negative reactions to an out-group member who was present in the contact situation" (p. 196). In this context, Hasson et al. (2018) had studied whether individuals with liberal political views differed from those with conservative views in their empathic disposition towards others. The researchers reported that "on average and across samples, liberals wanted to feel more empathy and experienced more empathy than conservatives did" (p. 1); however, the researchers also reported that "both liberals and conservatives wanted to feel less empathy toward outgroup members than toward ingroup members or members of a nonpolitical group" (p. 1).

In a study conducted in Arizona under the backdrop of a controversial anti-immigration bill, Bruneau and Saxe (2012) had explored the effects of empathic perspective taking (as well as empathic perspective giving)[5] on white Americans and Mexican immigrants towards each other. The researchers reported that perspective taking produced positive changes in attitude among the white Americans towards the Mexican immigrants; however, perspective giving was reported to produce better results among Mexican immigrants over perspective taking. Similar findings had been reported by Vescio et al. (2003) who had reported that "perspective taking promoted improved intergroup attitudes irrespective of stereotypicality; those encouraged to adopt the perspective of the target later reported more favourable intergroup attitudes than did those who remained detached and objective listeners" (p. 455).

Several countries have strong policies against immigration, especially illegal immigration; however, the human urge for a better life has led people to undertake dangerous attempts to break the law and enter certain countries through illegal means. These attempts are sometimes overseen by international criminal organizations who extract their pound of flesh and more from these hapless, poor people who feel that a fairyland awaits them across the border. This scenario is aptly witnessed in the Southern Borders of the United States where immigrants from Mexico continually attempt to breach international borders and enter the United States to chase an elusive American dream. The successive governments of the United States have been harsh with the immigrants and have often used the media to propagate falsehoods to create negative impressions about the migrants in an attempt to dehumanize the migrants and justify the inhuman treatment meted out to them. The result of such inhuman treatment has been catastrophic leading to countless deaths and the separation of thousands of children from their parents. Moore-Berg et al. (2021) found that empathy and dehumanization were strong independent predictors of the support for the anti-migration policies of the government as also the trust in the factually incorrect negative depiction of the migrants. The researchers found that the factually incorrect perceptions of the migrants further led to biases and lack of empathy towards them leading to a consequent dehumanization of migrants. The misperception about migrants was evident from the fact that the participants in the study estimated that approximately 15% of the migrants are involved with organized crime gangs while the reality is that only around 1% are involved with such illegal activities (Yount, 2021). The researchers found that if media interventions performed the dual role of enhancing empathy and correcting the wrong beliefs about migrants by humanizing them, it led to a decrease in support for antimigration polices.

In the background of the racist and xenophobic reactions that is witnessed against migrants in many parts of the world, empathic humanitarian behaviour towards the migrants presents as a complex phenomenon and the tendency of some people to help strangers has intrigued researchers. Many a times the humanitarian workers do not even meet the migrants that they help; for example, in the US-Mexico border, humanitarian workers leave bottles of water in the desert for the migrants, and when they return to find empty bottles, they understand that their work is done and lives have been saved by their action. Gomez et al. (2020) had developed a typology to describe the reactions (especially the humanitarian reactions) to migratory behaviour. The researchers categorized the positive empathic humanitarian behaviour towards migrants into four types: Missionary,

Good Samaritan, Do Gooder and the Activist. The Good Samaritan and the Missionary are guided by religious ideals and values while the do gooder and activist are guided by secular values. Further, Gomez et al. (2020) had categorized non-altruistic and negative attitudes and behaviour towards migrants into four categories: Militant, Crusader, Martyr and Humanitarian Tourist. The researchers explained that both the altruistic and the self-centred approaches are driven either by faith or by secular ideals though the core driver of the behaviour differs; in the case of the altruistic humanitarian approach, the core driver is empathy and a concern for the other, while in case of the non-altruistic approach, the core driver presents as concern for one self. The behaviour of the crusader and the Martyr are driven by faith while the Militant and the humanitarian tourist are driven by secular convictions. In an interesting analysis of the topology, Gomez et al. (2020) explained that the types that are presented within both aspects of the behaviour (altruistic and non-altruistic) are symmetric with each other; thus, the types militant and activist are symmetric while the types Good Samaritan and Martyr are symmetric, similarly Crusader and Missionary are symmetric and do gooder and humanitarian tourist are symmetric. The typology attempts to explain the seemingly contrasting behaviour of individuals and groups towards migrants. Several studies have been conducted on the relationship between empathy and altruistic behaviour. It has been widely reported that empathy is closely connected with altruistic behaviour (Krebs, 1975; Batson et al., 1997). In fact, Daniel Batson (1987, 1991) had developed the empathy-altruism hypothesis which "states that empathic emotion evokes altruistic motivation to benefit the person for whom empathy is felt" (Batson et al., 1995, p. 1042). The altruistic behaviour emanating from an empathic concern is termed as empathy-induced altruism. If the hypothesis put forward by Batson et al. (1995) is to be accepted, then the altruism shown by strangers towards migrants might be inferred to be motivated by empathic concern towards the migrants.

In the midst of the two radical points of view that are vehemently pro or anti-immigrant, a third ambivalent section exists in many societies. The ambivalent viewpoint presents as one of cautious optimism. Jaskułowski (2019) had studied the opinions of a section of Polish individuals who were ambivalent towards the reception of the Muslim refugees in Poland. This group of people exhibited two contradictory emotions when dealing with the matter of Muslim migrants in their country: that of fear and trepidation as well as empathy and humanitarianism for the migrants. The fear in this section of the polish populace was stoked by biased media reports which the ambivalent individuals seemed to recognize as stereotypical falsehood; however, the fear still remained alongside the desire to treat migrants with empathy. While some of these ambivalent individuals wanted only Christian refugees to be allowed, others wanted only a limited number of migrants and only for a limited time. The basic motivator that was driving the reactions was clearly the fear of the 'other'; the 'other' in this case was someone from a different religion and culture who could, in sufficient numbers, influence or even change the native Polish culture and way of life.

In order to promote an empathic approach to the management of migration in 2016, the General Assembly of the United Nations had adopted the New York declaration for refugees and migrants wherein it was mandated that a Global Compact for safe, orderly and regular migration be developed. The document that was adopted on the 13th of July 2018 asserts: "The Global Compact is based on international human rights law and upholds the principles of non-regression and non-discrimination. By implementing the Global Compact, we ensure effective respect, protection and fulfilment of the human rights of all migrants, regardless of their migration status, across all stages of the migration cycle. We also reaffirm the commitment to eliminate all forms of discrimination, including racism, xenophobia and intolerance against migrants and their families" (Global Compact for Safe, Orderly and Regular Migration, 2018, p. 4). The compact, though, non-legally binding is perceived as a step towards the recognition of the importance of empathic and humane treatment of migrants. However, as Maru et al. (2022) asserts, the issue of migration is complex, non-linear and often unpredictable; thus, "Such global compacts, which are central to western national framings of migration policy, are focused on risk management, predictability and stability. Despite being at the core of policy debates, they do not necessarily reflect the realities and lived experiences of migration" (Maru et al., 2022, p. 2).

The years preceding the writing of this book have produced haunting images of migration and the suffering of migrants from different parts of the world. The plight of the refugees from the Middle-East, the dehumanization and horrific treatment of the so-called illegal immigrants in the United States, the plight of hapless migrant workers in India who desperately tried to reach their homes when a hasty lockdown was declared in the country in the midst of the Covid pandemic in 2020, all bring forth the struggle of migrants and the need for empathic treatment of these fellow humans. It is ironic that the people who were carrying out the essential work during the Covid pandemic were mostly inadequately paid migrants; nurses, caregivers, delivery men, sanitization staff and a plethora of other workers who did not have the choice of working from home and were thus one of the most vulnerable sections at the frontline of the Covid war. The utter disregard of many governments for the migrants prompted Matteo de Bellis of Amnesty international to comment, "The fact that governments only remember migrants when they need them reveals an embarrassing lack of empathy for people particularly at risk during the pandemic" (de Bellis, 2020). During these trying times, in Greece, 34,000 asylum-seekers, including the elderly, children and pregnant women were confined in camps meant to hold only 6000 people. Countries like Italy and Malta closed their ports to refugees, and the migrants were thus effectively abandoned at sea; similar horrific instances of unempathic government treatment of migrants have been reported from Austria, Bosnia, Cyprus and Hungary among other places (de Bellis, 2020). Lockdowns and travel ban during the Covid pandemic led to large number of migrants being stranded away from home and often confined to crowded labour camps with enhanced risk of infection. An OECD report states that the risk of infection among the migrants in OECD countries was twice that of the native population of the countries (OECD, 2020). Further the remittances sent to home countries dropped significantly during the time, and a World Bank report of 2020 (The World Bank Group, 2020) had predicted that remittances to low- and middle-income countries would drop by 20% in 2020 from that of 2019.

The ultra-nationalist governments in many parts of the world have portrayed illegal migrants as enemies even dehumanizing them to points where they are called termites or locked up in cages with families split from each other, even children taken away from parents, all to create a narrative which plays on the inherent human fear of the other. The important role that migrants play in keeping important support systems running has been demonstrated aptly during the Covid epidemic. Empathic treatment towards the migrants and the issue of migration, while desirable and essential have been largely ignored by unempathic government policies. It is time that the inherent nature of humans to migrate and the positive impact of such migratory behaviour towards economic development and growth are recognized and celebrated.

Notes

1. At the time of writing this, the UNHCR reports that globally 82.4 million people have been forced to leave their homes of whom 26.4 million people are refugees and almost half of them are minors below the age of 18. In which case the organization emphasizes that 1 in 95 people on this planet have fled from their homes due to violent conflict or persecution. In addition, there are a million stateless people on earth who have been denied access to basic human rights and amenities for survival such as education, healthcare. See https://www.unhcr.org/figures-at-a-glance.html
2. Ravenstein himself was a migrant to England from Germany. He was born in Frankfurt in 1834, migrated to England in 1852, where he married an Englishwoman, while he spent his life in England, he died in Germany in 1913.
3. The term 'brain drain' was introduced by the British Royal Society. It was used to describe the migration of talented professionals and scientists from the United Kingdom to countries like the United States and Canada during the 1950s and 1960s. See Baptiste (2014).
4. In an accentuation to this point, it has been claimed that international remittances from migrants were projected to reach $596 billion in 2017 and $450 billion among this amount was projected to flow to developing countries; moreover, remittances accounted for almost 4% of the GDP of countries with low-income levels. See Ratha (n.d.).
5. Perspective giving refers to the act of one party, often the weaker entity, to make itself heard by the other, more dominant (and often more powerful) group. See Bruneau and Saxe (2012).

References

Atoyan, R., et al. (2016). Emigration and its economic impact on Eastern Europe. *IMF Staff Discussion Note*. Retrieved January 4, 2022, from https://www.imf.org/external/pubs/ft/sdn/2016/sdn1607.pdf

Baptiste, N. (2014). *Brain drain and the politics of immigration*. Retrieved January 7, 2022, from https://fpif.org/brain-drain-politics-immigration/

Batson, C. D. (1987). Prosocial motivation: Is it ever truly altruistic? *Advances in Experimental Social Psychology, 20*, *65–122*. https://doi.org/10.1016/s0065-2601(08)60412

Batson, C. D. (1991). *The altruism question: Toward a social-psychological answer*. Lawrence Erlbaum.

Batson, C. D., et al. (1995). Immorality from empathy-induced altruism: When compassion and justice conflict. *Journal of Personality and Social Psychology, 68*(6), 1042–1054. https://doi.org/10.1037/0022-3514.68.6.1042

Batson, C. D., et al. (1997). Is empathy-induced helping due to self-other merging? *Journal of Personality and Social Psychology, 73*(3), 495–509. https://doi.org/10.1037/0022-3514.73.3.495

Bauder, H. (2006). *Labor movement*. Oxford University Press.

Berndsen, M., et al. (2018). Resisting perspective-taking: Glorification of the national group elicits non-compliance with perspective-taking instructions. *Journal of Experimental Social Psychology, 79*, 126–137. https://doi.org/10.1016/j.jesp.2018.07.007

Bruneau, E. G., & Saxe, R. (2012). The power of being heard: The benefits of "perspective-giving" in the context of intergroup conflict. *Journal of Experimental Social Psychology, 48*(4), 855–866. https://doi.org/10.1016/j.jesp.2012.02.017

Camarota, S. A. (2003). *Immigration in a time of recession. An examination of trends since 2000*. Retrieved February 3, 2022, from https://cis.org/Report/Immigration-Time-Recession

Card, D. (1990). The impact of the Mariel boatlift on the Miami labor market. *Industrial and Labor Relations Review, 43*(2), 245–257. https://doi.org/10.2307/2523702

Carling, J. (2002). Migration in the age of involuntary immobility: Theoretical reflections and Cape Verdean experiences. *Journal of Ethnic and Migration Studies, 28*(1), 5–42. https://doi.org/10.1080/13691830120103912

Carling, J., & Collins, F. (2017). Aspiration, desire and drivers of migration. *Journal of Ethnic and Migration Studies, 44*(6), 909–926. https://doi.org/10.1080/1369183x.2017.13841

Castells, M. (1975). Immigrant workers and class struggles in advanced capitalism: The Western European experience. *Politics and Society, 5*(*1*), *33–66*. https://doi.org/10.1177/003232927500500102

Castles, S., & Kosack, G. (1973). *Immigrant workers and class structure in Western Europe*. Oxford University Press.

Chatterji, J. (2017). On being stuck in Bengal: Immobility in the 'age of migration'. *Modern Asian Studies, 51*(2), 511–541. https://doi.org/10.1017/S0026749X16000664

de Bellis, M. (2020). *Before coronavirus, Europe lacked empathy for migrants. The pandemic can teach us compassion*. Retrieved February 12, 2022, from https://www.euronews.com/2020/05/07/before-coronavirus-europe-lacked-empathy-for-migrants-pandemic-can-teach-compassion-view

de Haas, H. (2011). The determinants of international migration. Conceptualizing policy, origin and destination effects. In *DEMIG project paper, 2*. International Migration Institute.

Fischer, P. A., et al. (2000). Why do people stay? Insider advantages and immobility. In *HWWA discussion paper 112*. Hamburgisches Welt-Wirtschafts-Archiv (HWWA).

Global Compact for Safe, Orderly and Regular Migration. (2018). Retrieved February 11, 2022, from https://refugeesmigrants.un.org/sites/default/files/180713_agreed_outcome_global_compact_for_migration.pdf

Gomez, R., et al. (2020). Empathic humanitarianism: Understanding the motivations behind humanitarian work with migrants at the US–Mexico border. *Journal on Migration and Human Security, 8*(1), 1–13. https://doi.org/10.1177/2331502419900764

Haaland, I., & Roth, C. (2017). Labor market concerns and support for immigration. *SSRN Electronic Journal*. https://doi.org/10.2139/ssrn.3017420

Hasson, Y., et al. (2018). Are liberals and conservatives equally motivated to feel empathy toward others? *Personality and Social Psychology Bulletin, 014616721876986*, 1–11. https://doi.org/10.1177/0146167218769867

Jasini, A., et al. (2018). Feeling 'Right' when you feel accepted: Emotional acculturation in daily life interactions with majority members. *Frontiers in Psychology, 9*(1093). https://doi.org/10.3389/fpsyg.2018.01093

Jaskułowski, K. (2019). *The everyday politics of migration crisis in Poland*. Palgrave Macmillan.

Johnson, H. G. (1965). The economics of the "brain drain": The Canadian case. *Minerva, 3*(3), 299–311. https://doi.org/10.1007/bf01099956

Johnson, H. G. (1966). The economics of the "brain drain". *Minerva, 4*(2), 273–274. https://doi.org/10.1007/bf01584861

Kerr, S. P., & Kerr, W. R. (2011). Economic impacts of immigration. A survey. *Working paper 16736. NATIONAL BUREAU OF ECONOMIC RESEARCH*. Retrieved January 6, 2022, from http://www.nber.org/papers/w16736

Kidd, C. V. (1965). The economics of the "brain drain". *Minerva, 4*(1), 105–107. https://doi.org/10.1007/bf01585988

Klimecki, O. M., et al. (2020). The impact of empathy and perspective-taking instructions on proponents and opponents of immigration. *Humanities and Social Sciences Communications, 7*(91). https://doi.org/10.1057/s41599-020-00581-0

Koser, K. (2007). *International migration. A very short introduction*. Oxford University Press.

Krebs, D. (1975). Empathy and altruism. *Journal of Personality and Social Psychology, 32*(6), 1134–1146. https://doi.org/10.1037/0022-3514.32.6.1134

Lässig, S., & Steinberg, S. (2017). Knowledge on the move. *Geschichte und Gesellschaft, 43*(3), 313–346. https://doi.org/10.13109/gege.2017.43.3.313

Lee, E. S. (1966). A theory of migration. *Demography, 3*(1), 47–57. https://doi.org/10.2307/2060063

Leersnyder, J. D., et al. (2011). Where do my emotions belong? A study of immigrants' emotional acculturation. *Personality and Social Psychology Bulletin, 37*(4), 451–463. https://doi.org/10.1177/0146167211399103

Lüthi, B. (2018). Migration and migration history, version: 2.0. *Docupedia-Zeitgeschichte, 6.* https://doi.org/10.14765/zzf.dok.2.1178.v2

Mærsk, E., et al. (2021). Staying for the benefits: Location-specific insider advantages for geographically immobile students in higher education. *Population, Space and Place, 27*(5), 1–14. https://doi.org/10.1002/psp.2442

Maru, N., et al. (2022). Embracing uncertainty: Rethinking migration policy through pastoralists' experiences. *Comparative Migration Studies, 10*(5). https://doi.org/10.1186/s40878-022-00277-1

Mills, E. J., et al. (2008). Should active recruitment of health workers from sub-Saharan Africa be viewed as a crime? *The Lancet, 371*(9613), 685–688. https://doi.org/10.1016/s0140-6736(08)60308

Moore-Berg, S. L., et al. (2021). Empathy, dehumanization, and misperceptions: A media intervention humanizes migrants and increases empathy for their plight but only if misinformation about migrants is also corrected. *Social Psychological and Personality Science.* https://doi.org/10.1177/19485506211012793

OECD. (2020). *What is the impact of the COVID-19 pandemic on immigrants and their children?* Retrieved February 13, 2022, from https://read.oecd-ilibrary.org/view/?ref=137_137245-8saheqv0k3&title=What-is-the-impact-of-the-COVID-19-pandemic-on-immigrants-and-their-children%3F

Piore, M. J. (1979). *Birds of passage.* Cambridge University Press.

Portes, J. (2019). The economics of migration. *Contexts, 18*(2), 12–17. https://doi.org/10.1177/1536504219854712

Ratha, D. (n.d.). What are remittances? In *Finance and development. Back to basics* (pp. 76–77) Retrieved January 18, 2022, from https://www.imf.org/external/Pubs/FT/fandd/basics/pdf/ratha-remittances.pdf

Ravenstein, E. G. (1885). The laws of migration. *Journal of the Statistical Society of London, 48*(2), 167–235. https://doi.org/10.2307/2979181

Ravenstein, E. G. (1889). The laws of migration. *Journal of the Royal Statistical Society, 52*(2), 241–305. https://doi.org/10.2307/2979333

Schloss, D. F. (1891). Why working-men dislike piece-work. *The Economic Review, 1*(3), 312–326. Retrieved January 5, 2022, from http://tankona.free.fr/schloss91.pdf

The World Bank Group. (2020). *COVID-19 crisis through a migration lens.* Retrieved February 13, 2022, from https://openknowledge.worldbank.org/

bitstream/handle/10986/33634/COVID-19-Crisis-Through-a-Migration-Lens.pdf?sequence=5&isAllowed=y

Tilly, C. (1976). Migration in modern European history. *CRSO working paper #145*. The Center for Research on Social Organization. The University of Michigan. Retrieved January 3, 2022, from https://deepblue.lib.umich.edu/bitstream/handle/2027.42/50920/145.pdf?sequence=1

United Nations. (2012). *Toolkit on international migration*. Retrieved January 30, 2022, from https://www.un.org/en/development/desa/population/migration/publications/others/docs/toolkit_DESA_June%202012.pdf

Valsiner, J. (2022). We are all migrants. *Comparative Migration Studies, 10*(2). https://doi.org/10.1186/s40878-021-00276-8

Vescio, T. K., et al. (2003). Perspective taking and prejudice reduction: The mediational role of empathy arousal and situational attributions. *European Journal of Social Psychology, 33*(4), 455–472. https://doi.org/10.1002/ejsp.163

Vorauer, J. D., & Sasaki, S. J. (2009). Helpful only in the abstract? *Psychological Science, 20*(2), 191–197. https://doi.org/10.1111/j.1467-9280.2009.0

Wilkie, R. W. (1973). Toward a behavioral model of peasant migration: An Argentine case of spatial behavior by social class level. In *Publication series (Conference of Latin Americanist geographers), Vol. 2, POPULATION DYNAMICS of Latin America: A REVIEW AND BIBLIOGRAPHY* (pp. 83–114). https://doi.org/10.2307/25765441

Yang, A. A. (1979). Peasants on the move: A study of internal migration in India. *The Journal of Interdisciplinary History, 10*(1), 37–58.

Yount, A. (2021). *Correcting misperceptions about —And increasing empathy for—Migrants*. Retrieved January 30, 2022, from https://www.asc.upenn.edu/news-events/news/correcting-misperceptions-about-and-increasing-empathy-migrants

CHAPTER 10

Epilogue

It is not surprising, given the bloody history of human civilization that philosophers and thinkers have oftentimes resisted the urge to describe human behaviour with positive optimism. Thomas Hobbes, the British philosopher, had provided a dystopian description of human behaviour in his much-acclaimed book Leviathan which was published in the mid-seventeenth century (1651). Hobbes had written, "Whatsoever therefore is consequent to a time of war, where every man is enemy to every man, the same consequent to the time wherein men live without other security than what their own strength and their own invention shall furnish them withal. In such condition there is no place for industry, because the fruit thereof is uncertain: and consequently no culture of the earth; no navigation, nor use of the commodities that may be imported by sea; no commodious building; no instruments of moving and removing such things as require much force; no knowledge of the face of the earth; no account of time; no arts; no letters; no society; and which is worst of all, continual fear, and danger of violent death; and the life of man, solitary, poor, nasty, brutish, and short" (Hobbes, 1651, p. 78). Hobbes' solution to this violent and nightmarish situation was to apply strict government control to ensure civilized existence wherein people would not kill each at will. Sigmund Freud is reported to have had very similar views on human behaviour and had opined that societies have been created to ensure a rule of law so that humans do not indulge in uncontrolled behaviour in their

D. Roy, *Empathonomics*,
https://doi.org/10.1007/978-981-95-4033-4_10

pursuit of unbridled self-interest (Rifkin, 2009). Bertrand Russell was not positive about the selfless aspect of life either; he had commented, "Every living thing is a sort of imperialist, seeking to transform as much as possible of its environment into itself and its seed" (Russell, 1951, p. 31). Some other philosophers were more positive in their thoughts and had emphasized about the need for collective co-existence and the essence of empathy to such co-existence. In the early twentieth century, the British Sociologist Wilfred Trotter had proposed that human beings exist and thrive in herds and the natural instinct of humans thus is to protect each other in order to ensure individual and group survival (Rifkin, 2009).

In a similar vein, William McDougall, the early twentieth-century American psychologist of British origins, had described empathy to be "the cement that binds animal societies together, renders the actions of all members of a group harmonious, and allows them to reap some of the prime advantages of social life in spite of lack of intelligence" (McDougall, 2003, p. 85).[1]

The discussions within this book involved an analysis of the relationship of empathy to an important area of human activity: economics. It is widely accepted that economics helps in connecting diverse human societies and binding them to a common cause—that of a better life. No facet of human life from birth to death and everything in between including relationships, dreams, endeavours, knowledge, health, food, clothing, shelter and every other material, spiritual or abstract desideratum for survival and betterment of life can be contemplated upon in exclusion of economics. If William McDougall's description of empathy is to be broadly accepted, it would then render the discussions within this book, or least a significant part of it, relevant and crucial to the planning and implementation of economic interventions that seek to maximize the wellbeing of a large section of the human population.

This book was written in the backdrop of the tremendous suffering and misery that human beings around the world have endured over the past several years. A pandemic that cost millions of lives and extracted severe physical, psychological and economic cost from those who survived and lived might have demonstrated the importance of empathic behaviour to the human race. Intriguingly, however, the pandemic was used as an opportunity by many to further their ends; prohibitive hospital bills, hoarding and black marketing of essential goods and utilities like masks, sanitizers, toilet paper, medicines and even lifesaving equipment like oxygen cylinders and pulse oximeters were common. The rot seemed to stem right from the top and the shamelessly partisan manner in which vaccines were hoarded by the rich countries and prevented from being supplied to the relatively poorer nations, especially those in Africa, was an antithesis to empathic and civilized human behaviour. While the pandemic was a calamity of epic proportions, it was not an unprecedented disaster of the type that mankind had never witnessed, human civilization has endured many such calamities. However, evidently the human race has not learnt to prioritize empathic reactions to such calamities and seeks to use such situations to further selfish motives. This aspect of unempathic human behaviour was clearly demonstrated in the post-Covid world when a major war was thrust upon a section of humanity with the potential of major escalation including nuclear conflict. When the human race needed empathic support and a healing hand, war was an unthinking, selfish and entirely avoidable manmade disaster. While the war that closely followed the pandemic was abhorrent, it was not entirely surprising because historically war and pandemic often seem to be connected.[2]

It could be concluded through the discussions in the preceding chapters of this book that empathy or the lack of it has significantly influenced the path that mankind has taken to reach the present juncture in history. It might be argued that war, pandemic, illness, poverty, xenophobia, illiteracy, avoidable deaths, slavery, oppression, persecution, racism, asymmetric power and its abuse all have their source within unempathic behaviour or at times within a perverse exploitation of empathic understanding. Notwithstanding the instances of unempathic human behaviour towards fellow humans, it is oftentimes acknowledged that the human race has prospered and developed, at least in terms of some indicators. Global life expectancy has increased from 66.8 years in 2000 to 73.4 years in 2019 (Source WHO: https://www.who.int/data/gho/data/themes/mortality-and-global-health-estimates/ghe-life-expectancy-and-healthy-life-expectancy). Additionally, there has been a significant reduction in the rates of infant mortality. According to UNESCO, 86% of the world's population are now literate and know how to read and write, as compared to only 68% in 1979. (https://www.unesco.org/en/literacy/need-know). When the reality of the evidences of unempathic human behaviour is juxtaposed against the actuality of human progress, one might be justifiably confused. How can such an unempathic race ultimately progress to such heights of knowledge and wisdom? The answer might lie within a common thread that has linked much of the discussions in the chapters of this book: inequality. The progress that is visible overwhelmingly includes only the rich and powerful nations, some if not all of whom have progressed at the cost of the poorer nations. Even among the developed nations, it is the rich who can best enjoy the fruits of progress; the best schools and universities for children's education, the latest medical discoveries to cure life threatening diseases, healthy and nutritious food, clean and safe neighbourhood, pure air, luxury cars, extravagant hotels, flashy shopping malls, opulent apartment blocks, exclusive gated communities and the other indicators of economic progress and prosperity are thoroughly beyond the reach of the common people. Thus, while the world has become more comfortable, luxurious and plentiful for a section of the populace, progress if any, has been very slow for the vast majority. The result is apparent in the rapidly increasing economic gap between the rich and the rest of the populace. Moreover, what is termed, described and exhibited as indicators of human progress often presents only a shallow description of reality and not the fact in its entirety. For example, while progress has been made to improve levels of literacy around the world, UNESCO also reports that 771 million youngsters (of whom 250 million are children) in the world are still illiterate (https://www.unesco.org/en/literacy/need-know).

The discussions in the preceding chapters ultimately lead to a very pertinent and fundamental question. Why do some countries and individuals remain poor while others prosper? While the answer to the question is complex, an empathic understanding of the predicament eventually leads one to unravel the causes of poverty, thus reiterating the importance of empathy in economic thoughts and ideations. Nobel laureates Abhijit Banerjee and Esther Duflo tackled this question in their book *Poor Economics* (Banerjee & Duflo, 2011). The authors explained the quandary from the perspective of the poverty trap. Kraay and McKenzie (2014) had described a poverty trap "as a set of self-reinforcing mechanisms whereby countries start poor and remain poor: poverty begets poverty, so that current poverty is itself a direct cause of poverty in the future" (p. 127). A poverty trap might have a number of reasons, some of which could be climate, geographical location, prevalence of disease or even continued political unrest. Banerjee and Duflo (2011) had explained that there are two divergent views on poverty trap-one which accepts that it exists and one that does not. The economic interventions that are often implemented to tackle such predicaments are influenced heavily by these divergent views. While those that believe in the concept of a poverty trap emphasize on aid to push people and countries out of poverty, others that do not believe in the concept of a poverty trap do not believe in aids. Banerjee and Duflo (2011) had surmised, "There will be a poverty trap whenever the scope for growing income or wealth at a very fast rate is limited for those who have too little to invest, but expands dramatically for those who can invest a bit more. On the other hand, if the potential for fast growth is high among the poor, and then tapers off as one gets richer, there is no poverty trap" (p. 22). However, the authors presented such a theorization with a caveat that a 'grand universal answer' (Banerjee & Duflo, 2011, p. 23) to the question does not exist and analyses must be made on a case-to-case basis with a focus on ground reality. That point of view might be interpreted as an endorsement of the necessity for an empathic understanding of the situation. Economic analyses of such predicaments might involve explorations on savings behaviour, use of fertilizers by farmers, nutrition and food, health and hygiene, migration behaviour all of which need robust empathic understanding of the behavioural patterns of the target groups in order to know the reasons for the behaviour. It is thus evidentially clear that optimal economic decision making is dependent on an empathic understanding of the causes for the situations that are to be tackled. Banerjee and Duflo (2011) seemed to agree with this point of view when they opined, "To progress, we have to abandon the habit of reducing the poor to cartoon characters and take the time to really understand their lives, in all their complexity and richness" (p. 10).

In the light of the fact that the issues discussed in this book almost wholly relate to the economics of development and wellbeing of large sections of the population, it is pertinent to explore if governments around the world have acknowledged the importance of empathy in economic decision making. The importance of empathy in governmental decision making was emphasized by Wagaman and Segal (2014) who opined, "Nurturing empathy among those engaged in social welfare policy-making may support government efforts that are in the best interest of communities they are intended to help" (p. 91). Empathic understanding of the problems of section of the populace has led to very successful governmental interventions. An example of one such successful empathic intervention has been witnessed recently in India. Migrant workers in India faced a critical crisis during the Covid-19 pandemic when they could not access government ration schemes which provided cheap or free food grains. This was because the statutory ration card that was required for such access at that time was valid for use only in their native place. An empathic intervention from the Government of India in the form of the "one nation, one ration card" programme enabled countrywide access to subsidized food grains in India. The scheme has helped over 800 million beneficiaries of the program including 80 million migrant workers across India (Haq, 2021). While it is a common misperception that only the needy are beneficiaries of government help, the truth is that most citizens of a nation are helped by government policies and welfare in one way or the other. Consequently, if the argument that all citizens are beneficiaries of government policies is accepted, then the common criticism against social welfare, that of creating dependencies, is thereby rendered irrelevant (Wagaman & Segal, 2014).

Empathy, just as any other psychological construct, presents as a complex phenomenon. Humans are neither absolutely empathic nor are totally bereft of empathy; therefore, panoptic descriptions of humans as *Homo empathicus* have been avoided within the discussions in the preceding chapters. Economics, especially when viewed from the perspective of the complexities, unpredictability and irrationality of human behaviour, is complex too. When analysed within the perspective of a dyadic relationship, the complexities of the resultant phenomenon are enhanced significantly. Consequently, it might be acknowledged at this stage that there are no simplistic, immediate and algorithmic steps to implement empathic solutions to economic problems. The only common preliminary step to this effect could involve an honest effort to understand the problems objectively and dispassionately from the point of view of the empathy targets. Needless to say, such understanding is not an easy process, especially for individuals from divergent socio-economic or geographical background. Moreover, if such empathic understanding inadvertently ignores certain significant variables, then the resultant outcome might present as sub-optimal. Empathic perspective taking for economic decisions might involve a robust process of data collection, effective and efficient tools for such data collection and analysis as well as testing the quality of data that is collected. The next stage might involve interpretation of the data as well as the design and implementation of interventions which might be preceded by robust pilot studies. It is clear that the process involves an investment in resources especially in terms of time, skilled manpower and infrastructure. Moreover, empathic perspective taking for socio-economic interventions might require a reductive approach which results in a system design that is detailed, self-adapting and intelligent. The design, implementation and sustenance of such socio-economic systems might involve dedicated professionals who understand the empathy targets well.

The discussions that have been presented in the preceding chapters have illustrated how empathy is fundamentally embedded within the socioeconomic aspects of education, healthcare, migration, labour and welfare policies. However, as an extension to its descriptive and analytical value, empathy also presents a normative direction on how economies should be structured. In order to extend the discussions beyond a mere reflective appeal, it is pertinent to contextualize the arguments with established theorizations in economics and beyond.

The Capability Approach (Sen, 1999; Nussbaum, 2011) focuses on the morally important dimension of understanding individuals' capabilities to choose and achieve the life that they value and find worth living. Empathy serves to augment the capability approach by strengthening the understanding of the capabilities that are valuable and matter in peoples' lives. The capability approach provides a normative framework for freedom, justice and socioeconomic upliftment. However empathic perspective taking allows for the identification, valuation and prioritization of the capabilities as well as barriers. The emotional-cognitive attunement that empathy creates helps in the avoidance of abstract policy decisions or the imposition of alien values while amplifying focus on designing capability-enhancing interventions that are synchronous with people's lives and realities.

John Rawls's theory of justice (Rawls, 1971) prioritizes fairness through a veil of ignorance to eliminate bias. The veil of ignorance prevents individuals from recognizing their own positions in life. This leads to the unbiased recognition of the perspectives of those that need justice. Fundamentally this could be explained as an exercise in empathic perspective taking by grounding fairness in lived human experiences. Empathy in such an exercise motivates emotional and cognitive integration with the situations of others, thus ensuring that decisions that are taken behind the veil of ignorance are not merely rationally unbiased but are also morally attuned with the real-life suffering, dignity and aspirations of the people seeking justice.

The ethics of care (Gilligan, 1995) is a normative theory that prioritizes the moral importance of relationships and interdependence, thus emphasizing on the duty and responsibility to respond to the needs of others. The emphasis is not on impartial rules and contracts but on relationships, nurturing and responsiveness. Within the scope of this theory empathy is not merely a sentiment but a moral orientation that creates tangible and visible efforts of solidarity and love at family, societal or even international levels. Thus, empathy ensures that care is not merely perceived as a formal obligation but is context sensitive, attuned and based upon an appreciation of the lived experiences of those receiving the care or support.

These frameworks allow for a theorization of empathy not merely as a psychological disposition but as an important principled foundation for economic life. The fundamental normative claim of this book therefore is that even as efficiency and growth have historically guided economic reasoning, empathy should also be regarded as an equally important parameter for the evaluation of economic systems and institutions. Consequently, such socioeconomic systems and institutions should not only be evaluated by the goods and services that they produce but also how they help in sustaining dignity, reducing suffering and fostering mutual wellbeing.

The discussion in the preceding chapters refrains from inordinate prescriptive suggestions and focuses on the larger philosophy of the idea involving empathic economic decisions. Even while broadly advocating for empathic economic approaches, the discussions have not presented empathy as a wholly normative concept but in so far as possible an augmenter and catalyst for relevant normative socioeconomic theorizations which aim to improve human wellbeing. The effort was directed towards presenting an argument for empathy while recognizing the limitations of empathic models. Consequently, divergent points of view and arguments to and for relevant approaches and thoughts have been presented for the reader: after all a discussion of empathic economic thinking will hardly present as credible if the discussion itself is not empathic in its understanding of the divergent points of view. The author hopes that this humble work will inspire further thoughts, arguments and discussions on this important aspect of human behaviour and its relation to the field of economics and beyond; thus, stimulating research and theorizations which might lead to the establishment of economic models which are human-centric, efficient, effective and empathic. Such models will best serve to enhance the most important socio-economic outcome of all—human wellbeing.

Notes

1. McDougall had not used the word empathy in his description but had described empathic behaviour as "Sympathy of this crude kind." See McDougall (2003, p. 85).
2. Cooter (2003) had explained, "[T]here can be epidemics without wars, and wars without epidemics" (p. 285). While that might present as a rational

fact, every so often war and epidemics do present with a causal relationship and events involving the dyad are not always randomly coincidental. At the primarily level, war and epidemics are linked pathogenically; with the involvement of mass movements of troops, the chance of infections increases, thus facilitating the spread of an epidemic. One of the first instances of such an epidemic had been documented from the infamous plague of Athens which occurred in 430 BC, when, during the Peloponnesian War, the city of Athens was under siege by Sparta. It is claimed that between 75,000 and 1,00,000 people which comprised of 25% of the city's population died from the disease. (Littman, 2009). The 1918 influenza pandemic (also referred to as the Spanish flu) is posited to have been aided in its spread by World War I. Spanish flu said to have "spread along military pathways that had been carved out across the globe to sustain the war effort on the Western Front" (Humphries, 2014, p. 55). Gugushvili and Mckee (2022) had presented a bi-directional relationship between the Covid-19 pandemic and the ensuing war in Ukraine. The researchers claimed that the present war, as in the previous cases, was linked pathogenically to the pandemic, thus helping its spread; however, the relationship presented with an added level of complexity in this case. The researchers posited that the war was also incited and motivated by the xenophobia and militant nationalism that the pandemic had encouraged, thus motivating the armed conflict.

References

Banerjee, A., & Duflo, E. (2011). *Poor economics*. Public Affairs.

Cooter, R. (2003). Of war and epidemics: Unnatural couplings, problematic conceptions. *Social History of Medicine, 16*(2), 283–302. https://doi.org/10.1093/shm/16.2.283

Gilligan, C. (1995). Moral orientation and moral development. In V. Held (Ed.), *Justice and care: Essential readings in feminist ethics* (1st ed., pp. 31–46). Routledge. https://doi.org/10.4324/9780429499463

Gugushvili, A., & Mckee, M. (2022). The COVID-19 pandemic and war. *Scandinavian Journal of Public Health, 50*(1), 16–18. https://doi.org/10.1177/1403494821993732

Haq, Z. (2021). *Relief for migrant workers: 'One nation, one ration card' expands to 32 states*. Retrieved June 21, 2023, from https://www.hindustantimes.com/india-news/in-relief-for-migrant-workers-one-nation-one-ration-card-expands-to-32-states-101616094437932.html

Hobbes, T. (1651). *Leviathan*. Touchstone, 1997.

Humphries, M. O. (2014). Paths of infection: The first world war and the origins of the 1918 influenza pandemic. *War in History, 21*(1), 55–81. https://doi.org/10.1177/0968344513504525

Kraay, A., & McKenzie, D. (2014). Do poverty traps exist? Assessing the evidence. *Journal of Economic Perspectives, 28*(3), 127–148. https://doi.org/10.1257/jep.28.3.127

Littman, R. J. (2009). The plague of Athens: Epidemiology and paleopathology. *Mount Sinai Journal of Medicine: A Journal of Translational and Personalized Medicine, 76*(5), 456–467. https://doi.org/10.1002/msj.20137

McDougall, W. (2003). *An introduction to social psychology*. Dover Publications.

Nussbaum, M. (2011). *Creating capabilities. The human development approach*. Harvard University Press.

Rawls, J. A. (1971). *A theory of justice revised edition 1991*. Belnap Press of Harvard University Press.

Rifkin, J. (2009). *The empathic civilization*. Penguin Books.

Russell, B. (1951). *An outline of philosophy*. George Allen & Unwin Ltd.

Sen, A. (1999). *Commodities and capabilities*. Oxford University Press.

Wagaman, M. A., & Segal, E. A. (2014). The relationship between empathy and attitudes toward government intervention. *The Journal of Sociology & Social Welfare, 41*(4), 91–112. https://doi.org/10.15453/0191-5096.3984

Index

D. Roy, *Empathonomics*,
https://doi.org/10.1007/978-981-95-4033-4

Kolibri 360 GmbH
Ferdinand-Jühlke-Straße 7
99095 Erfurt, Deutschland
produktsicherheit@kolibri360.de